D1155067

Critical Essays on Robinson Jeffers

FIFTEEN CENTS (IN CANADA, 20c Reason: Tariff)
April 4, 1932
TIME
The Weekly Newsmagazine
Edward Weston
ROBINSON JEFFERS
"No imaginable
"Human presence here could do anything . . ."
(See Books)
Volume XIX
Number 14

Critical Essays on Robinson Jeffers

James Karman

G. K. Hall & Co. • Boston, Massachusetts

First published 1990.
10 9 8 7 6 5 4 3 2 1

Library of Congress Cataloging-in-Publication Data

Critical essays on Robinson Jeffers / [edited by] James Karman.
p. cm. — (Critical essays on American literature)
Includes bibliographical references and index.
ISBN 0-8161-8897-1
1. Jeffers, Robinson, 1887-1962—Criticism and interpretation.
I. Karman, James. II. Title. III. Series.
PS3519.E27Z578 1990
811′.52—dc20 90-36796
CIP

The paper used in this publication meets the minimum requirements of American National Standard for Information Sciences—Permanence of Paper for Printed Library Materials, ANSI Z39.48–1984. ∞™

Printed and bound in the United States of America

CRITICAL ESSAYS ON AMERICAN LITERATURE

This series seeks to anthologize the most important criticism on a wide variety of topics and writers in American Literature. Our readers will find in various volumes not only a generous selection of reprinted articles and reviews but original essays, bibliographies, manuscript sections, and other materials brought to public attention for the first time. *Critical Essays on Robinson Jeffers* contains the most comprehensive collection of scholarship ever published on this important American poet. The book contains both a sizable gathering of early reviews and a broad selection of modern scholarship, including essays by some of the most distinguished writers and scholars of the century. Among the authors of reprinted reviews and articles are Harriet Monroe, Mark Van Doren, Conrad Aiken, Morton Dauwen Zabel, Yvor Winters, Robert Penn Warren, Louise Bogan, Floyd Dell, and Gilbert Highet. In addition to an extensive introduction by James Karman, which provides an overview of Jeffers's career and the reaction to his work, there are also two original essays commissioned specifically for publication in this volume, new studies by Tim Hunt and Robert Zaller. We are confident that this book will make a permanent and significant contribution to American literary study.

James Nagel, GENERAL EDITOR

Northeastern University

For my parents
Chris and Roberta Karman

for Paula's parents
Carl and Georgia Anderson

and for Paula

CONTENTS

INTRODUCTION

The poet is dead.

*

Nor will ever again hear the sea lions
Grunt in the kelp at Point Lobos.
Nor look to the south when the grunion
Run the Pacific, and the plunging
Shearwaters, insatiable,
Stun themselves in the sea.

So ends William Everson's poem, "The Poet is Dead," which Albert Gelpi calls "one of the most powerful elegies in American literature."[1] The poem is powerful not just because it mourns the passing of Robinson Jeffers but because it does so in such a dramatic way. The forty-one strophes of the poem—read slowly, with full stops, as in a dirge—draw the reader or listener into dreamtime. Just as past, present, and future disappear in an archetypal quarantine—a period of forty years or forty days spent wandering, watching, or waiting—the forty marked stops of Everson's poem arrest the reader and carry him or her away. The pilgrim part of one's soul finds itself near the body of Jeffers, perhaps in the wee hours of the wake, addressed by a sentinel who says, again and again, the poet is dead: "The mouth is shut. I say / The mouth is clamped cold. / I tell you this tongue is dried." Life goes on, says the sentinel. Grunion run, hungry birds skim the roiling waves, the books of Jeffers vouchsafe a vision. But the poet himself has found "Finalness," entered the Absolute, "gone into death like a stone thrown in the sea."[2]

Everson's encomium is very restrained. Jeffers is simply acknowledged, never praised. But the compressed passion of the poem reveals Everson's profound sense of loss. From his perspective, as the title suggests, Jeffers was *the* poet of the modern age.

After Jeffers died, on 20 January 1962, other notices appeared. David Littlejohn's essay, published in *Commonweal*, is in spirit the farthest removed from Everson's poem. "Robinson Jeffers, the doom-shouting Inhumanist Poet of two generations," says Littlejohn, "died early this year at Tor House, his hand-built hermitage on the California coast. It took his death to remind most readers that he had in fact still been alive." Littlejohn condemns Jeffers for saying the same things over and over through the years: "The deficiencies, the idiosyncrasies, even the original, very personal strengths that one could accept in the early poems became tedious, empty, and unconvincing when repeated for the hundredth time." And with that, Jeffers, along with his books, is consigned to oblivion: "The big *Selected Poetry* has been out of print for twenty years; his little Modern Library collection slipped off the lists a year or two ago. And now he is gone."[3]

Between the despair of Everson and the disdain of Littlejohn, a full spectrum of responses to Jeffers's death appeared in print. In their otherwise straightforward announcements, the major magazines of the popular press played on familiar stereotypes. The "Transition" column of *Newsweek,* for instance, refers to Jeffers as the "misanthropic poet" whose works included a heralded translation of "Medea."[4] The "Milestones" section of *Time* describes Jeffers as a "solitary poet of gloom" who disliked civilization and who "wrote from the tower of a massive granite house that he built near the rugged Big Sur region of the California coast."[5] *Life* published a full-page picture of Jeffers sitting with a grandson. It was taken, says the accompanying text, during a moment when Jeffers "permitted himself a rare public display of warmth." The article goes on to say that Jeffers lived on a "bleak" point near Carmel, that he himself was "tall and gaunt," and that his poetry "bore the stamp of his dark and troubled credo: that man is only a passing evil defiling the eternal beauty of nature."[6]

The obituaries that appeared in major newspapers were more inclined toward praise. Although the *New York Times* admits that Jeffers "was a profoundly pessimistic poet, absorbed with tragedy and attracted to the doom-haunted Greek epics," it refers to him as "one of the most honored of American writers and poets" and goes on to offer a balanced summary of his life and work.[7] An essay in the *New York Times Book Review* by William Turner Levy attempts to correct mistaken impressions of Jeffers by describing him as "the most affectionate of men" and "far from gloomy." His stony disposition, if that is what seriousness of purpose should be called, was shaped in part by his desire to tell the truth about the world, especially the modern world. His "examinations of darkness," says Levy, offer wisdom; they "serve to temper alike our hopes and despairs, helping us reclaim an age he had feared lost." Such an accomplishment deserves admiration and gratitude, which future generations of readers will no doubt freely express. Indeed, claims Levy, the house Jeffers built on the edge of the Pacific "may one day be visited with the same sense of debt with which we visit Wordsworth's Dove Cottage or Hardy's Max Gate."[8] The *San Francisco Chronicle* also praised the poet. The front-page announcement of Jeffers's death describes him as "one of America's foremost poets." Additional stories on following days refer to Jeffers as "one of the great figures of his generation," perhaps one of "the greatest American poets of the day," without question "a fierce and original talent."[9]

Friends and admirers honored Jeffers in a variety of other ways. Residents of Carmel gathered at the local Golden Bough Theater for a memorial reading of Jeffers's poems. Edward Weston and Brett Weston dedicated a selection of photographs to Jeffers that they published, along with excerpts from his work, in *Ramparts.*[10] Mark Van Doren, a critic who had watched Jeffers's career unfold from the beginning, included a eulogy in the *Proceedings* of the annual meeting of the American Academy of Arts and Letters. After listing some of the great loves in the poet's life—truth, the Carmel coast, his wife, Una, and solitude—he describes Jeffers as "a man of improbable, grim, abstracted beauty, indeed a hawk, a figure of granite, rather than a man at all." He adds, however, that to those who knew him, Jeffers was also "affectionate and humorous, warm-hearted and courtly," in every way a gentleman. Above all, says Van Doren, Jeffers was a man who said what he had to say—about God, the universe, and human destiny—and who never backed away from nor toned down his position. Van Doren's eulogy ends with a prediction: "If Jeffers was wrong he will be wrong forever, and he would be the first to admit this. Right or wrong, however, his poems have power. And this power, at a guess, will last into other centuries than this one which he thought so pitifully mistaken."[11]

Van Doren's prediction appears to have been justified. One index of continued popularity is the rare-book market, where first editions by Jeffers are among the most expensive of any modern author. Another index is the trade market, where books by Jeffers are still on the lists. Despite Littlejohn's assertion to the contrary, for instance, Jeffers's *Selected Poetry* has been in print since it was first published by Random House in 1938. *The Women at Point Sur, Dear Judas,* and *The Double Axe* were reissued by Liveright in 1977 and are still available. In 1987, Random House published *Rock and Hawk,* a new anthology of Jeffers's poems edited by Robert Hass. In the same year, new anthologies also appeared in England and Germany. Insofar as posterity is concerned, however, the most important Jeffers publication came out in 1988, when Stanford University Press released the first of its handsomely designed, beautifully printed four-volume *Collected Poetry,* edited by Tim Hunt.

William Turner Levy seems to have been correct as well. Jeffers's home was placed on the National Register of Historic Places in 1976 and was purchased by the Tor House Foundation soon thereafter. The foundation maintains the property and opens it to the public for tours. Hundreds of people from all over the world visit each year.

Nevertheless, Jeffers has not yet secured his niche in the canon of American literature. He is, in fact, one of the most neglected major poets of the twentieth century. Why this is so reveals much about Jeffers but even more about modern criticism.

2

John Robinson Jeffers was born 10 January 1887. He was named after John Robinson, a prosperous banker from Sewickley, Pennsylvania, who helped raise Annie Tuttle, Jeffers's mother, after she and her sister were orphaned. Mr. Robinson and Annie's father were first cousins; they belonged to a family that had been in America almost from the beginning and that included Jonathan Edwards among its more illustrious ancestors. Mr. Robinson and his wife Philena had no children of their own so they were happy to give Annie and her sister the best possible home. It was in the Robinson home, in fact, that Annie became acquainted with the man she married—William Hamilton Jeffers, A.B., D.D., LL.D., a guest pastor at the Robinsons' church (where Annie played the organ), a senior professor at Western Theological Seminary in Pittsburgh, and a widower nearly twice her age. Annie was twenty-five in 1885, the year of her marriage; Dr. Jeffers, forty-seven. She was a refined and intelligent young woman who shared her husband's love of travel. After a second trip to Europe, the couple returned home for the birth of their first child.[12]

Robin, as he was called, was raised by parents committed to education. The elder Jeffers was a scholar of Greek, Latin, Hebrew, Aramaic, Syriac, Arabic, Babylonian, and Assyrian. He taught courses in ecclesiastical history, Old Testament literature, and the history of doctrine. To open their son's mind as wide and as soon as possible, Dr. and Mrs. Jeffers took him on extensive tours of Europe when he was four and five, enrolling him in private schools first in Zurich and then in Lucerne. With English as his first language and German as his second, Robin moved on to Greek and Latin, both of which were learned in rigorous daily lessons with his father. The family returned to Europe when Robin was eleven and again when he was twelve. He studied first in Leipzig, where instruction was in German, and then in Vevey, where instruction was in French. As his childhood came to a close, Robin could read, write, and speak three modern languages with equal fluency and could work commandingly with both classical ones. Two more years of private school in Lausanne and Geneva completed his European education.

Dr. Jeffers retired from teaching in 1903 and moved his family across the country to southern California. Robinson entered Occidental College with advanced standing and graduated, at the age of 18, in 1905. After a year of graduate studies at the University of Southern California, he returned to Europe with his parents and entered the University of Zurich, where he took a broad range of graduate courses in history, literature, and philosophy. Back in America the next year, he worked for a family physician as a translator of German medical papers. This experience prompted him to enter the University of Southern California Medical School, where he remained for three years. Though he was considered the top student in his class, he abandoned medicine in 1910, moved to Seattle, and entered the School of Forestry at the University of Washington.

Jeffers's lack of direction at this time was caused in part by an unbridled love of learning. His father had grounded him in the humanities, making sure he obtained a scholar's familiarity with the history and literature of Western civilization, but he had also inspired in his son a love of science. Jeffers himself says that "my father was a clergyman but also intelligent, and he brought me up to timely ideas about origin of species, descent of man, astronomy, geology, etc."[13] As a result, Jeffers felt inwardly compelled to read widely in many different fields.

Jeffers' restlessness was also caused by his love for Una Call Kuster, whom he met during his first year of graduate studies at the University of Southern California. Una was a beautiful, spirited, intellectually gifted woman married to a prominent young attorney. Although she and Robinson tried, at times, to stay away from each other, the attraction was too strong. After an ordeal that lasted seven years, Una obtained a divorce and married Robinson. The couple hoped to move to the southern coast of England but the outbreak of World War I forced them to stay home. On the advice of a friend, they settled in Carmel, California.

Marrying Una and moving to Carmel transformed Jeffers's life. Una was for Jeffers, as he himself says, "more like a woman in a Scotch ballad, passionate, untamed and rather heroic—or like a falcon—than like an ordinary person." She "excited and focused" his otherwise "cold and undiscriminating" nature and, in doing so, taught him new ways to see and think and feel. Carmel was untamed, too. The "savage beauty" of the seacoast, where people lived "amid magnificent unspoiled scenery—essentially as they did in the Idyls or the Sagas, or in Homer's Ithaka," offered Jeffers a chance to live a "contemporary life that was also a permanent life."[14] Civilization was transcended there for something more primeval. After twin sons, Garth and Donnan, were born, Robinson and Una purchased property on the windblown edge of the ocean, built a stone cottage along with a tower, and crafted a simple existence for themselves—the wild fruit of which was Jeffers's art.

Jeffers began reading and memorizing poetry very early in life; his Greek and Latin lessons necessitated that. A youthful enthusiasm for verse, which centered on Horace, La Fontaine, Longfellow, and others, was intensified by a gift from his father of a book by Dante Gabriel Rossetti.[15] Jeffers received the collection of poems when he was fourteen or fifteen and wore it out from repeated readings within a year. The book thrilled him deeply and provided what Jeffers called the "passionate springtime" in his lifelong love of literature, a love which compelled him to embrace or at least encounter almost everything of merit in the Western tradition and much from the East.

He began writing poetry during childhood and continued through adolescence. At sixteen, he contributed poems to the *Aurora,* the campus magazine of Occidental College. The following year, when the name of the magazine was changed to the *Occidental,* Jeffers served as literary editor. He also sold his first poem when he was seventeen—"The Condor," which was published in the *Youth's Companion.* During graduate and medical studies at the University of Southern California, he contributed to the *University Courier.*

Though Jeffers read widely in his youth and took himself seriously as a writer, he was not a pale or bookish intellectual. A cousin who had come to California for an extended vacation recalled meeting Jeffers after not seeing him for many years. He expected to find someone a bit younger than himself "who would act years older" and who would no doubt be "homely, stooped, and boringly literary." What he found, however, "was a mighty good-looking fellow, tall, well set up, charming and quiet in manner, and full of fun."[16] Perhaps too full of fun. Jeffers belonged to a fraternity at the University of Southern California, dressed well, and enjoyed late-night parties. He smoked his own hand-rolled cigarettes, drank hard, and caroused not just with classmates but with friends who were longshoremen. A fine athlete, he excelled at such endurance sports as ocean swimming, mountain climbing and hiking, long-distance running, and wrestling. He also enjoyed the company of women.

The women he courted often received love poems. Jeffers addressed them to "Helen," which meant he could use the same lines more than once. In 1912, with several dozen poems in his sheaf and money in his pocket from a small inheritance, Jeffers decided to publish his first book. He paid the Grafton Publishing Company to print and bind 500 copies of a collection called *Flagons and Apples.*

Jeffers not only published his first book but also reviewed it, at the invitation of a friend who worked at the *Los Angeles Times.* Willard Huntington Wright signed his name to "The Subtle Passion," an essay written by Jeffers and published in the 8 December 1912 edition.[17] If one is in on the joke, one can smile at Jeffers's boldness and wry sense of humor, especially when he refers to the book as "a maiden blush, a premiere, a debut, a blooming forth" and adds that it "shows great promise." Irony aside, the review contains several interesting statements. Jeffers anticipates, for instance, a charge that will be leveled against him throughout his career—that he is sometimes reckless with the technical aspects of poetic composition. Also interesting is Jeffers's identification of foreign influences, specifically W. B. Yeats, Algernon Charles Swinburne, and Heinrich Heine. Finally, one perceives complex emotional dynamics at work when Jeffers singles out one poem in particular for praise. "Launcelot to Guinevere" is described as a "tragic sequence" which, though "perfervid and melodramatic," contains "some of the best poetry . . . seen in a dog's age." When one considers that the poem is about his relationship with Una, the woman who by this time had eclipsed all others in his life, one senses considerable anxiety in his self-mocking affirmation. The poem represents an attempt by Jeffers to place his love for Una in an archetypal context and to find the language for his very real suffering.

Within a year of publication, *Flagons and Apples* was all but forgotten. Jeffers had more important things on his mind: he and Una were married in August 1913; a daughter, who only lived for a day, was born the following May; the move to Carmel occurred in November 1914; and Jeffers's father died in December. With these changes came resolve. Jeffers was determined to become a legitimate author.

As he and Una settled into their new life together, which she described as "full and over-full of joy from the first,"[18] Jeffers found ample time for writing. Hours spent at his desk were balanced by chores around the house, long walks with Una along the beach, and hikes into the mountains. Evenings found the couple beside the hearth, reading to each other. This routine, established early, sustained them throughout their long, intense, and star-crossed marriage.

Part of the pleasure of living in Carmel came from exploring the rugged countryside and hearing stories about the people residing there. Soon after arriving, for instance, Robinson and Una took a coach ride down the coast and marveled as the driver pointed out unusual features of the landscape—like the trunk of an albino redwood struck by lightning.[19] Tales of lost dreams and demented passion also absorbed them as the driver described a dying old man in one cabin and a murderer in another. These and other stories expressed for Jeffers, as he said with William Wordsworth in mind, "the still small music of humanity," which was all but lost in the din of waves crashing against the shore and in the sacred calm of mountain forests. Here, Jeffers realized, one needed the cry of a hawk to be heard.

Although Jeffers himself could not yet make that cry, he worked hard to record the stories and repeat them in conventional poetic forms. He prepared a manuscript, sent it to the Macmillan Company, and soon received a favorable reply. *Californians*, his first book released by a major publisher, appeared in October 1916. It did not find a large audience but it was reviewed and critics were generally impressed. Most noted a certain immaturity in his work mixed with unmistakable power. They welcomed him as a new and important talent but wondered what would happen next. "Has Mr. Jeffers the patience and humility which will loose his evident force from its no less obvious incumbrances?" asks a critic in the *Nation*. "All turns on the answer to that question."[20]

Jeffers wondered about his future, too. As he said later, looking back on this period in his life, he was all too aware that he "had written many verses, but they were all worthless." He had "imitated and imitated, and that was all."[21] In trying to chart a new course for himself, he considered paths his contemporaries were taking, such as the one laid out by Mallarmé. The more he thought about the avant-garde move toward abstraction, however, the more discouraged he became. "It seemed to me that Mallarmé and his followers, renouncing intelligibility in order to concentrate the music of poetry, had turned off the road into a narrowing lane. Their successors could only make further renunciations; ideas had gone, now meter had gone, imagery would have to go; perhaps at last even words might have to go or give up their meaning, nothing be left but musical syllables." Every advance, he realized, "required the elimination of some aspect of reality," and this was a direction in which he could not go. He felt "doomed to go on imitating dead men," unless some "impossible wind" should blow him "emotions or ideas, or a point of view, or even mere rhythms" that had not occurred to others.[22]

He had to wait a long time (eight years, in fact, before the publication of his next book), but when it came, the wind was fierce. Meanwhile, he kept writing, his sons were born, he suffered through divided emotions about the war, his lifelong dwelling place was built, and his mother died.

Tor House, located on a bluff just fifty yards above the sea, was constructed out of local granite boulders in the summer of 1919. In helping the masons, Jeffers learned their craft; and so was able to continue working on his own when the house was finished. In the next few years, he added a stone wall around his property and the four-story, freestanding structure called Hawk Tower. "As he helped the masons shift and place the wind and wave-worn granite," says Una in a letter, "I think he realized some kinship with it and became aware of strengths in himself unknown before." Thus, she says, referring to an important moment of transformation, "there came to him a kind of awakening such as adolescents and religious converts are said to experience."[23]

From that moment on, Jeffers knew who he was as an artist and understood the project laid out before him. He resolved "not to tell lies in verse"—not to feign any emotion he did not feel; not to pretend to believe in optimism or pessimism, or unreversible progress; not to say anything because it was popular, or generally accepted, or fashionable in intellectual circles, unless he himself believed it.[24] These negatives limited the field, he knew, but were necessary for the kind of success he wanted, which involved fulfilling a vocation as a poet, not adopting a pose. He also resolved to continue writing narrative poetry, which provided ample room for drama, description of landscape, and the expression of mythic, scientific, and philosophical ideas. Finally, he resolved to concern himself with "things that a reader two thousand years away could understand and be moved by"—permanent things in nature and human experience that unite the present with the past and future. The aim behind these resolutions was not "to open new fields for poetry, but only to reclaim old freedom."[25]

Jeffers's prophetic antiquarianism was empowered by a profound religious vision. From the moment of his awakening, he wrote as a man inspired, at times as a man possessed. A succinct summary of his views can be found in a letter to a reader.

> As to my "religious attitudes"—you know it is a sort of tradition in this country not to talk about religion for fear of offending—I am still a little subject to the tradition, and rather dislike stating my "attitudes" except in the course of a poem. However, they are simple. I believe that the universe is one being, all its parts are different expressions of the same energy, and they are all in communication with each other, influencing each other, therefore parts of one organic whole. (This is physics, I believe, as well as religion.) The parts change and pass, or die, people and races and rocks and stars, none of them seems to me important in itself, but only the whole. This whole is in all its parts so beautiful, and is felt by me to be so intensely in earnest, that I am compelled to love it, and to think of it as divine. It seems to me that this whole alone is worthy of the deeper sort of love; and that there is peace, freedom, I might say a kind of salvation, in turning one's affections outward toward this one God, rather than inward on one's self, or on humanity, or on human imagination and abstractions—the world of spirits.
>
> I think that it is our privilege and felicity to love God for his beauty, without claiming or expecting love from him. We are not important to him, but he to us.
>
> I think that one may contribute (ever so slightly) to the beauty of things by making one's own life and environment beautiful, so far as one's power reaches. This includes moral beauty, one of the qualities of humanity, though it seems not to appear elsewhere in the universe. But I would have each person realize that his contribution is not important, its success not really a matter for exultation nor its failure for mourning; the beauty of things is sufficient without him.
>
> (An office of tragic poetry is to show that there is beauty in pain and failure as much as in success and happiness.)[26]

Jeffers is calm here. He writes with stoic gracefulness about the divine beauty of the universe and the relative insignificance of humankind. His philosophy, which he called *Inhumanism*, is prescriptive: overcome self-centeredness and enlightenment can be found.

The calm that comes with conviction is at the core of most of Jeffers's poems. It is one of the qualities that three editors no doubt found attractive in poems Jeffers submitted for publication. In 1925, George Sterling, Genevieve Taggard, and James Rorty prepared an anthology of West Coast authors for the Book Club of California. Jeffers was invited to contribute because of the book he published with Macmillan. Five of his poems were selected, including "Continent's End," which became the title piece for the book as a whole.

"Continent's End" is a poem about rhythm—cosmic, human, and poetic. It begins with a reference to the vernal equinox, "when the earth was veiled in a late rain, wreathed with poppies, waiting spring." Rebirth within the ancient cycle is about to occur again. This temporal threshold is matched by a spatial one. Jeffers, standing on the shore, refers to the vast American continent spread behind him and the enormous ocean stretched out before him. And these thresholds bring to mind a third. The journey that began when life first emerged from primal water and continued, after eons of evolution, through human migration, ends once again at the water line. Where, Jeffers asks implicitly, can Western civilization go from here? Acknowledging kinship and dependence, he addresses the ocean as "mother" and says "the tides are in our veins." He adds, however, that he possesses a faculty of perception that is "older and harder than life and more impartial," an "eye that watched before there was an ocean." He identifies himself with stone—that once-molten cosmic matter that cooled down on the surface of the earth and formed the basins for the sea. Although, as a poet, his "song's measure" is like the "surf-beat's ancient rhythm," the pounding of his line does not come from ocean waves. "Before there was any water there were tides of fire," he says to the Pacific; "both our tones flow from the older fountain."[27]

As he stands between winter and spring, land and sea, and past and future, Jeffers acknowledges his participation in the rhythms of existence, but by identifying himself with stone, he claims for himself transcendent wisdom. Long since settled down, stone recollects the fury of creation and destruction (the Big Bang was both at once). For now, however, it endures and observes all change with dispassion.

The eye through which Jeffers gazed throughout his career was like the all-seeing eye of Horus, or the third eye of Siva, or the eye of the Buddha at the moment of awakening. It is like the "inward eye" of William Blake functioning at the fourth or anagogic level of vision. It is identical to the organ of insight described by mystics everywhere—the mode of awareness through which ultimate truth and pure beauty can be seen, by which union with the divine can be achieved.

Those who have this awareness sometimes withdraw from the world and sit absorbed; sometimes they seek to share it. Jeffers, more the artist than the monk, sought to capture his experience in words. As a man of passion, however, this was not easy. What he felt with his two hands, what he saw with his ordinary eyes, what he heard and smelled and tasted, stirred him deeply. His experience of the One occurred via an intense encounter with the Many.

The calm one finds in his poems, therefore, is both the source of his vision and a difficult goal to be attained. His lyric poems often show no evidence of struggle; his best ones are uttered with breathless detachment. His long narratives, however, reveal the full extent of his ordeal. With energies like those Blake describes unleashed in his psyche, Jeffers the mystic had to work against the storm created by Jeffers the artist; he had to spiral in and down as the centrifugal force of a long poem, like a whirlwind, ripped his inner world apart. The calm he strove for was the calm at the whirlwind's heart.

Jeffers was a dervish, perfectly centered and composed, whirling with knives in his hands. The "ice within the soul, the admonisher / of madness when we're wildest, the unwinking eye / That measures all things with indifferent stare,"[28] looked on impassively as he himself, the characters he created, and eventually his readers got gashed. Given the world in which he lived, however, and his own commitments as an artist, there was nothing he could do. As he says, referring to the violence of life in the twentieth century, "the day is a poem: but too much / Like one of Jeffers's, crusted with blood and barbaric omens, / Painful to excess, inhuman as a hawk's cry."[29]

By 1920, the hawk's cry he wanted as a poet had come to him on the wind he had been waiting for. Soon thereafter, he began work on a long narrative called *Tamar,* which tells the story of a restless girl who seduces a shiftless brother. To conceal the pregnancy that ensues, Tamar seduces a young neighbor. She soon discovers that incest (used here and throughout Jeffers's work as a symbol for human introversion) is part of her family history, for her now-debilitated, Bible-thumping father had once carried on a similar romance with his sister. The ghost of this woman haunts the isolated Cauldwell home, as does the ghost of Tamar's mother. A clairvoyant aunt and a demented aunt complete the cast of main characters, all of whom die at the end of the poem in a fury-filled fire.

Although Jeffers was proud of *Tamar,* he did not think it could be published. No book-length manuscript of his had been accepted since *Californians.* Rather than sending it to a regular publisher, therefore, he decided to pay for the printing himself. In 1924, he ordered 500 copies from the firm of Peter G. Boyle in New York. Boyle liked the finished product and even sent complimentary copies to reviewers and friends, but no one took any notice. Jeffers soon received a crate containing 450 volumes of *Tamar and Other Poems,* which he stored in his attic.

It was at just this time that selections were being made for *Continent's End,* the anthology commissioned by the Book Club of California. Among the poems by Jeffers accepted by the editors was an excerpt titled "Invocation to Tamar." Thinking James Rorty might want to read the poem as a whole, Jeffers enclosed a copy of his book along with other correspondence. He also sent a copy to George Sterling. These men, both influential in their respective spheres, had never seen anything like it.

Rorty was a poet, author, and social critic who, as one of the founders of the *New Masses,* became a leader of the radical movement in America. Soon after receiving his copy of *Tamar and Other Poems* he reviewed it in the *New York Herald Tribune.* In praising the "extraordinary virtuosity" of the poem, he serves blunt notice to the East Coast literary establishment: "The net effect of *Tamar* is that of a magnificent tour de force. It is enough. Nothing as good of its kind has been written in America."[30]

George Sterling was equally enthusiastic. As a disciple of Ambrose Bierce, close friend of Jack London, and key poet of the bohemian circle that lived in Carmel before Jeffers's time, Sterling was considered a leading West Coast writer. His more florid endorsement of Jeffers comes with a word of warning: "If you are by chance so squeamish that the theme of incest is too much for you, if you are such a sensitive plant that you shrink from the hidden horrors of life, have nothing to do with *Tamar.* It is the strongest and most dreadful poem that I have ever read or heard of, a mingling of such terror and beauty that for a symbol of it I am reminded of great serpents coiled around high and translucent jars of poison, gleaming with a thousand hues of witch-fire."[31]

Other reviews, more thoughtful perhaps but hardly more restrained, were written by leading critics for national magazines. "Few recent volumes of any sort have struck me with such force as this one has," says Mark Van Doren in the *Nation.* "Few are as rich with the beauty and strength which belong to genius alone."[32] Babette Deutsch, describing her first encounter with Jeffers in the *New Republic,* "felt somewhat as Keats professed to feel, on looking into Chapman's Homer."[33] James Daly, writing in *Poetry,* says he finds "a beauty and vigor" in Jeffers which he dares to think is "unsurpassed by any other poet writing today in English."[34]

The simultaneous explosions of interest in Jeffers—east, west, and across the country—made him famous overnight. Unfortunately, however, no one had any books to sell. The 450 volumes Jeffers had in his attic were shipped back to New York and sold immediately. Peter Boyle was reluctant to take on a larger second printing so he negotiated on Jeffers's behalf with Boni and Liveright. The company accepted the manuscript and prepared to publish an expanded trade edition.

Roan Stallion, Tamar and Other Poems appeared in November 1925. It was greeted with the same acclaim. Percy Hutchison, writing in the *New York Times,* questions "whether there is another poet writing in America today—or in England for that matter—who can, when he so desires, write in so indelible a fashion as the author of *Tamar.*" Hutchison goes even further by placing Jeffers among the immortals: "To us it seems that there are in this book pages, many, many pages, which are equalled only by the very great."[35]

Harriet Monroe expresses some doubts in her review, especially concerning Jeffers's themes. Neither a love of Greek mythology nor the most accomplished artistry can excuse for her "the deliberate choice of so revolting a subject" as that found in *Roan Stallion,* where a woman expresses a physical and spiritual longing for a horse.[36] Such caveats, however, only increased Jeffers's fame.

In 1926, Boni and Liveright rushed into print a short biography of Jeffers written by George Sterling, who by this time had become a very close friend. "This book," says the jacket note, "will satisfy the great interest aroused in the life of the genuinely great American poet, whose emergence after years of obscurity, is the outstanding literary event of a decade." A paean of praise from beginning to end, *Robinson Jeffers: The Man and the Artist* was the last book written by Sterling before he died.

As praise heaped on the scales of public opinion lifted Jeffers toward Olympus, stones of condemnation were being gathered to lower him down. Floyd Dell, writing in the *Modern Quarterly,* criticized not only Jeffers but his readers. Admiration for his degenerate, nihilistic poetry, he concludes, is a symptom of mental disease caused, perhaps, by shell shock: "The current enthusiasm for these poems would seem to indicate that the spiritual wound inflicted upon the American intelligentsia by the World War has been even greater than we have been willing to recognize."[37]

The publication of his next book was all that was needed to bring Jeffers back to earth and send him plummeting toward Hades. *The Women at Point Sur,* which appeared in 1927, concerns a mad preacher who, before taking his own life, commits a number of transgressions, including the rape of his daughter. Although Mark Van Doren admits to having experienced "thrills of pleasure" while reading the long poem, he wonders whether Jeffers should keep going in this direction—"he seems to be knocking his head to pieces against the night."[38] Babette Deutsch felt the same way. "For all the metaphysical meat of its content," she says, "for all the lightning-like visions which streak certain passages with a glory, the poem leaves one with the feeling of having witnessed a Pyrrhic victory."[39] But such reservations were mild compared to Genevieve Taggard's bitter attack. As one of the editors of *Continent's End,* she was one of the first to discover Jeffers. Since Jeffers makes no mention of sending her a copy of *Tamar,* however, she appears to have been denied full participation in the excitement concerning him. Perhaps because of this slight, she went after Jeffers with a vengeance. Writing in the *New York Herald Tribune,* she describes his work as "stupendous wreckage," "a ridiculous, belated second flowering" of Nietzsche, "terrific nonsense," and preoccupied with cruelty. "After a long search for the secret of his failure," she concludes that Jeffers is perverse, sadistic, and self-deceived. She ends her review by saying, "The world is probably not as sick as Jeffers feels it to be. If it were sick enough to accept Jeffers, it could hardly live long enough to do so."[40]

From here on, the scales were balanced. There were those who thought of Jeffers as one of the greatest poets who ever lived and those who thought of him as a despicable fraud. And there were those who divided their opinion between the two.

Since Jeffers's principal aim was to be true to himself and his own vision, he neither sought praise nor felt disturbed by scorn. He states his position in a poem titled "Soliloquy" which appeared in his next book, *Cawdor and Other Poems,* published in 1928. Framed as a dialogue with himself—a form that defiantly underscores his feeling of independence, for rather than speaking to his critics, Jeffers merely allows them to listen in—Jeffers ponders reasons why readers might not like him. "August and laurelled poets" are content to speak for the age in which they live, he says, and are rewarded for their "pious fidelity," but he has "defeatured time for timelessness" and measured his age against a more universal standard. The most highly revered poets celebrate beauty and heroism in human life, but he invokes "the slime in the skull / The lymph in the vessels." Other poets tell stories in which the longings of people are fulfilled, but "nothing / Human seems happy" in his world. As a result, people will undoubtedly reject him. Looking into the future he sees that, though he will not be forgotten, he also will not be loved. People will call him "heartless and blind." But that does not change the facts of life as he understands them nor can it alter what he feels compelled to say. "Laired in the rock" of his own personality, which "sheds pleasure and pain like hailstones," he must, by temperament and necessity, remain oblivious to acclaim and condemnation.[41]

Many critics were willing to accept Jeffers on his own terms. Not since Whitman had there been a poet in America who spoke so convincingly in the vatic mode. In his review of *Cawdor and Other Poems,* Morton Dauwen Zabel refers to Jeffers's "oracular aloofness" and "seer-like omnipotence." Unaffected by "the mandates of his readers and eager to complete a body of work which he outlined long ago," Jeffers simply stands alone.[42] For Anne Singleton, standing alone means standing at the top. "It seems to me," she says, reviewing the same book, "that here Robinson Jeffers is writing the most powerful, the most challenging poetry of this generation."[43]

When *Dear Judas and Other Poems* was published in 1929, Rolfe Humphries titled his review "Poet or Prophet?"[44] This reflects the ambiguity of Jeffers's place in American letters. Although Humphries was inclined to answer "neither one" to his own question, Theodore Morrison was more impressed. "No one has guessed the depth, the height, the power of contemporary poetry," he says, until he or she has experienced some of the passages contained in the book.[45] Yvor Winters, however, attacked the volume mercilessly. In an influential review published in *Poetry,* Winters describes Jeffers's writing as "loose, turgid, and careless." His "insistence on . . . his own aloofness" is dismissed as an embarrassing pose. "One might classify Mr. Jeffers as a 'great failure,' " he concludes, "if one meant by the phrase that he had wasted unusual talents; but not if one meant that he had failed in a major effort, for his aims are badly thought-out and are essentially trivial."[46]

Despite the heavy-handedness of that blow, Jeffers was still regarded as a major figure. In his review of *Descent to the Dead,* a small volume of lyrics that appeared in 1931, William Rose Benét expresses some doubts about Jeffers but acknowledges his greatness. "We have to judge him by higher standards than we apply to most poets," he says. "The range of his pondering and the power of his language necessitate that." Whatever may be the truth about him, he adds, "he is one of the most striking poets of our period."[47]

This is reflected in the fact that Jeffers appeared on the cover of *Time* in 1932. The accompanying review of *Thurso's Landing and Other Poems* even goes so far as to report that a considerable public thinks of Jeffers as "the most impressive poet the U.S. has yet produced."[48] Love him or hate him, says Louis Untermeyer in the *Yale Review*, the fact remains that Jeffers's poetry "is like nothing else of which we are proud to boast"; it "vibrates with a reckless fecundity."[49] Once again, however, Yvor Winters demurred. Although he can see "an attempt at some sort of coherent narrative" in *Thurso's Landing*, "the result is merely dogged and soggy melodrama." The "brute clumsiness and emptiness" of Jeffers's writing "can hardly be equalled," Winters says. "The book is composed almost wholly of trash."[50]

It is sometimes said that Jeffers's reputation reached its peak with *Thurso's Landing* and declined thereafter. That is not quite true. Although more and more critics were willing to state their objections concerning the style or content of Jeffers's work, he continued to command attention. When Liveright, his publisher, declared bankruptcy in 1932, thirteen companies offered new contracts. According to Bennett Cerf, Jeffers "had become a topic of conversation because of his passionate poetry" and, along with Eugene O'Neill, another Liveright author, "there was great prestige in publishing him."[51] A special trip by Cerf to Carmel persuaded Jeffers to sign with Random House.

Give Your Heart to the Hawks and Other Poems came out in 1933. It too contained a poem in which Jeffers talked to himself about his isolation. If one should tell people the truth about the world, he says in "Crumbs or the Loaf," they would not understand; if they understood they would not believe; if they understood and believed they would call the person a "hater of men" and accuse him of diminishing the value of their lives. Even so, says Jeffers, one must harden oneself and continue—knowing full well that fewer and fewer people will follow. He was right insofar as the critical response to this book was concerned. Although Henry Seidel Canby liked what he saw, he agreed with Jeffers. A poet who writes "like some morbid Hebrew prophet" can expect to lose his readers.[52] Rightly so, says Eda Lou Walton, when the message is so out of touch with the times: "Most men . . . moving with the age, will find in Jeffers no message and no solace. The poet, entrenched in his personal religion, will be more and more a voice in the wilderness, crying out to no purpose whatsoever."[53]

What some critics regarded as a weakness, others saw as a strength. Reviewing *Solstice and Other Poems*, which appeared in 1935, Percy Hutchison praises Jeffers's power while acknowledging his uniqueness: "Those who have come to find in the startling poetic genius of Robinson Jeffers something not akin to the elder poets or to the general run of poetry turned out today will not be disappointed in this new collection." *Solstice,* he says, is written "in the true Jeffers manner."[54] For Robert Penn Warren, this is exactly what is wrong with the book. *Solstice,* he argues, "contains a great deal of self-imitation"; if the message has been delivered, why repeat it again and again?[55]

As successive books appeared, more and more critics wondered the same thing. Although Louis Untermeyer admired *Such Counsels You Gave to Me and Other Poems,* published in 1937, he describes the philosophy contained therein as "an annotated restatement" of familiar themes.[56] *Time,* blown in a new direction by the prevailing wind, turned to ridicule. "The book as a whole," says the magazine, "reveals no new juxtaposition of the parts of Jeffers's hybrid nature, but rather a wearied division between them—with the aging prophet still hell-bent on emitting clouds of sulphur and smoke, and the poet simultaneously becoming more and more corner-loving and mealy-eyed."[57]

Time maintained this tack with its response to *The Selected Poetry of Robinson Jeffers,* published in 1938. The 600-page distillation of Jeffers's life work is dismissed as a mess of "semi-scientific platitudes, non-poetical intensities, and—for the pay-off—mental exhaustion."[58] Dudley Fitts praises the grandeur found in some of the poems but sees the book as a whole as, finally, laughable.[59] Sherman Conrad, writing in the *Nation,* argues that the repetition of the same spectacle in poem after poem—namely, murder, madness, and mayhem—"results in something as grotesque and boring as a sideshow of freaks. In a collection of these works, such as this book, Jeffers's crippling limitations are completely revealed."[60]

Despite these attacks, Jeffers was still a very popular and highly respected author. In April 1939, the *Saturday Review* reported the results of its unofficial survey concerning the best books of 1938. The magazine had sent ballots to professional reviewers and literary editors throughout the United States asking, "What books do you nominate for the Pulitzer Prize awards?" In the poetry category, Jeffers's *Selected Poetry* led the field by a margin of 2 to 1. Other choices included *Air Raid* and *Land of the Free* by Archibald MacLeish, *Collected Poems* by e. e. cummings, *Collected Poems* by William Carlos Williams, and *Collected Poems* by Mark Van Doren. When the prizes themselves were announced and John Gould Fletcher won with his *Selected Poems,* the editors of *Saturday Review* were livid: "We have no choice but to revive the annual battle-cry of these columns, and protest once more that Robinson Jeffers has been neglected. The number of minor poets who have won Pulitzer Prizes in years when Jeffers had books in the field is a serious reflection on the standards of the poetry award."[61]

One can understand why many critics turned on Jeffers in the 1930s. With the economic crisis early in the decade and tension abroad toward the end, Jeffers's pessimism (or realism) was difficult to endure. As the

1940s dawned, however, it was clear that even the direst of Jeffers's predictions would fall short of the mark. The sword had been drawn and the young men of the world had been set to hacking once again. The title poem of Jeffers's next book, *Be Angry at the Sun and Other Poems*, published in 1941, sums up his response to the situation. "Be angry at the sun for setting / If these things anger you"—violence comes to human life as surely as darkness falls. One cannot stop the wheel of the world from turning. One can only watch with pity, awe, revulsion, and dread. As a poet, bound to the wheel, one can only write with the hope of evoking the same emotions. Stanley Kunitz appreciated Jeffers's effort. His work, he says, "has always had the force and torment of great art." Poems in this latest book, he adds, contain "virtues for which he had not consistently prepared us: beauty of form; imagination of a high order; a style economical, just, bone-clean." One poem in particular, *The Bowl of Blood*, wherein Hitler plays the major role, was regarded by Kunitz as a stunning but troublesome success—"I am even tempted to call it the greatest masque since *Comus*."[62] Other critics were equally impressed. As R. Ellis Roberts said, "The whole book will confirm any intelligent reader that here is one of the few major poets now writing in English. . . ."[63] According to Benjamin Miller, Jeffers's book contained "what will in all probability stand as the strongest and most profound verses to come out of this war."[64]

For the next few years, Jeffers was silent. What could he say that people did not read in the newspapers? In 1946, however, Random House released his adaptation of Euripides's *Medea*. Literary critics, for the most part, regarded the book as a failure; Jeffers was accused of misappropriating the original for his own ends. In fact, the story of a woman who kills her own children served Jeffers particularly well; Medea's murderous jealousy and rage provided him with a perfect symbol for the fury unleashed by World War II. Writing in the *New York Times Book Review*, Donald Stauffer dismisses the book; grudgingly, however, he admits that "the play might act well, for with proper lighting and an ambitious actress it could explode uncompromising horror in the heart."[65] That, of course, is exactly what happened the next year when John Gielgud staged the play on Broadway with Judith Anderson in the title role. In what turned out to be one of the season's biggest hits and a landmark for the American stage, Anderson gave, night after night, "a burning performance in a savage part."[66]

As the applause died down, Jeffers released another book—*The Double Axe and Other Poems*, published in 1948. This time, rather than concealing his feelings about the war by expressing them through ancient myth, Jeffers spoke directly. He swung his *Double Axe* at the leaders of America, the people duped by those leaders, Western civilization, and humanity as a whole. His condemnation was so extreme and so gruesome in places that Saxe Commins, his editor at Random House, was moved to object. Commins went so far as to insist on the inclusion of a "Publisher's Note" in the book, wherein he informs readers that "Random House feels compelled to go on record with its disagreement over some of the political views pronounced by the poet in this volume."[67] It hardly mattered, however, for in the flush of life-affirming optimism following the war, readers were not very interested in what Jeffers had to say. Selden Rodman, though admitting that Jeffers "remains as close to a major poet as we have," calls the book "totally irresponsible, politically, poetically, humanly."[68] Robert Fitzgerald says, "It is a sorry exhibition for a responsible poet to have made."[69] Jeffers himself knew exactly where he stood. He compared himself, in one of the poems contained in the book, to Cassandra, the tormented daughter of Priam whose prophecies were fated to fall on deaf ears. "Poor bitch, be wise," he says. "No: you'll still mumble in a corner a crust of truth, to men / And gods disgusting.—You and I, Cassandra."[70]

Six more years passed before Jeffers was heard from again. The aging poet was slowing down. Una died during this time and Jeffers, unable to imagine life without her, was left "waiting for death, like a leafless tree / Waiting for the roots to rot and the trunk to fall."[71] He pressed on, however, and published *Hungerfield and Other Poems* in 1954. Although "Jeffers has not lost the gift of biting language and the ability to communicate the phantasmagoria of terror," says Louis Untermeyer in his review of the book, some passages are "all the more moving for being uncannily calm."[72] Horace Gregory notices and praises the same thing. "Something that is not resignation yet has the serenity of self-knowledge" can be found in many of the poems, he says. "In taking the road beyond middle age few poets have stepped so far with a more deeply expressed humility and courage."[73]

Hungerfield was the last book Jeffers saw published. He continued writing, however, until he died in 1962. Poems composed in this period appeared the following year in *The Beginning and the End and Other Poems*. True to his vision, his last words were the same as his first—humans must overcome self-centeredness and turn outward toward the wild, beautiful God who is the universe. And true to his vocation, he was still willing to endure disintegration for the sake of enlightenment—"The poet cannot feed on this time of the world / Until he has torn it to pieces, and himself also."[74] Even if one rejects his philosophy, says William Turner Levy in his review of the book, Jeffers "instructs us how our minds might be exalted in beauty—and so share in the divine quality and fabric of all creation."[75] According to Stephen Spender, Jeffers's last poems "may well be his best"; they have "imaginative grandeur."[76]

3

Although David Littlejohn was wrong in 1962 when he said that Jeffers's books were out of print, and though he exaggerated when he said, "It took his death to remind most readers that he had in fact still been alive," he was correct in saying that very little was being written about him. Major scholars and critics had long since abandoned Jeffers. Winfield Townley Scott, noting this in his review of *The Beginning and the End*, says that, not many years before, people were calling Jeffers one of the greatest poets who ever lived—"But there has been a long hiatus of critical neglect and even at times contempt. People now write whole surveys of American poetry without finding any necessity to mention him. Other people have peered up over their little quatrains to sneer at him." Nevertheless, he says, calling the literary establishment to task, Jeffers's unique voice is "far more important in American poetry than the critics in latter years have supposed it to be."[77]

Nine years earlier, Horace Gregory expressed a similar concern about the neglect of Jeffers in his review of *Hungerfield*. "A man from Mars," he says, "or less remotely, a visitor from Europe might well ask those who talk of poets and poetry in the United States a pertinent question: 'Why does so much deep silence surround the name of Robinson Jeffers?' "[78]

The question, of course, is difficult to answer—all the more so because Gregory describes the silence surrounding Jeffers as "deep," which suggests something uncanny. In fact, if one sets aside the notion that Jeffers was a poor poet and that the silence was deserved, one struggles to find the language to describe what happened. One could say that Jeffers's poetry was like a spectacular explosion, so bright and loud that witnesses were blinded for a time, deafened, and made mute. Or one could refer to Freud's theory of repression. Whatever an individual or a culture cannot face gets buried. Silence, in this regard, is a symptom of disturbance. And the farther down something is pushed into the unconscious, the more profound the silence grows. Gregory himself had a simpler explanation. Jeffers's name dropped out of fashion because "in critical circles, right, left, or center, his candid opinions, plainly said in verse" were unpopular. Critics knew, or thought they knew, where Jeffers stood on important issues and dismissed him accordingly. Furthermore, when critics discovered that Jeffers did not fit into any of their hermeneutical circles, that "his writing cannot be analyzed by the use of critical formulae," they turned away from him.[79] And in an age of competing ideologies, where critics worked hard to define the tradition and canonize particular authors (primarily for college reading lists), that spelled doom.

Whatever the reason for the silence surrounding him, Jeffers was easy to marginalize, for his work was nothing if not singular. He understood early on which way modern poetry was heading and decided to go, or found himself going, in another direction. The studied obscurity employed by many of his contemporaries, the tendency toward abstraction, and the use of irony were abandoned by Jeffers in favor of forthright declaration. Impersonality, innuendo, a preference for evocative description, and countless other techniques employed to make an object of a poem, an object that could belong to anyone, were replaced with a radical subjectivity. Readers found Jeffers himself in all of his poems. While the short lyric gained in popularity, Jeffers poured much of his energy into long narratives. Others who worked in large formats (such as Ezra Pound, T. S. Eliot, William Carlos Williams, and Hart Crane) expressed ideas or shared impressions in fragments, often arranged haphazardly. Jeffers, however, told stories in a traditional way, with characters and carefully developed plots. The solipsism bemoaned yet celebrated by modernists, whereby people create the world in the act of perceiving it and thus live within closed systems, was countered by Jeffers's insistence on transcendence. Truth can be found, he believed, if and when human consciousness is cracked open. In these and many other ways, Jeffers demonstrated his independence. Perhaps, therefore, one needed Fernand Braudel's sense of the *longue durée* in order to appreciate him fully. At close range, Jeffers's place in and importance for the Western tradition could not be seen; it could not be seen, that is, by critics who approached him with specific agendas in mind.

What, for instance, was a new humanist to make of Jeffers? Critics like Paul Elmer More, Irving Babbitt, and Norman Foerster built careers on the notion that "the proper study of mankind is man." For Jeffers, such anthropocentricity was a sign of insanity. The new humanists attacked romanticism, naturalism, or any other philosophy that diminished human autonomy, but Jeffers argued throughout his career that humans were not just animals but in many ways a lower form of life. When the humanists looked back to Greece for the virtues they admired—such as reason, order, and restraint—they saw Apollo. Jeffers, equally rooted in the classics, experienced the *enthousiasmos* of Dionysus. When the humanists turned toward the future, they foresaw—if only culture could get people back on track—a new Golden Age. Jeffers looked forward to the fall of civilization and eventually the complete obliteration of humankind. Clearly, there was no common ground.

Long after new humanism lost influence as a critical school, the American Humanist Association included Jeffers in a survey. He and many other writers were asked about the relevance of the term *humanism* for their personal philosophies. The responses, published in the *Humanist,* were prefaced by a statement concerning the association's own position. Given a number of choices (such as classical, theistic, and atheistic), the association preferred naturalistic humanism, which included among its tenets faith in the supreme value and self-perfectability of human personality, optimism, relative agnosticism rather than absolute atheism, rejection of any form of supernaturalism, and opposition to any belief not founded upon the freedom and significance of the individual. Jeffers's response sums up the difference between himself and those who sought the meaning of life primarily among people; it also reveals some of the reasons why humanists of any sort might have been repelled by Jeffers and his poetry.

> The word Humanism refers primarily to the Renaissance interest in art and literature rather than in theological doctrine; and personally I am content to leave it there. "Naturalistic Humanism"—in the modern sense—is no doubt a better philosophical attitude than many others; but the emphasis seems wrong; "human naturalism" would seem to be more satisfactory, with but little accent on the "human." Man is a part of nature, but a nearly infinitesimal part; the human race will cease after a while and leave no trace, but the great splendors of nature will go on. Meanwhile most of our time and energy are necessarily spent on human affairs; that can't be prevented, though I think it should be minimized; but for philosophy, which is an endless search for truth, and for contemplation, which can be a sort of worship, I would suggest the immense beauty of the earth and the outer universe, the divine "nature of things," is a more rewarding object. Certainly it is more ennobling. It is a source of strength; the other of distraction.[80]

Marxist critics, also influential, had problems with Jeffers as well. They appreciated his condemnation of modern life but disliked his lack of enthusiasm for social reform. V. F. Calverton, for instance, finds Jeffers useful only as an example of "the breakdown of consciousness and the rapid deterioration of rationality." As he argues in *The Liberation of American Literature*, the collapse of petty bourgeois ideology, "the violent toppling-ruins of a dying civilization," could clearly be seen in Jeffers's pessimistic, pathological, "desperately dooming . . . mad, chaotic, crucifying verse."[81] In *The Great Tradition*, Granville Hicks applauds Jeffers for saying that the present world order "not only will perish but deserves to," but he censures him for not proclaiming that a new and better "world may take its place."[82] Indeed, Jeffers had no such expectation. In a questionnaire sent to him by the *New Masses*, Jeffers was asked, "What attitude should the artist take to the revolutionary labor movement? Is there any hope of a new world culture through the rise of the workers to power?" In his response, Jeffers says that the revolutionary labor movement, if successful, will probably not create a world worth living in: "A really new culture could arise only beyond the Lethe of a new dark ages."[83] In a letter to James Rorty, a founding editor of the magazine, Jeffers develops his ideas further.

> I don't think industrial civilization is worth the distortion of human nature, and the meanness and lack of contact with the earth, that it en-

> tails. I think your Marxist industrialized communism—if it were ever brought into existence—would be only a further step in a bad direction. It would entail less meanness but equal distortion, and would rot people with more complete security. What I think on the subject is only academic, of course. Civilization will have to go on building up for centuries yet, and its collapse will be gradual and tragic and sordid, and I have no remedy to propose, except for the individual to keep himself out of it as much as he can conveniently, as you are doing, and as I am doing, and exercise his instincts and self-restraints and powers as completely as possible in spite of it.[84]

Rorty, more engaged in the struggle for reform than Jeffers believed, disapproved of his *laissez faire* approach to current affairs. In his review of *Give Your Heart to the Hawks,* Rorty takes Jeffers to task for his lack of involvement. Because "the world struggle is not a part of him nor he of it," he says, "the drive of his art is becoming, if anything, increasingly tangential."[85]

Jeffers responded to the Marxists and alienated them further by denigrating the movement in poems. "The proletariat for your Messiah," he says questioningly, "the poor and many are to seize power and make the world new"—not likely, Jeffers answers himself, for "they cannot even conduct a strike without cunning leaders." And the leaders themselves, like Stalin, are only pursuing the age-old dream of power. "This is not quite a new world," Jeffers says scornfully; Caesars have taken control many times before.[86] And anyone who joins the so-called revolution is but a different kind of slave. "Is it so hard for men to stand by themselves," he asks in another poem, "they must hang on Marx or Christ, or mere Progress?" Truly, it is hard, for in dark times, when the wolves come, sheep follow sheep, people "flock into fold."[87]

Although neither humanists nor Marxists could make or break Jeffers's career, there was one group of critics who had the power to do so. John Crowe Ransom, Allen Tate, R. P. Blackmur, Robert Penn Warren, Cleanth Brooks, Yvor Winters, and others exercised considerable authority from about 1930 on as proponents of the New Criticism. This movement, primarily an academic enterprise, valued the close reading of literary objects, preferably short poems. Social, biographical, or historical concerns, though recognized as important, were set aside in favor of a careful analysis of the artifact itself. The words of a poem were studied for multiple meanings; clever devices—like ambiguity, irony, and paradox—were therefore prized. Add to these interests a conservative value system that was at least moralistic if not specifically Christian, and the standards of judgment become clear. Broadly speaking, from the perspective of New Criticism, Emily Dickinson is a better or more interesting poet than Walt Whitman. Robinson Jeffers is not a poet at all. Yvor Winters set the tone for criticism of Jeffers in pronouncements made first in journal articles and then repeated in *Primitivism and Decadence.* "Mr.

Jeffers," he says, "has abandoned narrative logic with the theory of ethics, and he has never, in addition, achieved a distinguished style: his writing, line by line, is pretentious trash. There are a few good phrases, but they are very few, and none is first-rate."[88] R. P. Blackmur responded to Jeffers in a similar way. In a survey of modern poetry titled "Lord Tennyson's Scissors: 1912–1950," he praises Eliot, Yeats, and Pound for their ability to make music with words. A. E. Housman, Walter De la Mare, John Masefield, Robert Frost, Edwin Arlington Robinson, William Empson, W. H. Auden, Robert Graves, Marianne Moore, H. D., Sturge Moore, Herbert Read, and Thomas Hardy are described by Blackmur as being less successful in uniting meter and rhythm. "But all of them," he says, "are better than the flannel-mouthed inflation in the metric of Robinson Jeffers with his rugged rock-garden violence."[89] More typical of New Criticism, especially as the years passed, was the approach of John Crowe Ransom. In his survey titled "The Poetry of 1900–1950," which contains lists of major and minor poets, Jeffers is simply left out.[90]

One cannot fault a critic for having prejudices; in many ways, that is what criticism is all about. But the New Critics took on a different and more important responsibility. They not only sought to elevate criticism to the status of a profession (practiced by scholars of English in colleges and universities); they also endeavored to define Britain's and America's literary canon. The extraordinary impact of the movement can be gauged by David Daiches's observation. New Criticism, he says, "taught a whole generation to read."[91] It taught a whole generation of students, some of whom later became professors who taught more students, not just how to read but what to read—and Jeffers was excluded. When R. W. Lewis, Cleanth Brooks, and Robert Penn Warren assembled their two-volume, 4,000-page comprehensive textbook titled *American Literature: The Makers and the Making,* Jeffers was not mentioned. For the professors who used the anthology, therefore, and for the students whose understanding of American literature was shaped by it, Jeffers did not exist—and that is criticism taken to the extreme.

The all-pervasive influence of New Criticism can be seen in an essay by Kenneth Rexroth published in the *Saturday Review.*[92] Using the standard terminology of the movement, though not identifying with it in any way, he condemns Jeffers for belaboring the pathetic fallacy in his descriptions of landscape and for indulging in emotional falsehood, sentimentality, and intellectual dishonesty. He attacks Jeffers for his "unscrupulous use of language," where "no regard whatever" is displayed for the actual meaning of words. And he rails at him for coarsening the sensibility of ancient literature. Jeffers's "reworkings of Greek tragic plots" make Rexroth "shudder at their vulgarity." License to vent such spleen came from Yvor Winters, who is credited with ruining Jeffers's career. "Many years ago," says Rexroth, referring to the essay that appeared in *Hound and Horn,* Winters wrote "one of the most devastating attacks in modern criticism, and Jeffers' reputation, then at its height, never recovered, but entered a slow decline." Today, Rexroth adds, writing in 1957, "young people simply do not read him. Few young poets of my acquaintance, and I know most of them, have ever opened one of his books, and know only the anthology pieces, which, I am afraid, they dislike. This is true even in San Francisco where I live, and where Jeffers once had a tremendous following." This, of course, was not true. Indeed, if a case needed to be made for hysterical blindness in postwar criticism of Jeffers, Rexroth's comments would be evidence enough, for almost all the poets Rexroth knew were reading Jeffers and one of the poets closest to his heart, William Everson, considered himself a disciple.

Everson discovered Jeffers in 1934 when he was 22. He picked up a collection of his poetry from a campus library and took it home, not knowing what he would find. The words in the book hammered into him, "one after another—terrible, devastating blows"; his "whole inner world began to tremble," and tears poured down his face.[93] The experience was so important to Everson that he refers to it as a religious conversion, intellectual awakening, and artistic birth. "The indoctrination took so thoroughly," in fact, that years had to pass before he could speak as a poet with his own voice. When New Directions published a volume of his early work in 1948, the editor "carefully screened out" those poems that still revealed the "pervasive Jeffersian influence"; that way, no one would know who had fathered him.[94] Everson's acquiescence here is important to note, for it reveals that silence concerning Jeffers was not just a response of those who hated him. The impulse to ignore his presence, conceal his influence, or efface his memory was found in those who loved him, too. Before the *mysterium tremendum*—whether one experiences it with fear and trembling, anger, awe, or bliss—the mouth is stopped. Everson himself said virtually nothing, except to friends (like Rexroth), until after Jeffers died. An essay titled "A Tribute to Robinson Jeffers," published in the *Critic*, represented an attempt to publicly acknowledge his debt and pay his "birth-dues." The floodgate was not fully opened, however, until Everson composed "The Poet is Dead" for the San Francisco Poetry Festival of 1962. The poem emerged from the darkest chambers of his heart and the experience of sharing it with a stunned audience was cathartic. After that, Everson could stand on his own as a poet *and* speak for Jeffers. He went on to become a leading Jeffers critic and scholar. In 1968 he published a book of essays titled *Robinson Jeffers: Fragments of an Older Fury.* In the 1970s, in addition to writing introductions to or commentaries on books by Jeffers, he reissued *Californians* and brought into print two books of early work that had never been seen, *The Alpine Christ and Other Poems* and *Brides of the South Wind: Poems 1917–1922 by Robinson Jeffers.* In 1988 he published *The Excesses of God: Robinson Jeffers as a Religious Figure.*

Everson lived within a hundred miles of Jeffers most of his life and never met him. The pull of Jeffers was so strong, he had to stay away. Gary Snyder, another poet associated with the Beat movement and the San Francisco Renaissance, had a similar experience. Although he had the opportunity to visit Jeffers or at least to see where the poet lived, he avoided Tor House whenever he was in Carmel because he did not want to see it surrounded by other homes. He needed to keep an image in his mind—of Jeffers alone—pure. Snyder saw Tor House for the first time in 1987 when he participated in a celebration honoring the 100th anniversary of Jeffers's birth. On that occasion, he talked about what he has never fully written down—the profundity of Jeffers and the impact he has had on him. Other poets who attended the celebration, such as Diane Wakoski and William Stafford, shared their feelings about Jeffers as well. Stafford recounted how, fifty years before, he hitchhiked with almost no money from El Dorado, Kansas, to California in search of Jeffers and his tower. Although he made it all the way to Carmel, he never approached the poet's door. He stopped on a path that might have taken him to it, thought for awhile, and headed home.

How can you measure influence like that? It certainly never shows up in poems, Stafford's or anyone else's. It is like the "certain Slant of light" that Emily Dickinson refers to, the illumination that oppresses: "Heavenly Hurt, it gives us— / We can find no scar, / But internal difference, / Where the Meanings, are."[95] Although it may seem strange to mention Dickinson here, in many ways she is the perfect foil for Jeffers; her microcosmic universe is like his macrocosm insofar as both open to infinity. And what difference is there, after all, between a robin and a hawk when both are hungry and feed upon the world? What difference does it make whether a poet wields a scalpel or a double-bladed axe when both can cut the human heart? The greatest poets always hurt their readers—deep inside, where the Meanings are.

When Ansel Adams was introduced to Jeffers in 1926, he found that "quiet and shy in manner, he possessed a strange presence with his rugged features and relentless glance." Adams wanted to meet the man who, in his opinion, had written "much of America's greatest poetry." As he says in his autobiography, "Jeffers's poetry deeply affected me, not so much because of the narrative complexities of the epic poems, or the stern messages involved in many of them, but the extraordinary grandeur of the images invoked and the profound music of his lines."[96] Throughout his life Adams sought to do with a camera what Jeffers did with words. In a letter to Alfred Steiglitz, dated 12 August 1945, he describes his mission: "I am going to do my best to call attention to the simplicities of environment and method, to 'the enormous beauty of the world,' as Jeffers writes. Pray for me."[97] Again, how can you measure influence like that? How can you gauge what happens in the blink of an artist's eye?

Edward Weston was also affected by Jeffers. After spending a day photographing him, the impression captured in his journal reveals what he was looking for, or what he found, in the portrait that appeared on the cover of *Time*.

> I made three dozen negatives of Jeffers,—used all my magazines: and developed the moment I got home. It was another grey day, but I now realize, knowing him better, that Jeffers is more himself on grey days. He belongs to stormy skies and heavy seas. Without knowing his work one would feel in his presence, greatness. His build is heroic—nor do I mean huge in bulk—more the way he is put together. His profile is like the eagle he writes of. His bearing is aloof—yet not disdainfully so—rather with a constrained, almost awkward friendliness. I did not find him silent—rather a man of few words. Jeffers' eyes are notable: blue, shifting—but in no sense furtive—as though they would keep their secrets,—penetrating, all seeing eyes. Despite his writing I cannot feel him misanthropic: his is the bitterness of despair over humanity he really loves.[98]

Weston introduced Loren Eiseley to Jeffers. Although the circumstances of the meeting in Carmel faded from his mind, Eiseley never forgot "the haunting presence of his features, lined and immobile as a Greek mask." In the time he spent with Jeffers, he felt as if he "stood before another and nobler species of man whose moods and ways would remain . . . inscrutable" to him. Decades later he could say, "I have never again encountered a man who, in one brief meeting, left me with so strong an impression that I had been speaking with someone out of time, an oracle who would presently withdraw among the nearby stones and pinewood."[99] The oracle had a message for Eiseley that rang in his ears throughout his life and helped shape his distinguished career as a writer and naturalist.

Joseph Campbell had a similar experience, not with Jeffers himself but with his work. Insight gained from his early reading of Jeffers stayed with him and became, as he says, "very important for my own understanding of the life of art."[100] His understanding of art—human creativity in all its forms—informed his theories concerning myth. It is no wonder, then, that Campbell quotes Jeffers in most of his major books and considered him "one of the really great poets of the century."[101] Like Eiseley, Weston, Adams, and many others who enriched the modern world in fields outside of literature, Campbell valued the experience of being opened by Jeffers, as he had been opened by other visionaries, to the beauty of nature and the mystery of the cosmos as a whole. It should be noted, too, that during his sojourn in Monterey, Campbell was a close friend of the young John Steinbeck. It was with Steinbeck and his circle that Campbell stayed up through long nights discussing *Roan Stallion* and other of Jeffers's poems. And so, the hidden influence grows. If one counts the ecology movement in America, spearheaded by David Brower, the Sierra Club, and others, the influence of Jeffers can be seen to pervade the culture. It certainly leaps the little fences of literary criticism.

Robert Bly's attempt to open a wider field for modern poetry in *News of the Universe* is helpful here. He describes the breakdown of an old way of looking at the world and the creation of a new order. The "old position," according to Bly, peaked in the eighteenth century; it emphasized the superiority of humans and celebrated the power of reason. God was pushed out of the world and nature was emptied of significance. Toward the end of that century, an explosive reaction occurred that came to be known as *romanticism*. Hölderlin, Novalis, Goethe, Wordsworth, Blake, and others sought to revivify nature, recapture an intense experience of God (or the gods), and think deeply through feeling and imagination. To clarify the difference between the old and the new, Bly suggests that the one can be seen as daylight-oriented, male, orderly, dry, and rational, while the other draws its adherents into the night, the female, the wild, moist, and unconscious.

Modern poets—those who came of age early in the twentieth century—could draw from either side. In a world that was becoming increasingly mechanized and urban, however, and at a time when poetry had almost no audience outside the classroom, attention was given primarily to poetry inspired by the old position. As Bly says, an important and "genuine tradition of modern poetry begins with the ironic and sarcastic poems of Corbière and La Forgue, and continues through Eliot, Auden, Cummings and Pound." But the Novalis-Hölderlin-Goethe tradition is also there, even in some of these same poets, and demands acknowledgment. In fact, says Bly, the suppressed tradition is "the major one" and he urges his readers "to reconsider what 'modern' poetry is."[102]

If one does so, then a new and different place has to be found for Jeffers—somewhere near the center, somewhere near the top.

Even without Bly's categories in mind, a reassessment is called for. At the very least, Jeffers's powerful voice, added to those already being heard, should be identified as one which deepens the sad, resplendent music of the modern world.

In making my selections for this collection, I tried to pick the most representative texts. In the case of reviews, I chose the ones that best reveal the response Jeffers received as his books appeared. Articles and essays are also arranged chronologically, with at least one text coming from each decade between 1920 and the present. Unfortunately, much of value has been left out. Many prominent Jeffers scholars, both from America and abroad, are excluded—not for lack of distinction but for lack of space. To redress this problem in some measure, suggestions for further reading are found in the section titled "Supplementary Selections." The primary focus of this section is on essays written after 1950, but here again omissions abound. Researchers who require more exhaustive reading lists should consult *A Bibliography of the Works of Robinson Jeffers* by S. S. Alberts, *Robinson Jeffers and the Critics 1912–1983: A Bib-*

liography of Secondary Sources with Selective Annotations by Jeanetta Boswell, and the especially valuable *The Critical Reputation of Robinson Jeffers: A Bibliographical Study* by Alex A. Vardamis.

Minor editorial changes have been made in the articles and essays. For consistency throughout the text, titles of plays and long narrative poems by Jeffers have been italicized, mistakes in quotations have been corrected, and, on occasion, spelling and punctuation have been modernized.

When I began work on this project, several scholars and friends offered advice and encouragement. I wish to thank James Nagel, the general editor of the Critical Essays series, Robert Brophy, David Downes, Tim Hunt, Robert Kafka, William Nolte, Lawrence Clark Powell, Robert Ian Scott, Alan Soldofsky, Alex Vardamis, Diane Wakoski, and Robert Zaller.

At California State University, Chico, I am grateful to Donald Heinz, Dean of the College of Humanities and Fine Arts, Elaine Wangberg, Dean of the Graduate School and Vice Provost for Research, and Jeff Wright and Robert Bakke in the Office of Sponsored Projects for their enthusiastic support of my work. I would also like to thank the staff of Meriam Library, especially Ilona Toko, Sylvia Jones, Lorraine Mosley, and Nancy Amour for helping me secure copies of the texts.

At G. K. Hall several people deserve thanks: Gabrielle McDonald, India Koopman, Lewis DeSimone, and Michael Sims for the special care they have given this project, and Carla Thompson, for her exceptional editing.

Finally, I would like to express my gratitude to Carolyn Livingston for her expert typing of the preliminary manuscript and to Paula Karman for her careful proofreading and perceptive criticism.

JAMES KARMAN

California State University, Chico

Notes

1. William Everson, *The Excesses of God: Robinson Jeffers as a Religious Figure* (Stanford: Stanford University Press, 1988), x.

2. Everson, 171–78.

3. David Littlejohn, "Cassandra Grown Tired," *Commonweal* 77 (7 December 1962): 276–78.

4. Transition, *Newsweek*, 5 February 1962, 57.

5. Milestones, *Time*, 2 February 1962, 62.

6. "Rare Moment of Peace for Robinson Jeffers," *Life*, 2 February 1962, 38.

7. "Robinson Jeffers Dead at Age of 75," *New York Times*, 22 January 1962, 23.

8. William Turner Levy, "Speaking of Books," *New York Times Book Review*, 3 June 1962, 2.

9. "Robinson Jeffers Is Dead at 75," *San Francisco Chronicle*, 22 January 1962, 34; 24 January 1962, 31.

10. Edward Weston and Brett Weston, "A Robinson Jeffers Memorial," *Ramparts* 1 (September 1962): 66–72.

11. Mark Van Doren, "Robinson Jeffers 1887–1962," *Proceedings* of the American Academy of Art and Letters and the National Institute of Arts and Letters, second series, no. 13 (5 December 1962): 293–97.

12. For a more detailed account of Jeffers's life and work, see my *Robinson Jeffers: Poet of California* (San Francisco: Chronicle Books, 1987).

13. Ann N. Ridgeway, ed., *The Selected Letters of Robinson Jeffers 1897–1962* (Baltimore: The Johns Hopkins Press, 1968), 255. It is important to note, in this regard, that Jeffers's only sibling, a younger brother named Hamilton, became a professional astronomer.

14. Robinson Jeffers, *The Selected Poetry of Robinson Jeffers* (New York: Random House, 1938), xv–xvi.

15. S. S. Alberts, *A Bibliography of the Works of Robinson Jeffers* (Rye, New York: Cultural History Research, Inc., 1961), xv–xvi.

16. Melba Berry Bennett, *The Stone Mason of Tor House: The Life and Work of Robinson Jeffers* (Los Angeles: The Ward Ritchie Press, 1966), 53.

17. " 'The Subtle Passion': A Review by John Robinson Jeffers," *Robinson Jeffers Newsletter* 47 (December 1976): 8–9.

18. Bennett, 70.

19. Robinson Jeffers and Horace Lyon, *Jeffers Country: The Seed Plots of Robinson Jeffers' Poetry* (San Francisco: The Scrimshaw Press, 1971), 9–11.

20. O. W. Firkins, "Chez Nous," *Nation* 105 (11 October 1917): 401.

21. Robinson Jeffers, *Roan Stallion, Tamar and Other Poems* (New York: Random House, 1935), viii.

22. Jeffers, *Roan Stallion*, ix–x.

23. Ridgeway, 213.

24. Jeffers, *Selected Poetry*, xv.

25. Jeffers, *Selected Poetry*, xv.

26. Ridgeway, 221–22.

27. Jeffers, *Selected Poetry*, 87–88.

28. Jeffers, *Selected Poetry*, 75.

29. Robinson Jeffers, *Be Angry at the Sun and Other Poems* (New York: Random House, 1941), 126.

30. James Rorty, "In Major Mold," *New York Herald Tribune Books*, 1 March 1925, 2.

31. George Sterling, "Rhymes and Reactions," *Overland Monthly* 83 (November 1925): 411.

32. Mark Van Doren, "First Glance," *Nation* 120 (11 March 1925): 268.

33. Babette Deutsch, "Brains and Lyrics," *New Republic* 43 (27 May 1925): 23.

34. James Daly, "Roots under the Rocks," *Poetry* 27 (August 1925): 280.

35. Percy A. Hutchison, "An Elder Poet and a Young One Greet the New Year," *New York Times Book Review*, 3 January 1926, 24.

36. Harriet Monroe, "Power and Pomp," *Poetry* 28 (June 1926): 160–61.

37. Floyd Dell, "Shell-Shock and the Poetry of Robinson Jeffers," *Modern Quarterly* 3 (September–December 1926): 273.

38. Mark Van Doren, "First Glance," *Nation* 125 (27 July 1927): 88.

39. Babette Deutsch, "Or What's a Heaven For?", *New Republic* 51 (17 August 1927): 341.

40. Genevieve Taggard, "The Deliberate Annihilation," *New York Herald Tribune Books,* 28 August 1927, 3.

41. Robinson Jeffers, *Cawdor and Other Poems* (New York: Random House, 1928), 147.

42. Morton Dauwen Zabel, "The Problem of Tragedy," *Poetry* 33 (March 1929): 337.

43. Anne Singleton, "A Major Poet," *New York Herald Tribune Books,* 23 December 1928, 5.

44. Rolfe Humphries, "Poet or Prophet?", *New Republic* 61 (15 January 1930): 228–29.

45. Theodore Morrison, "A Critic and Four Poets," *Atlantic Monthly* 145 (February 1930): 26.

46. Yvor Winters, "Robinson Jeffers," *Poetry* 35 (February 1930): 282, 285, 286.

47. William Rose Benét, "Round about Parnassus," *Saturday Review of Literature* 8 (16 January 1932): 461.

48. "Harrowed Marrow," *Time,* 4 April 1932, 63.

49. Louis Untermeyer, "Five Notable Poets," *Yale Review* 21 (June 1932): 817.

50. Yvor Winters, "Poets and Others," *Hound and Horn* 5 (July–September 1932): 684.

51. Bennett Cerf, *At Random* (New York: Random House, 1977), 86.

52. Henry Seidel Canby, "North of Hollywood," *Saturday Review of Literature* 10 (7 October 1933): 162.

53. Eda Lou Walton, "A Poet at Odds with His Own Civilization," *New York Herald Tribune Books,* 8 October 1933, 6.

54. Percy Hutchinson, "Three New Books of Poetry," *New York Times Book Review,* 20 October 1935, 28.

55. Robert Penn Warren, "Jeffers on the Age," *Poetry* 49 (February 1937): 280.

56. Louis Untermeyer, "No Escape," *Saturday Review of Literature* 16 (9 October 1937): 11.

57. "California Hybrid," *Time,* 18 October 1937, 87.

58. "Nine and Two," *Time,* 26 December 1938, 41.

59. Dudley Fitts, "Tragedy or Violence?", *Saturday Review of Literature* 19 (22 April 1939): 19.

60. Sherman Conrad, "Robinson Jeffers," *Nation* 148 (3 June 1939): 652.

61. "Critics Vote on Best Books of 1938," *Saturday Review of Literature* 19 (22 April 1939): 6–7; "The Pulitzer Prizes," *Saturday Review of Literature* 19 (6 May 1939): 8.

62. Stanley Kunitz, "The Day Is a Poem," *Poetry* 49 (December 1941): 151–52.

63. R. Robert Ellis, "Lonely Eminence," *Saturday Review of Literature* 25 (25 April 1942): 8.

64. Benjamin Miller, "Spring Is Far Off," *Christian Century* 49 (3 June 1942): 729.

65. Donald A. Stauffer, "California Euripides," *New York Times Book Review,* 21 April 1946, 7.

66. Brooks Atkinson, "At the Theatre," *New York Times,* 21 October 1947, 27.

67. For more information about Commins's objections see Dorothy Commins, *What Is an Editor? Saxe Commins at Work* (Chicago: The University of Chicago Press, 1978), 120–31.

68. Seldon Rodman, "Transhuman Magnificence," *Saturday Review of Literature* 31 (31 July 1948): 13.

69. Robert Fitzgerald, "Oracles and Things," *New Republic* 119 (22 November 1948): 23.

70. Robinson Jeffers, *The Double Axe and Other Poems* (New York: Random House, 1948), 117.

71. Robinson Jeffers, *Hungerfield and Other Poems* (New York: Random House, 1954), 4.

72. Louis Untermeyer, "A Grim and Bitter Dose," *Saturday Review* 37 (16 January 1954): 17.

73. Horace Gregory, "The Disillusioned Wordsworth of Our Age," *New York Herald Tribune*, 24 January 1954, 5.

74. Robinson Jeffers, *The Beginning and the End and Other Poems* (New York: Random House, 1963), 39.

75. William Turner Levy, "The Theme Is Always Man," *New York Times Book Review*, 5 May 1963, 5.

76. Stephen Spender, "Rugged Poetry Imbued with Spirit of the Hawk," *Chicago Tribune Magazine of Books*, 12 May 1963, 3.

77. Winfield Townley Scott, "Jeffers: The Undeserved Neglect," *New York Herald Tribune Books*, 16 June 1963, 10.

78. Gregory, 5.

79. Gregory, 5.

80. Warren Allen Smith, "Authors and Humanism," *Humanist* 11 (October 1951): 200–201.

81. V. F. Calverton, *The Liberation of American Literature* (New York: Charles Scribner's Sons, 1932), 472, 474.

82. Granville Hicks, *The Great Tradition* (New York: The Macmillan Company, 1933), 264.

83. Alberts, 139.

84. Alberts, 139.

85. James Rorty, "Robinson Jeffers," *Nation* 137 (20 December 1933): 712.

86. Jeffers, *Selected Poetry*, 592.

87. Jeffers, *Selected Poetry*, 458.

88. Yvor Winters, *In Defense of Reason* (Denver: Alan Swallow, 1937), 34.

89. R. P. Blackmur, "Lord Tennyson's Scissors: 1912–1950," *Kenyon Review* 14 (Winter 1952): 11.

90. John Crowe Ransom, "The Poetry of 1900–1950," *Kenyon Review* 13 (Summer 1951): 445–454.

91. David Daiches, "The New Criticism," in *A Time of Harvest: American Literature 1910–1960*, ed. Robert E. Spiller (New York: Hill and Wang, 1962), 105.

92. Kenneth Rexroth, "In Defense of Jeffers," *Saturday Review* 40 (10 August 1957): 30.

93. Lee Bartlett, *William Everson: The Life of Brother Antoninus* (New York: New Directions, 1988), 16.

94. William Everson, "A Tribute to Robinson Jeffers," *Critic* 20 (June–July 1962): 15–16.

95. Thomas H. Johnson, ed., *The Complete Poems of Emily Dickinson* (Boston: Little, Brown and Company, 1960), 118.

96. *Ansel Adams: An Autobiography* with Mary Street Alinder (Boston: Little, Brown and Company, 1985), 86.

97. Mary Street Alinder and Andrea Gray Stillman, eds., *Ansel Adams: Letters and Images 1916–1984* (Boston: Little, Brown and Company, 1988), 160.

98. Nancy Newhall, ed., *The Daybooks of Edward Weston: Volume II, California* (New York: Horizon Press, 1961), 124–125.

99. Loren Eiseley, "Foreword," *Not Man Apart* (New York: Ballantine Books, 1965), 15.

100. Joseph Campbell, interview by Pauline Pearson, 28 November 1983, transcript, John Steinbeck Archives, John Steinbeck Library, Salinas, California.

101. Joseph Campbell in conversation with Michael Toms, *An Open Life* (Burdett, N.Y.: Larson Publications, 1988), 103.

102. Robert Bly, *News of the Universe: Poems of Twofold Consciousness* (San Francisco: Sierra Club Books, 1980), 80.

Book Reviews

Flagons and Apples (1912)

The Subtle Passion

Willard Huntington Wright*

It is no easy task to say anything new about the good old illusion of love: yet Jeffers, in his slender volume of melancholy lyrics, *Flagons and Apples,* has several times come close to turning the trick. Especially in such poems as "The Quarrel," or "End of Summer," there is a distinctly novel and individual touch—not lascivious, be it noted, but psychologic. Noteworthy also is the tragic sequence entitled "Launcelot to Guinevere," which, though perfervid and melodramatic, contains some of the best poetry I've seen in a dog's age—except, of course, my own.

Flagons and Apples is a first volume, a maiden blush, a premiere, a debut, a blooming forth. Therefore let me hasten to say that it shows great promise. And more! Jeffers's verse has a finish rarely found in virgin volumes. But the verse in this volume, though it has for the most part an individuality of its own, shows very distinct traces of foreign influence. This bard has evidently sniffed the fragrance of Yeats and Swinburne, and especially of Heinrich Heine. Several of the lyrics—"Ebbtide" and "Last Spring" for example—might well be taken for translations of hitherto unpublished poems by the Parisian German Jew. And the rather deprecatory "Epilogue" is flagrantly Swinburnian.

However, Jeffers's language is fluent, and his metrical form usually correct; but he is sometimes reckless in the matter of rhyme; as, for instance, when "you" be forced to jingle with "ago," or "wind" with "friend," and, shortly afterward, with "blind." Also, the rhyming of "one" with "own" is a very egregious mésalliance.

*From the *Los Angeles Times Review: Holiday Book Number,* a magazine supplement to the *Los Angeles Times,* 8 December 1912, 17. Copyright, 1912, *Los Angeles Times.* Reprinted by permission. Most of this review was written by Jeffers himself. See the introduction to this volume, 6–7.

CALIFORNIANS (1916)

Concerning Another California Poet

Marguerite Wilkinson*

It is not at all strange that we are able this week to make mention of another California poet—an authentic poet. California has been destined to breed poets. Hot color, mighty spaces, splendid contrasts, gardens of lavish bloom, deserts of utter silence, all these, bordering on the greatest of all the seven seas, make richly fertile the minds of those capable of producing poetry under the conditions California offers and enflame the temperaments that can find in her their fruition.

Robinson Jeffers, whose book, *Californians,* has just been published by The Macmillan Company, is a new poet. He is young. He was born in Pittsburg in 1889 [*sic*] and educated, as he says, "to most purpose" in Switzerland. He knows all the coast cities of California and is now living in Los Angeles. His work has never been published in magazines nor had he submitted his manuscript elsewhere before The Macmillan Company accepted it. Therefore we must bring to the reading of this book minds prepared for something quite new. And we shall find it.

Mr. Jeffers shows a very real and steadfast love of "the golden state" although he indulges in no tourist raptures over poppies and mission bells. His California is not a California placarded with trite effusions about pepper trees and "everlasting sunshine." Nor is it the California of Bret Harte, of Joaquin Miller, of George Sterling, of Ina Coolbrith. And most emphatically it is not the California of vivid realism that we find after crossing the desert, when we enter into the sunny, vigorous daytime of the cities of the Southwest. Mr. Jeffers would give us a California of romance, and from beginning to end of the volume his mood is romantic. His cool-toned rhythms that sometimes chime like silver cast a spell like twilight upon the brilliant land that we love. Out of this twilight emerge romantic personalities, old men dwelling alone in mountains and young lovers meeting under the sequoias or in coves by the ocean, Emilia, a young girl like a wood nymph who makes a revel with the rain, and Dorothy Atwell, a child who loves a great white horse and dreams of the

*Reprinted from the *Los Angeles Graphic* 49 (11 November 1916): 4.

ghost stabled in the deep caverns of the sea, after she learns that the horse has been drowned.

Mr. Jeffers is not a modern. He is too young to be quite a modern, although many poets of his age seem to have left the past far behind. I mean that he is too young in mood and interest. But his philosophy, when it is expressed, is modern. His technique belies his philosophy and unites him spiritually to the poets who were writing twenty-five years or more ago. He is fond of the old "poetry words." He loves to make an occasional inversion, even if it be somewhat awkward, for the sake of a rhyme. He enjoys the use of "thee" and "thou" forms. Sometimes, moreover, in his enjoyment of a story that he is telling, he forgets to be a poet and lapses into rather flat prose which betrays itself in spite of the fact that his rhythm moves on over the prosiness, apparently unvexed. If he had published work in magazines—as he certainly could have done—he might have been helped, perhaps, by an occasional bit of canny and friendly criticism from the overworked editor. But perhaps, as it is, he has been able to preserve the better his intellectual freedom and his individual gift.

But it is not churlish to complain of flaws when such excellence is offered as lines like these:

> Bacchanalian, silver-footed, gleamed and glanced
>
> In the slant window-glimmer the sweet rain,
> And hissed among the leaves, and pattered on
> The ghostly gravel walks; and like a stain
> Across the radiance of the moon was drawn
> In luminous clouds; and failed; and fell again,
> Wetting the tall-stemmed dahlias autumn-wan;
> And from the eave-troughs with a gurgling sound
> Gushed; and was sucked in by the thirsty ground.

And what of these lines from "The Three Avilas"? Do they not fix themselves firm in memory? "Be strong, seeing Life's crown-jewels remain these three—/To have strength, and to love much, and to be free."

Let me repeat that I believe that Mr. Jeffers is an authentic poet, a man of genuine talent, who should be heartily welcomed in California. And let me quote the four closing stanzas of "Stephen Brown," a poem that tells the story of a consumptive cured in the hill country, who remains in the hills, a kind of hermit for love of them.

> "I'd always loved the trees; and half a year
> Was half a year; and it was springtime then.
> I'd always loved the mountains; I came here,
> But soon, instead of dying, I lived again.
> I like my hill, though it is far removed
> From the sweet looks and kindly help of men."

—The old man spoke now as if in words approved
By lingering thought: "We grow to be what we have loved."

Now when I went my way I wondered still
What he had meant in saying, "We grow to be
What we have loved." Was it, that in the hill
Buried, he would grow into earth and tree,
And briar and fern? Or did he rather mean
That, by such love uplifted and made free
From common fears, he had become serene
As Nature's darling children evermore have been?

The mighty peaks that bathe in viewless air,
The pines that murmur by the mountain streams,
What thoughts have they? We know they do not share
Our passions, the disturbance of our dreams.
But as I looked about me treading slowly
The canyon trail, the curtain of what seems
Was lifted, and my heart grew glad and lowly:
"O happy earth," I cried, "O fearless, O most holy!"

Then I remembered with no change of mood
That aged man whose wisdom was serene.
—He stands now in my memory, as he stood
Upon his cabin threshold, and between
The door-posts of rough pine, to say good-by.
A little man, scant-bearded, old and lean;
A man at home in the world to live or die.
Self-stationed, self-upheld as the all-beholding sky.

In the Realm of Bookland

Anonymous*

The landscape and atmosphere of California naturally leads to the development of artistic temperament. It is the land of adventure in new ideas. Robinson Jeffers is one of the new poets, and in this volume he sings his first poems. There is inspiration and a fine note of rare charm in his lines, a harbinger of the songs that count in all lands and all people. As would be expected, California is the background of many of his themes. His bent is toward the descriptive narrative which he handles with fine sense. His work is worth while.

*Reprinted from the *Overland Monthly* 68 (December 1916): 570.

Chez Nous

O. W. Firkins[†]

Mr. Jeffers is distinguished from many brethren in art by the compass, pungency, and resonance of the nature he portrays with masculine fervor. The personages in his tales are hills and pines and eucalyptuses; the men and women are a kind of undergrowth. If by chance he succeeds in human sketches, as in "The Old Farmer" and "The Mill Creek Farm," it is with some man whose heart is lusting for a river or a creek. There is something mildly symbolic in the fact that Mr. Jeffers's localism should have thrust its roots so piercingly into the soil that breeds sequoias. Willis said that Emerson's voice had a shoulder in it. There is a shoulder in Mr. Jeffers's verse, something muscular, hardy, and a trifle cumbrous. His failings are many and grave. He rhymes with a fine boldness and a crisp bravado; his grammar is unconcerned; his construction is *bushy;* he envelops, smothers, his idea in language, and the last deity to whom he could be coaxed to erect an altar is the god Terminus. Has Mr. Jeffers the patience and the humility which will loose his evident force from its no less obvious incumbrances? All turns on the answer to that question. I shall not mock him with the word "promising"; promise is half ominous in our day.

[†]From a review of six poets in the *Nation* 105 (11 October 1917): 400–401. Reprinted by permission of The Nation Company, Inc.

Tamar and Other Poems (1924)

In Major Mold

James Rorty*

Tamar is published by a New York linotyper, who happens to possess both imagination and courage. It exhibits the maturity of a remarkable talent, which critical opinion will have to take account of and measure at leisure. I am convinced that no poet of equal potential importance has appeared on the American scene since Robinson.

The title poem of the volume is a narrative in some two thousand lines of sinewy and beautifully controlled free verse. The brilliant cymbal strokes with which it opens suggest and imply the symphonic scope and power of the poem as a whole:

A night the half-moon was like a dancing-girl,
No, like a drunkard's last half-dollar
Shoved on the polished bar of the eastern hill-range,
Young Cauldwell rode his pony along the sea-cliff;
When she stopped, spurred; when she trembled, drove
The teeth of the little jagged wheels so deep
They tasted blood; the mare with four slim hooves
On a foot of ground pivoted like a top,
Jumped from the crumble of sod, went down, caught, slipped;
Then, the quick frenzy finished, stiffening herself
Slid with her drunken rider down the ledges,
Shot from sheer rock and broke
Her life out on the rounded tidal boulders.

The night you know accepted with no show of emotion the little accident;
    grave Orion
Moved northwest from the naked shore, the moon moved to meridian, the
    slow pulse of the ocean
Beat, the slow tide came in across the slippery stones; it drowned the
    dead mare's muzzle and sluggishly
Felt for the rider. . . .

*From the *New York Herald Tribune Books*, 1 March 1925: 1–2. I. H. T. Corporation. Reprinted by permission.

Mr. Jeffers has proved that free verse—*his* free verse—is a swift and powerful vehicle for narrative. He has even proved that for him at least it is a better vehicle than the eighteen syllabled rhymed couplets which he uses with extraordinary virtuosity, but with less effect in another long narrative poem included in the same volume, *The Coast-Range Christ.*

Concerning the subject matter of *Tamar,* it is enough to say that it probably represents a more or less conscious transplantation and adaptation of the Greek tragic formulae designed to let life burn and char itself, and so reveal its essential structure. But the spiritual conflagration released in *Tamar,* in the progress of which incest and murder are mere incidents, does not appear to be wholly the spontaneous act of nature. These people are destroyed not alone by the forces within them, but by a will-to-die operating from the outside. And that will, one is convinced, is the author. Never does he quite permit his puppets to walk the stage alone. They live and struggle, because they are sustained by a narrative style of extraordinary intensity and resourcefulness; yet their features are blurred, and their blood is not their own, but is that of their maker. Never does the blown glass of this gorgeous and terrible fiction quite leave the pipe of the blower.

So that the net effect of *Tamar* is that of a magnificent tour de force. It is enough. Nothing as good of its kind has been written in America.

In the shorter pieces Mr. Jeffers deepens the impression of his sharp individuality, his developed and powerful style. A single quotation will have to suffice:

Continent's End

At the equinox when the earth was veiled in a late rain, wreathed with
 wet poppies, waiting spring,
The ocean swelled for a far storm and beat its boundary, the ground-swell
 shook the beds of granite.

I gazing at the boundaries of granite and spray, the established seamarks,
 felt behind me
Mountain and plain, the immense breadth of the continent, before me the
 mass and doubled stretch of water.

I said: You yoke the Aleutian seal-rocks with the lava and coral sowings
 that flower the south,
Over your flood the life that sought the sunrise faces ours that has
 followed the evening star.

The long migrations meet across you and it is nothing to you, you have
 forgotten us, mother.
You were much younger when we crawled out of the womb and lay in the
 sun's eye on the tideline.

It was long and long ago; we have grown proud since then and you have grown bitter; life retains
Your mobile, soft, unquiet strength; and envies hardness, the insolent quietness of stone.

The tides are in your veins, we still mirror the stars, life is your child, but there is in me
Older and harder than life and more impartial, the eye that watched before there was an ocean.

That watched you fill your beds out of the condensation of thin vapor and watched you change them,
That saw you soft and violent wear your boundaries down, eat rock, shift places with the continents.

Mother, though my song's measure is like your surf-beat's ancient rhythm I never learned it of you.
Before there was any water there were tides of fire; both our tones flow from the older fountain.

There are at least eight other short poems as good as this in the collection. There is not a single undistinguished piece in the volume.

The scene in "Tamar," as in practically all the poems in the collection, is the coast of California, where for ten years Mr. Jeffers has lived on a point of land opposite the mouth of the Carmel River.

Out of the eight-point machine-set type of the cheaply printed volume, the great hills of the coast range rise and take their places, the brown earth cracks beneath the glare of the California sun, the "earth-ending" waters of the Pacific heap themselves upon the lava beds. California has another great writer to place beside John Muir. America has a new poet of genius.

First Glance

Mark Van Doren*

The most rousing volume of verse I have seen in a long time comes, it appears, from California. I am told that *Tamar and Other Poems*, by Robinson Jeffers (New York: Peter G. Boyle), attracted no attention whatever when it was published here last summer. I did not see it then, and I am able to understand how those who did cast a glance at it failed to get very far. For the paper is coarse and the type is so small as to be painful. Yet the neglect of the book is decidedly to the discredit of New York criticism, as the necessity of its being printed at the author's expense is a dis-

*From *Nation* 120 (11 March 1925): 268. Reprinted by permission of The Nation Company, Inc.

grace to American publishing. Few recent volumes of any sort have struck me with such force as this one has; few are as rich with the beauty and strength which belong to genius alone.

The imagination of Mr. Jeffers seems to have ripened between the mountains and the sea, but its fruit is no common thing; it hangs on no simple tree. In the shadow of hard ranges and within the hearing of deep waters it has blackened like time itself, and the juices under the rind remember the sap that ran through the first roots of the world. But Mr. Jeffers says this better himself in the long, free lines of a lyric with which he closes his volume:

> At the equinox when the earth was veiled in a late rain, wreathed with wet poppies, waiting spring,
> The ocean swelled for a far storm and beat its boundary, the ground-swell shook the beds of granite.
>
> I gazing at the boundaries of granite and spray, the established sea-marks, felt behind me
> Mountain and plain, the immense breadth of the continent, before me the mass and doubled stretch of water. . . .
>
> The long migrations meet across you and it is nothing to you, you have forgotten us, mother.
> You were much younger when we crawled out of the womb and lay in the sun's eye on the tide line. . . .
>
> The tides are in our veins, we still mirror the stars, life is your child, but there is in me
> Older and harder than life and more impartial, the eye that watched before there was an ocean. . . .
>
> Mother, though my song's measure is like your surf-beat's ancient rhythm I never learned it of you.
> Before there was any water there were tides of fire, both our tones flow from the older fountain.

There are a dozen short poems in the book which go like that, but two long narrative pieces are its real contribution. I must skip *The Coast-Range Christ,* though it too is worth talking about, and come directly to the title-poem, *Tamar,* which seems to me to point a new path for narrative verse in America. The rhythms, for one thing, are variable and free; now crabbed and nervous, now copious and sweeping, they get their story told as few are told—with style. And their story, though it is anything on earth but pleasant, was magnificently worth telling. Tamar, the heroine, begins by being like the Tamar who figures in the thirteenth chapter of II Samuel, but she develops in an ampler strain. It is obvious that Mr. Jeffers's inspiration has been Greek rather than Hebrew; the House of Cauldwell is the House of Atreus, and the deeds done there are such as have rarely been attempted in song since Aeschylus petrified an audience with his Clytemnestra and his Furies. Tamar Cauldwell takes three lovers, two of them incestuous; and the tale ends with her burning the hateful house with all of them in it—not to speak of the Cassandra of the piece, old idiot Jinny, who is "the bloodhound / To bay at the smell of what they're doing in there." This sounds horrible, and so it is. Doubtless it is too horrible. But it is never ridiculous, and I must confess that I am both pleased and impressed by a poet these days who plunges into thunder—provided he can write with haunting power.

Brains and Lyrics

Babette Deutsch*

In Robinson Jeffers we find a poet concerned, like Muir, with the cosmos in which man is but a momentary flicker, but the magnificent strophes of this strangely obscure poet show a richer maturity. This reviewer, reading Jeffers, felt somewhat as Keats professed to feel, on looking into Chapman's Homer. Nothing is discoverable of the man save that he lives on the Pacific coast and was published by a New York linotyper, Peter Boyle, whose name should go down laurelled in the annals of American literature. The opening poem, *Tamar,* is a powerful dramatic narrative on the stern Greek model, given a native setting and written in a free verse that has in it the long roll and swing of the elder seas. Jeffers has his own style, which is worthy of his high moods and gnarled thinking. For there is thinking in these lyrics, which lifts them out of the category attractive to Mr. Moore, and on to the plane of great writing. It is possible not to share the Oriental philosophy expressed in certain of his poems, but it is impossible to have strong poetry without the force of some equal conviction beating like a heart in its body. Jeffers himself tells us what the stuff of a poem must be:

> Permanent things are what is needful in a poem, things temporally
> Of great dimension, things continually renewed or always present.
>
> Grass that is made each year equals the mountains in her past and future;
> Fashionable and momentary things we need not see nor speak of.
>
> Man gleaning food between the solemn presences of land and ocean,
> On shores where better men have shipwrecked, under fog and among
> flowers,
>
> Equals the mountains in his past and future. . . .

*From a review of six poets in the *New Republic* 43 (27 May 1925). 23–24. Reprinted by permission.

Permanent things—bound together in a cosmic pattern, as Jeffers binds them—permanent things, edged with the light of our new knowledge of the world—permanent things torn up from the sea-floor of emotion and giving off the aromatic odors of fossil resin in the fires of the poet's mind. That is what one is granted in such work as this—work that is hard and cool and precious as amber, and like amber, charged with electricity. Here is a solitary example:

The Cycle

The clapping blackness of the wings of pointed cormorants, the great
    indolent planes
Of autumn pelicans nine or a dozen strung shorelong,
But chiefly the gulls, the cloud-calligraphers of windy spirals before a
    storm,
Cruise north and south over the sea-rocks and over
That bluish enormous opal; very lately these alone, these and the clouds
And westering lights of heaven, crossed it; but then
A hull with standing canvas crept about Point Lobos . . . now all day long
    the steamers
Smudge the opal's rim; often a sea-plane troubles
The sea-wind with its throbbing heart. These will increase, the others
    diminish; and later
These will diminish; our Pacific have pastured
The Mediterranean torch and passed it west across the fountains of the
    morning;
And the following desolation that feeds on Crete
Feed here; the clapping blackness of the wings of pointed cormorants,
    the great sails
Of autumn pelicans, the gray sea-going gulls,
Alone will streak the enormous opal, the earth have peace like the broad
    water, our blood's
Unrest have doubled to Asia and be peopling
Europe again, or dropping colonies at the morning star: what moody
    traveller
Wanders back here, watches the sea-fowl circle
The old sea-granite and cemented granite with one regard, and greets my
    ghost,
One temper with the granite, bulking about here?

Roots Under the Rocks

James Daly*

When Robinson Jeffers' *Californians* (Macmillan Co.) appeared in 1916, its most appreciative critics were somewhat dismayed by the con-

*From *Poetry* 27 (August 1925): 278–85. Copyrighted by The Modern Poetry Association and reprinted by permission of the Editor of *Poetry.*

trast between his philosophy, which was modern, and his technique, which belonged to a period thirty years past. They greeted him as an authentic poet, a fine fruition of the land he celebrated; but they pointed out that he did not hesitate to make awkward inversions for the sake of rhyme, and that he seemed over-fond of *thee* and *thou.* The strength that came shouldering through the highly conventional metres of poems like "Emilia," "The Three Avilas," "Ruth Alison," and "Dorothy Atwell" showed that here was a poet whose development called chiefly for a resolute avoidance of the established, the ready-made, in verse.

Mr. Jeffers himself must have realized this. *Tamar and Other Poems,* published last summer, proves that in these eight years he has learned to be splendidly resolute. In many of the poems he has contrived to "shear the rhyme-tassels from verse." In others he uses rhyme but does not let it tempt him into inversions. And except in the sonnets—to me the least successful poems in the book—he forgets his own verse-forms. The first poem in the book is an interesting instance. Seeing that the customary measure of blank verse moves too rapidly for the slow pulse of many of his rhythms, Mr. Jeffers thought of doubling the lines, as a lyrical trimeter was doubled to make hexameters; he then had ten bars to the line instead of five. But fearing that this measure alone would prove too heavy for the long contemporary story he wished to tell, he sought the variety of a further tidal recurrence by alternating a succession of ten-bar lines with a succession of five-bar ones. And then, to ease the transitions and to satisfy his inner ear, he granted himself the Elizabethan playwright's license to leave many lines irregular; so many, in fact, that the result frequently is a thing Mr. Jeffers probably never expected to find himself writing—free verse! And it is free verse of a high order.

This later book shows marked growth in other ways. Retaining the richly indigenous quality of *Californians,* his work has flowered into a rare force and naturalness of articulation. "Between the solemn presences of land and ocean" all that was halting and tentative in his earlier approach has matured into a mastery that seldom fails him. Without effusive raptures over mission-bells and pepper-trees and "eternal sunshine," Mr. Jeffers gives us California—its "boundaries of granite and spray," its "foreland cypresses," its "moss-grown boulder stone." Most of his poems seem to come, inevitably as "the low flower called footsteps of the spring" from what can be seen, doubtless, through the windows of his house in Carmel: "the wild Pacific pasture," or "oak-trees thrusting elbows at the wind," or "pine-crested Santa Lucian hills." The land has rewarded his steadfast devotion by making him part of its primal fertility; his power seems superbly ripened.

One could say that he has "found" himself. That, though, would be a tame and easy thing to say, and the poet who has given us Tamar, "that wild girl whose soul was fire," is not one to be spoken of tamely. Many people find themselves whose discovery can be of no great moment to others. The important thing about Mr. Jeffers is that through finding himself he has written in a way that makes imperative and unforgettable our own finding of him.

I remember that day last summer when I opened his book. I had no especial anticipation; the work and the man were both unknown to me, the book was privately printed, the paper is coarse and the type too small. But before I had read a page my listlessness was gone, I was tense with excitement. Here was writing that seemed to spring from genius of a deep poetic compulsion, writing that had what one rarely finds in contemporary poetry—genuine passion. Here, page upon page, was a nuggeted ruggedness of imagery. Here was magnificent rhythm, responsive to the spur and rein of the thought riding it. And here were a beauty and vigor and objective immediacy of phrase—prolific, seemingly unpremeditated, yet restrained—which I dared to think unsurpassed by any other poet writing today in English.

It was the title-poem that roused these responses in me. "The strong will thrive on bitter food," Mr. Jeffers wrote in "Dorothy Atwell." There are few, I fear, who will not find *Tamar* bitter food. A long narrative, it gives us "a dotard and an idiot, / An old woman puffed with vanity, youth, but botched with incest."

Not a pretty story; but to me it is, as Mr. Jeffers tells it, tremendously worth the telling. The first half of it is told so well that one hesitates to use the superlatives which a just praise of it would require. Everything leading up to and surrounding Tamar's dance on that shore of "gross and replete shadows" stands out crystal clear. Afterwards, Mr. Jeffers unfortunately loses his grip a little; there is often a confusing indistinctness of focus. This indistinctness comes not from a weakness in design, but rather from a blurring of incident within the design. Perhaps it is that the poet is lured out of his earlier detachment: in some of the later pages he seems crowded into rooms with the people he is writing about; and these pages have, I feel, an hysteria beyond that of the characters, an hysteria which makes for bewilderment. Luckily in the very last pages Mr. Jeffers extricates himself into his earlier high vividness and clarity. Even the partial failure in control of the latter half of his story, however, cannot greatly weigh against the proportions of his achievement. It would be egregiously unfair to him if this comparison were taken to have implications beyond those which it states; but his tale (although by its relentless inclusiveness, its determination to tell everything at first hand, shirking neither blood nor fire, it foregoes the austerity of its ancient prototype) has the intensity of suspense, the unswerving strength of design, the atmosphere of cumulative violence and doom, of a Greek tragedy. And we are made to accept the doom, to welcome it. It seems almost a happy thing when fire takes the house and everyone in it, leaving "A hollowed lawn strewn with a few black stones / And the brick of broken chimneys."

So far I have been dealing with *Tamar* as a narrative. It is no less engrossing as a poem. To the lover of imagery its every page will be an adventure. From the poem's store of opulent and piercing beauty one longs to quote profusely. A few scattered passages, though, will be enough to illustrate its quality. On the first page is the description of a death:

. . . . the mare with four slim hooves
On a foot of ground pivoted like a top,
Jumped from the crumble of sod, went down, caught, slipped;
Then, the quick frenzy finished, stiffening herself,
Slid with her drunken rider down the ledges,
Shot from sheer rock and broke
Her life out on the rounded tidal boulders.

Pages later, to Helen, the ghost, "flitting / The chilly and brittle pumice-tips of the moon," Tamar describes "the beauty and strangeness of this place":

Old cypresses
The sailor wind works into deep-sea knots
A thousand years; age-reddened granite
That was the world's cradle and crumbles apieces
Now that we're all grown up, breaks out at the roots;
And underneath it the old gray-granite strength
Is neither glad nor sorry to take the seas
Of all the storms forever and stand as firmly
As when the red hawk wings of the first dawn
Streamed up the sky over it: there is one more beautiful thing—,
Water that owns the north and west and south
And is all colors and never is all quiet,
And the fogs are its breath and float along the branches of the cypresses.
And I forgot the coals of ruby lichen
That glow in the fog on the old twigs.

And when Tamar is made to dance "between the tidemarks on the rocks," we see her:

Tamar drew her beauty
Out of its husks; dwellers on eastern shores
Watch moonrises as white as hers
When the half-moon about midnight
Steps out of her husk of water to dance in heaven:
So Tamar weeping
Slipped every sheath down to her feet, the spirit of the place
Ruling her, she and the evening star sharing the darkness,
And danced on the naked shore
Where a pale couch of sand covered the rocks,
Danced with slow steps and streaming hair,
Dark and slender
Against the pallid sea-gleam, slender and maidenly,
Dancing and weeping . . .

Tamar comprises almost half the book. A number of shorter poems, many of them of striking beauty and strength, and another long narrative poem, make up the rest of it. *The Coast-Range Christ* is told in couplets, ten bars to a line. Here too Mr. Jeffers proves that he knows how to tell a story. In the matter of selection and pace, even of dialogue, there are few novelists who could not learn something from him. He is able to venture into most untoward and refractory regions of human conduct and remain psychologically credible and convincing; able to achieve high flights of poetry without ceasing to be dramatic. And he can create dimensional people, can "characterize": few of the characters in either story could be called normal, yet it would be hard indeed to doubt their reality; his women especially are memorably vivid and real.

I wish to praise, but not unstintedly. There are flaws, of course; lapses into prose, for instance—at times through a stumbling of the rhythm, at times through a flat tonelessness of phrase, at times through both. In poems of such length it would be little short of miraculous if there were not these lapses. And there are, occasionally, bad images. The first three lines of *Tamar*—"A night the half-moon was like a dancing-girl,/ No, like a drunkard's last half-dollar / Shoved on the polished bar of the eastern hill-range"—although right in intention, are to me unfortunate. It is natural enough to follow the image of a dancing-girl with that of a drunkard's last half-dollar. The trouble is that the semi-circular is likened to the circular; the inner eye rebels. And Mr. Jeffers' work will in most instances disappoint readers who require of a contemporary poet that he be, in a special sense, modern; that is, that he divorce poetry from subject, giving them poems which in firm clarity of design attain to a complete existence independent of death, love, nature, or God. I can take delight in such sheer technical excellence, but I have full sympathy for a poet like Mr. Jeffers who is so old-fashioned as to forego this exclusive perfection for a passionate portrayal of "the essence and the end" of life. Indeed, when I began to read it Mr. Jeffers' work filed over the arsenaled contours of some finely modern poems I had been reading as, in one of his poems,

> over the tiled brick temple buttresses
> And the folly of a garden on arches, the ancienter simple and silent tribe of the stars
> Filed.

For it seemed, and it still seems, the work of one who, like Tamar, knows "the muddy root under the rock of things." He may write of "one girl's beauty and one girl's mouth," lyrically exultant over the sensual no less than the sensuous aspects of love; or he may write of "the sea that the stars and the sea and the mountain bones of the earth and men's souls are the foam on." But always he writes as one who has dared to go down into the deep pits of the mind where the imagination's ultimate eyes, confronting "the central fire," are blinded into knowledge.

Rhymes and Reactions

George Sterling*

I am wondering how many of our readers have seen *Tamar*, that terrific poem by Robinson Jeffers, given long reviews by James Rorty in the *New York Herald Tribune*, and by James Daly in *Poetry*, the first edition was immediately exhausted, nor do I know how many copies came to California.

However, the good news comes that it is to be issued by Boni and Liveright as a part of Mr. Jeffers' new volume, *Roan Stallion*, and those of you who have not read that unforgettable poem will now have their chance. A word of warning, though: if you are by chance so squeamish that the theme of incest is too much for you, if you are such a sensitive plant that you shrink from the hidden horrors of life, have nothing to do with *Tamar*. It is the strongest and most dreadful poem that I have ever read or heard of, a mingling of such terror and beauty that for a symbol of it I am reminded of great serpents coiled around high and translucent jars of poison, gleaming with a thousand hues of witch-fire. For Mr. Jeffers has put everything into his poem, and its huge rhythms are those of the very ocean on which his tower of granite looks forth. I have not at hand Mr. Rorty's very able review, but read what James Daly has to say of it in *Poetry*. It is what I should have liked to say, and can now at least echo.

"The first half of it is told so well that one hesitates to use the superlatives which a just praise of it would require. . . . To the lover of imagery its every page will be an adventure. From the poem's store of opulent and piercing beauty one longs to quote profusely."

And again: ". . . a beauty and vigor and objective immediacy of phrase—prolific, seemingly unpremediated, yet restrained—which I dared to think unsurpassed by any other poet writing today in English." Mr. Daly could quite as well have put it "unequalled." But we will let that pass.

As to *Roan Stallion*, I have not yet seen it, and am somewhat in doubt as to what its effect will be on the Rev. John A. Sumner, since it uses the Pasiphaë theme. It is true that one can "get away with murder" in verse, and I am hoping that the book will have that much luck, for even in Moronia all things are possible, if not probable.

*Reprinted from the *Overland Monthly* 83 (November 1925): 411.

Roan Stallion, Tamar and Other Poems (1925)

An Elder Poet and a Young One Greet the New Year

Percy A. Hutchison*

In the year 1642 the Puritan glacier, in the course of its ponderous but invincible progress toward the Commonwealth, closed the London theatres. So powerful had the Puritans become that they would have brought about this closing even had it not been for the additional excuse offered in the plays of John Ford. But Ford's plays removed, in the Puritan mind, whatever shred of justification the theatres might have advanced for continued leniency. And not from the time of Ford until Shelley wrote his Beatrice Cenci was the essential theme of the Oedipus trilogy again attempted in English letters. It is sincerely to be hoped, for the cause of poetry in general, and of American poetry in particular, that no heavy hand will descend upon Robinson Jeffers's *Tamar.* That "the curse of Pelops' line," as handled by Sophocles in the Oedipus trilogy, may be lifted into the realm of art, can any one deny? The sole question at issue is—has the transformation into art, the fusion of matter and expression, been accomplished in a manner sufficiently lofty so that the attitude toward the result may be one of utter detachment? This is the test, the sole test; and by this test must *Tamar* be judged.

Jeffers's *Tamar* was printed privately last year; it is now, for the first time, given to the public, together with the other poems of the volume including it in the title. Whether by design that it might serve as an introduction to *Tamar,* or whether it was as a mere bit of experimentation that Mr. Jeffers wrote a long dramatic poem, making use of a large part of Sophocles's material, he does not state. But the fact remains that *The Tower Beyond Tragedy* must, since Sophocles may everywhere be found in translation, completely disarm the possible censor of *Tamar.* In the latter poem, the scene of which is laid in California, the "curse" is in no wise remitted, and madness ultimately engulfs the house of Cauldwell as effectually as it engulfed the line of Pelops.

It will be unnecessary to follow in any detail the story of *Tamar*; suf-

*From a review subtitled "Thomas Hardy's Powers Undiminished—Robinson Jeffers Displays a Remarkable Gift" in the *New York Times Book Review,* 3 January 1926, 14, 24.

fice it to say that by the sheer power of his poetic inspiration and execution Jeffers has attained and maintained the degree of detachment requisite to the theme. In short, in this respect the poem is remarkable in that the narrative seems quite as legendary as the Greek story, while, at the same time, it is vividly in and of the present. Mr. Jeffers, although writing in what must be termed blank verse, in that it is without rhyme, has developed a line peculiarly his own. It is as long as the familiar Whitman line, but without the Whitman surge, which would have been totally unfitted to the purpose. It is a line not lending itself to pleasing setting within the narrow lateral confines of a newspaper column. Of different texture and, if anything, of even sharper projection, is the short introduction to the main theme, and this will be quoted:

> A night the half-moon was like a dancing-girl,
> No, like a drunkard's last half-dollar
> Shoved on the polished bar of the eastern hill-range,
> Young Cauldwell rode his pony along the sea-cliff;
> When she stopped, spurred; when she trembled, drove
> The teeth of the little jagged wheels so deep
> They tasted blood; the mare with four slim hooves
> On a foot of ground pivoted like a top,
> Jumped from the crumble of sod, went down, caught, slipped;
> Then, the quick frenzy finished, stiffening herself
> Slid with her drunken rider down the ledges,
> Shot from sheer rock and broke
> Her life out on the rounded tidal boulders.

This is not Mr. Jeffers's best verse by any means. But it has sufficed to indicate his great power of portrayal; and if it also indicates that the reader may expect no softening of realistic detail, it will have served still another useful purpose. If one desires to know what Jeffers can do in a more purely romantic way, this stanza, torn bodily from the middle of another long narrative piece, with its final verse that might have been by Swinburne, will give convincing evidence:

> And Nais, with laughter like the drippings of
> The little waxen chambers of wild bees:
> "O nicely! You are at ease
> In your nice fort of honor and know not love,
> You men, that is free wind on sweet wild seas."

Indeed, it may be questioned whether there is another poet writing in America today—or in England for that matter—who can, when he so desires, write in so indelible a fashion as the author of *Tamar.* Where, for instance, will this be matched? ". . . and surely her face / Grew lean and whitened like a mask, the lips/Thinned their rose to a split thread." Or, "And the sea moved, on the obscure bed of her eternity." Or, finally: looking down he saw "... the barn-roofs and the house roof / Like ships' keels in the cypress tops."

Robinson Jeffers is not a poet for the adolescent; he is not a poet for the Puritan; he is not a poet whose conception of poetry is confined to the honeyed lyric and to conventional themes. Our guess is that when Dr. Collins turns his light on *Roan Stallion, Tamar and Other Poems* he will find the writer a little out of bounds. But it was a theory of the ancient Greeks that genius was akin to madness; and perhaps it makes little difference which of the two words is placed first. To us it seems that there are in this book pages, many, many pages, which are equaled only by the very great.

Robinson Jeffers's Poetry

Edwin Seaver*

The appearance last Spring of *Tamar and Other Poems* announced an utterly new and vigorous voice in contemporary American poetry. Suddenly, out of obscurity, almost—one felt convinced—by divine right, Robinson Jeffers declared himself in the thin ranks of our major poets. It was as if America, having done with broken and muddled songs, with intellectualized escape and the wistful lyricism of children among machines, had conceived out of her instant need a poet lofty and rugged and imperturbable as the granite and cypresses among which he lived.

No one who had the opportunity to read Jeffers's first offering, privately published and launched unpretentiously into an indifferent *milieu,* no one, I think, can forget the thrill of discovery that heightened as page after page of *Tamar* revealed an overwhelmingly poetic imagination, a firm grasp of dramatic values, a profound seriousness, and a fecundity that danced at white heat through his "mighty line." It was an experience not soon to be forgotten. And this, not only because of the amazing poetry, but because here was the rare poet come among us who neither accepted nor rejected his America, but faced it for exactly what it was worth to him and used it as material for a more important end, for his visioned song.

Primitive—that was the word that best fitted Robinson Jeffers, as one who conceived form not as a mold into which the fluid substance is poured and from which it takes shape, but as that which *informs* the substance, which identifies it and makes it choate. Form as spirit, form as imagination, form as life force. By this mark the poems of Robinson Jeffers published last Spring announced their creator a true primitive.

*From the *Saturday Review of Literature* 2 (16 January 1926): 492. Reprinted by permission.

To these poems have been added a new dramatic poem, *Roan Stallion*, and more lyrics, the sum heightening the totality of confidence we felt unshaken after several readings of the earlier volume. Serener than *Tamar*, more definite in line and more economical in conception, *Roan Stallion* is a magnificent achievement. Only once does Jeffers depart from the intense objectivity of his narrative, and then it is to leap into a characteristically frenzied and dancing strophe:

Humanity is the
start of the race; I say
Humanity is the mould to break away from, the crust to break through,
the coal to break into fire,
The atom to be split.
Tragedy that breaks man's face and a white fire flies
out of it; vision that fools him
Out of his limits, desire that fools him out of his limits, unnatural crime,
inhuman science,
Slit eyes in the mask; wild loves that leap over the walls of nature, the
wild fence-vaulter science,
Useless intelligence of far stars, dim knowledge of the spinning demons
that makes an atom,
These break, these pierce, these deify, praising their God shrilly with
fierce voices: not in a man's shape
He approves the praise, he that walks lightning-naked on the Pacific,that
laces the suns with planets,
The heart of the atom with electrons: what is humanity in this cosmos?
For him, the last
Least taint of a trace in the dregs of the solution; for itself the mould to
break away from, the coal
To break into fire, the atom to be split.

This is the burden of all of Jeffers's song, over against "coldness and the tenor of a stone tranquility; slow life, the growth of trees and verse." This, and the knowledge that

all the arts lose virtue
Against the essential reality
Of creatures going about their business among the equally
Earnest elements of nature.

It is obvious from these and other lines that Robinson Jeffers is one of Walt Whitman's "poets to come" whom the earlier primitive hailed on the horizon, "expecting the main things" from them. But whereas Whitman sang of an advancing republic rejoicing in its youth, Jeffers faces a "perishing republic" from the heights of a tougher reality.

Power and Pomp

Harriet Monroe*

Tamar and all the final three-fifths of this book were exhaustively reviewed by James Daly in *Poetry* last August, so that the present writer need only record her hearty agreement with that review, her recognition of the "deep poetic compulsion" in Mr. Jeffers' usually distinguished art. All the more is it to be regretted that the title-poem of this larger book, if not 'prentice-work dug up and retouched, as I suspect, is of a quality quite unworthy of the author of *Tamar.* But it is doubtful whether even the most accomplished artistry would excuse the deliberate choice of so revolting a subject. Apparently Mr. Jeffers wanted to see how far he could go with himself and his newly acquired public; and we may be permitted to express a hope that the poet has now registered his final limit in a direction so repellant to modern taste.

Mr. Jeffers was brought up on classic literature, his father being a professor of Greek; therefore the class of subjects under discussion may come to his mind more naturally than to another's. But whereas to the Greek poet all the pagan energies of life were open ground for his spirit, ground almost sanctified by his myth-haunted religion, to a poet of our time and country it is impossible to explore certain jungles in the old simple and natural way. He has to force himself in; he is conscious of breathing noxious vapors in a dark melodrama of evil. The Greek audience accepted quite simply the horror as well as the beauty of its inherited myths; but the world has lived a number of centuries since then, and all the dark power of Mr. Jeffers cannot quite persuade us to swallow his modern tales of abnormal passion with the simple inherited faith of a more primitive time. The danger is that such a preoccupation may make his majestic art an anachronism, without vitality enough to endure.

In *The Tower Beyond Tragedy* the subject is appropriately Greek—the Clytemnestra story—and the poet's version, while too expansive, has passages of splendid eloquence, done in huge pounding rhythms like the Pacific at Carmel. Here are nine lines of Cassandra's despair:

> For me there is no mountain firm enough,
> The storms of light beating on the headlands,
> The storms of music undermine the mountains, they stumble and fall inward.
> Such music the stars
> Make in their courses, the vast vibration
> Plucks the iron heart of the earth like a harp-string.
> Iron and stone core, O stubborn axle of the earth, you also
> Dissolving in a little time like salt in water. . . .

*From *Poetry* 28 (June 1926): 160–64.

This Cassandra ranges over the centuries; her prophecies reach out to the day "when America has eaten Europe and takes tribute of Asia, when the ends of the world grow aware of each other."

One turns with relief to the shorter poems which follow these. Here we have a stern and stately beauty, the expression of a harsh loneliness of soul which has studied the world afar off as it communed with sea and mountains. Perhaps this brief one, "Joy," will suggest the sweep of this poet's imagination and the temper of his spirit; also his way of striking off vivid images in lines of mournful music:

Though joy is better than sorrow, joy is not great;
Peace is great, strength is great.
Not for joy the stars burn, not for joy the vulture
Spreads her gray sails on the air
Over the mountain; not for joy the worn mountain
Stands, while years like water
Trench his long sides. "I am neither mountain nor bird
Nor star; and I seek joy."
The weakness of your breed: yet at length quietness
Will cover those wistful eyes.

Not that Mr. Jeffers has been unobservant of passing events, or unpitiful of human agony. In "Woodrow Wilson," a dialogue between "It" and the hero's death-enfranchised soul, we have a really noble tribute, a high recognition of tragedy. Here are the first two of the eight stanzas:

It said "Come home, here is an end, a goal,
Not the one raced for, is it not better indeed? Victory you know requires
Force to sustain victory, the burden is never lightened, but final defeat
Buys peace: you have praised peace, peace without victory."

He said "It seems I am traveling no new way,
But leaving my great work unfinished how can I rest? I enjoyed a vision,
Endured betrayal, you must not ask me to endure final defeat,
Visionless men, blind hearts, blind mouths, live still."

I should like to quote lengthily from "Night," with its proud recognition of newly discovered immensities of space—

A few centuries
Gone by, was none dared not to people
The darkness beyond the stars with harps and habitations.
But now, dear is the truth. Life is grown sweeter and lonelier,
And death is no evil.

"The Torch-bearer's Race" shows man "at the world's end," where, all coasts and jungles explored, he is daring the air, "feet shaking earth off." But the poet reminds him:

In the glory of that your hawk's dream
Remember that the life of mankind is like the life of a man, a flutter from darkness to darkness
Across the bright hair of a fire.

Brooding on his rock over "the deep dark-shining Pacific," this poet has watched the course of stars and nations, and the music of his verse has acquired large rhythms. What he thinks of his own nation in its hour of splendor he tells in the poem "Shine, Perishing Republic," which may be quoted as of immediate interest, and representative of his art in one of its less detached moods:

While this America settles in the mould of its vulgarity, heavily thickening to empire,
And protest, only a bubble in the molten mass, pops and sighs out, and the mass hardens,

I sadly smiling remember that the flower fades to make fruit, the fruit rots to make earth.
Out of the mother; and through the spring exultances, ripeness and decadence; and home to the mother.

You making haste haste on decay: not blameworthy; life is good, be it stubbornly long or suddenly
A mortal splendor: meteors are not needed less than mountains: shine, perishing republic.

But for my children, I would have them keep their distance from the thickening center; corruption
Never has been compulsory, when the cities lie at the monster's feet there are left the mountains.

And boys, be in nothing so moderate as in love of man, a clever servant, insufferable master.
There is the trap that catches noblest spirits, that caught—they say—God, when he walked on earth.

A poet of extraordinary power is Mr. Jeffers, with perhaps a purple pride in the use of it.

The Women at Point Sur (1927)

First Glance

Mark Van Doren*

Greater attention has been paid, I fancy, to the astounding manner of Robinson Jeffers's poetry than to its still more astounding matter. It was, of course, natural that the critics of *Tamar* and *The Tower Beyond Tragedy* should speak chiefly of those long lines which on first inspection might seem to be the work of a loose writer yet which proved to be so tightly packed with explosive that only disciplined and courageous readers ever understood them all. But it is time, now that Mr. Jeffers has published a third long poem, *The Women at Point Sur*, to consider what it is he is saying. Floyd Dell did with some disgust consider the bearings of "The Tower Beyond Tragedy" in an issue of the *Modern Quarterly*—leaving, however, the last thing unsaid. Mr. Dell found Mr. Jeffers to be a hater of humanity, and charged the generation of readers which likes him with shell-shock. There is nothing social in Mr. Jeffers, said Mr. Dell. But there is, if society be taken to mean the company of all things that live—stones, worms, lightning, mountains, the Pacific Ocean, as well as men and women. And it is worth while to ask why Mr. Jeffers handles his men and women as he does.

He sees them not in themselves—which he says would be madness and which Mr. Dell implies would be the only sanity—but in their relation to the whole conscious universe. And this is how they strike him:

> . . . The old rock under the house, the hills with their hard roots and the
>   ocean hearted
> With sacred quietness from here to Asia
> Make me ashamed to speak of the active little bodies, the coupling
>   bodies, the misty brainfuls
> Of perplexed passion. Humanity is needless.

*From the *Nation* 125 (27 July 1927): 88. Reprinted by permission of The Nation Company, Inc.

Humanity, says Mr. Jeffers both in his last book and in this one, is "something to break away from." It is the starting-point of discoveries, something to make a bonfire of in the hope that something hard and perfect will be found in the ashes.

I say that if the mind centers on humanity
And is not dulled, but remains powerful enough to feel its own and the
    others, the mind will go mad.
. . . I will show you the face of God.
He is like a man that has an orchard, all the boughs from the river to the
    hill bending with abundance,
Apples like globes of sunset, apples like burnt gold from the broken
    mountain: . . . the man is a madman.
He has found a worm in one of the apples: he has turned from all the
    living orchard to love the white worm
That pricks one apple. I tell you . . . that God has gone mad . . . he has
    turned to love men.

No wonder, then, that the hero of the present poem, Dr. Barclay, runs crying from his pulpit to wander in the wilderness of the mountains and call upon mankind to burn, break, annihilate mankind.

. . . Annihilation, the beautiful
Word, the black crystal structure, prisms of black crystal
Arranged the one behind the other in the word
To catch a ray not of this world.

And no wonder that he can look with the disinterested eyes of a madman upon the perplexed passions of those about him—passions which lead to murder, incest, suicide, sadism, infanticide, adultery, lesbianism, and rape. All of these things Dr. Barclay sees with something like glory in his face—they are the bonfire; and all of them Mr. Jeffers shows us with a satisfaction that Mr. Dell would certainly call unsocial.

But there is no need of thundering against Mr. Jeffers. For in the first place he is a powerful poet and hears thunder naturally—thunder that we could not make if we tried. And in the second place his ideas carry their own death. If it is madness to consider humanity in itself, as doubtless it is, it is also madness to consider humanity out of itself. Mr. Jeffers thus far has found no way of resolving the great paradox. That he feels it so strongly is evidence of his quality as an artist. That he cannot get round it is evidence that he may, if he keeps on, give us poems we cannot bear to read. *The Women at Point Sur* is unbearable enough. I have read it with thrills of pleasure at its power and beauty, and I shall read everything else Mr. Jeffers writes. But I may be brought to wonder whether there is need of his trying further in this direction. He seems to be knocking his head to pieces against the night.

Again, Jeffers

Anonymous[*]

The story of a parson outgrowing his profession, turning bitterly on his congregation with the news that Christianity is outlived, that God has left his church and returned to the fire and whirlwind, is one that might, almost any day nowadays, provide a sensation for the outspoken U.S. press. Particularly if there were violent or sexual details would the public be served to surfeit, until a very real crisis in one man's life became a vulgar byword, grossly misinterpreted.

Poet Jeffers unfolds just such a story with the high seriousness of a prophetic pantheist. He follows the Rev. Dr. Barclay, a man of 50, from a deserted pulpit southward down the Pacific coast from Monterey. Common sanity is dropping from him like a cloak that he may carry or not. His spirit runs naked to the spirit of the hills, of the "iron wind" on the sea promontories. He will be possessed of a god beyond the old ethic, "good and evil."

The region around Point Sur is already crowded with psychic disturbances. While dry winds blew, followed by a night "striped with lightning" and a day of yellow floods, two boys crucified a hawk; their brother, a visionary, saw the Virgin walking on the sea, mountain tall, mourning her lover; a ranch girl fled to her man to slake her fear of death; the lighthouse keeper's daughter, Faith Heriot, went in a famine of unnatural love to Natalia Morhead, whose husband's act unsexed Faith Heriot two years before. Morhead is not back from the War. Faith nurses his crippled father under the old rooftree, moving about the house "like a restless fire." Natalia mistrusts everything but her child.

An unseen multitude surrounds Dr. Barclay approaching Point Sur—his disciples; minds at any distance aware of his power. The women at Point Sur,—even Maruca, the squat half-breed whom he uses as deliverance from a 15-year chastity—vaguely understand his announcements: "God thinks through action. . . . Nothing you can do is wicked."

His complete deliverance lies through an act for normal men the most unthinkable. When his young daughter, April, comes to Point Sur to fetch him for her mother, he forces her, passing through incest to the full exaltation of godhood.

People follow him into the mountain, their camp-fires lighting weird scenes of license and ecstasy. He moves above them, brooding on the dark ridges. There is an earthquake.

Down at the house, Morhead returns, made more bestial by War. The women are drawn to the God, "the black maypole," on the mountain, which now is scourged to the north by fire from the camps. Natalia smothers her child to preserve its innocence. April, informed with her

[*]From *Time*, 1 August 1927, 31–32.

dead brother's spirit, smuggles out a pistol to kill her father but quails at sight of him, shoots herself instead. He roams back into the burnt hills, fasting, escaped from human automatisms, inexhaustible, thirsting to create. . . .

The significance of Robinson Jeffers as a poet is, by critical consensus, that of one to rank with the greatest poets of all generations. Homer and Sophocles have not been held too lofty comparisons for him—yet he remains distinctly a product of this continent. Inhuman in his intensity—he says "Humanity is needless"; calls men "the apes that walk like herons"—he repels people who seek comfort in poetry. He takes the race as a starting point—". . . the coal to kindle,/The blind mask crying to be slit with eye-holes—" and seeks tracks for its life force to reunite with the cosmic force of the impersonal universe, in "the hollow darkness outside the stars and the dark hollow in the atom."

The nerves of his writing are taut under elemental strains—the strain of the Pacific against its granite boundaries, of a mountainous coast verging on earthquake, of oil tanks about to explode and consume themselves, of brains splitting with a daemon. His greatest word is

> . . . Annihilation, the beautiful
> Word, the black crystal structure, prisms of black crystal
> Arranged the one behind the other in the word
> To catch a ray not of this world.

Like all poets, he finds language inadequate; is forced back upon "match-ends of burnt experience human enough to be understood." But from his match-ends he extracts white heat, terrific convulsions, monstrous images, without more linguistic violence than a harsh ellipsis and radical translations of character. He pictures "the coast hills, thinking the thing out to conclusion." The strata of the continental fault are ". . . tortured and twisted/Layer under layer like tetanus, like the muscles of a mountain bear that has gorged the strychnine." The sun is "the day's eyeball," and elsewhere, "The yellow dog barking in the blue pasture,/ Snapping sidewise."

The Poet

Born in Pittsburgh, 40 years ago, he was schooled in Europe until 15. His parents moved to California where he studied medicine at various universities but never with the deep interest he had in poetry. His early work, *Californians,* is of a surprisingly flat, "native son" variety.

He married Una Call Kuster in 1913. They have twin boys. Lean, athletic, needing solitude, he built a house of sea-boulders on a headland near Carmel, Calif. Falcons nested in his tower of "hawk-perch" stones. Some years ago he offered *Tamar and Other Poems* to Manhattan publishers but only an obscure Irish printer, Peter G. Boyle, would risk handling such inflammable material as a tragedy of incest (*Time,* March 30, 1925). Reviews soon brought him to a notice for which he has small regard but which must become, despite the book world's busy piddlings, nationwide and perpetual.

"Or What's a Heaven For?"

Babette Deutsch*

The work of Robinson Jeffers is striped with diverse colors: the tawny and saffron and blue burning of the stars; the savage rust of ancient bloodstains on one crawling planet; the bitter green of scorn; the protean fires nesting in that most dazzling crystal—imagination. He is possessed by the apparently interminable tragedy enacted by the human race. He struggles to wrench his eyes from that spectacle. He leaps into a surge of perverse passions as though to cleanse himself from the scurf bred by stale decencies. He shakes those waters from him and is off again, a panting hound of Heaven. His latest book—a lengthy narrative poem—shows him in this guise more clearly than his earlier work.

Its theme is the struggle of a man toward godhood. The man is a broken old minister, who lost his son in the War, and lost his faith thereafter—a half-crazed man groping for the ultimate reality, and dreaming he will find it by committing some monstrous act. The questions old Dr. Barclay wrestles with when he first wanders off from his pulpit are the questions that torment every mind in those hours when the soul plumbs its own ignorance: Is there any spirit of the universe? Is there one life informing the whole? ". . . is anything left after we die but worm's meat?" ". . . how should men live?" The old man comes to believe that God is taking possession of his own withered flesh. But questions continue to boil up in him—there is no peace in this Power. What are God's thoughts but action? How lay hold on God save by becoming Him? How contain Him save by passing beyond good and evil? Barclay roams the Pacific coastal hills, gathering his disciples, preaching the God who is to overthrow the limited moralities of thousands of years. He infects the unhappy ignorant wretches about him with strange lusts and queer dreams. He utters terrible prophecies. He commits incest with his virginal young daughter. He ends his uncertain pilgrimage at the mouth of a dead coal-mine, muttering through baked lips at the last: "I want creation. The wind over the desert/Has turned and I will build again all that's gone down./I am inexhaustible." Certainly Jeffers never handled a richer subject. Even thus barely outlined, it presents, to those who know the poet's stride, an intimation of magnificent achievement. And yet, for all the metaphysical

*From the *New Republic* 51 (17 August 1927): 341. Reprinted by permission.

meat of its content, for all the lightning-like visions which streak certain passages with a glory, the poem leaves one with the feeling of having witnessed a Pyrrhic victory. Its profundities are too often obscure. Its drama is moiled with an irrelevant sordidness. There are too many persons, too many conflicts, that seem to have no organic relation to the whole. It is not sufficiently stripped and bare.

The author's power is unquestionable. Perhaps because his reach is enormous, it has exceeded, for once, his grasp. He has the large allusiveness, the shining plunges, the strenuous beauty, that are possible only to a searching, supple, tough-fibered mentality. What is lacking here is a sterner self-discipline, a more reticent expressiveness. Then might pity flower out of horror. Then might a hard grain of wisdom be left in the clenched fist of desperation.

The Deliberate Annihilation

Genevieve Taggard*

Most artists show their work to the world a little before it begins to die. The work flowers, and then the death that lies curled at the center cuts the stem's structure and we see the slow withering. Robinson Jeffers we discovered late, because he discovered himself late. The terrific death he is now experiencing is our only knowledge of him. What he was like before destruction overtook him we cannot very well know. His power is gigantic, but now it is consumed in death-lashings. Was there power in him before these acute death pangs? That is hard to tell. Birth and death, for him, seem to be almost simultaneous.

This has happened before in other lives, but perhaps never in such a dramatic manner in such a poet. John Keats, facing physical annihilation, wrote his great odes with all the force of life meeting death, in clear realization of his extremity: "knowing I must die/Like a sick eagle looking at the sky."

Jeffers used the metaphor of the crucified hawk. The difference is a telling one. For what has happened to Jeffers is not physical death, but a deliberate celebration in the service and worship of cruelty. All this he knows; he himself announces it.

Perhaps the story of the long poem will explain what would otherwise seem an unnecessarily morbid opinion of this poet. For it is Robinson Jeffers that will interest the world, not Robinson Jeffers's poetry. That is saying, as simply as possible, that his work has failed. His poems will interest us in the future chiefly by being related to him. Poetry that has been given a life of its own allows the poet himself only a secondary glory.

*From the *New York Herald Tribune Books*, 28 August 1927, 3. I. H. T. Corporation. Reprinted by permission.

Jeffers's poetry keeps relating itself back to him, and yet—so intricate and troubled is the connection—we only care to sit out the tragedy of the man because his work, in its stupendous wreckage, suggests something that might have been supreme.

This poem, a volume in length, tells, as did the three others in a previous volume, the story of human beings who break what Jeffers calls the mold of humanity. By incest, murder, rape, adultery and animal worship they shatter their innate human lawfulness and escape into chaos, the new world. Spirits of the past and the unseen, unborn multitudes of the future assist at this horrid surgery, cutting the unborn soul of the Jeffers superman from the body of our time.

> But why should I make fables again? There are many
> Tellers of tales to delight women and the people.
> I have no vocation. The old rock under the house, the hills with their hard
>   roots and the ocean hearted
> With sacred quietness from here to Asia
> Make me ashamed to speak of the active little bodies, the coupling
>   bodies, the misty brainfuls
> Of perplexed passion. Humanity is needless.
> I said: "Humanity is the start of the race, the gate to break away from, the
>   coal to kindle,
> The blind mask crying to be slit with eyeholes."
> Well, now it is done, the mask slit, the rag burnt, the starting-post left
>   behind: but not in a fable.
> Culture's outlived, art's root-cut, discovery's
> The way to walk in. Only remains to invent the language to tell it.
>   Match-ends of burnt experience
> Human enough to be understood,
> Scraps and metaphors will serve. The wine was a little too strong for the
>   new wine skins. . . .

All this was implicit before. But now there is no mistaking the new philosophy. *Roan Stallion*, *Tamar*, and *The Tower Beyond Tragedy* left us wondering at the symbols of terror. Our questions are answered in *Women at Point Sur*, in the language of Friedrich Nietzsche—a ridiculous, belated second flowering of *Thus Spake Zarathustra*. But this time, instead of objective men and women who play out the parts assigned them, Jeffers gives us a minister of the gospel, who preaches outright a philosophy only half uttered before. The poem is often realistically dull—is dull as *Main Street*. . . . "*Human enough to be understood.*"

All the novelists were playing with this theme a decade ago. The Rev. Dr. Barclay, who has just lost his young son in the great war, faces his congregation one Sunday morning and declares that for years he has been preaching lies. Then he announces his intention to create a new religion.

So far very like Upton Sinclair or Harold Frederick, Barclay leaves his daughter and wife, and goes to a farm near Point Lobos (the pantheistic hero of all Jeffers's work), and here he elaborates his vision. A woman with a young child, called Nathalia; her husband, Edward, a returned soldier; the strange Faith Heriot, who is in love with Nathalia, and companion to her father-in-law; an Indian servant, and eventually Barclay's daughter, April, and his wife, Audis, all become either his unwilling disciples, or fall under his lust of destruction after murdering the child and desecrating each other. Barclay has succeeded in the necessary act of assaulting his daughter—an act that breaks, as he terms it, the last remaining fetter in his mind, and makes him God. April, possessed by the spirit of her dead brother, goes to avenge her wrong of Barclay, and cannot.

Of such terrific nonsense is this poem made.

Jeffers is a better poet than his minister. Hardly a line worth remembering comes from Barclay's mouth. His attempts at superlative mysticism are vapid: hardly any one living could succeed in writing as badly. We may conclude, therefore, that Jeffers does not entirely feel or believe what he is trying to profess. The great passages in this book hang on the thread of the philosophy only as if the meaning were invented in order to give the poet cause for dwelling on his old obsessions—repeated almost literally in each succeeding poem. Nearly always the highest attainment of his verse comes with the description of cruelty. The crucified hawk on the barn wall is marvelous and unforgettable. The terrible language of the returned husband to his wife; the words of that embodiment of hate, Faith Heriot; the description of Nathalia opening and shutting the dresser drawers after she has killed her child, and the loud weeping of Edward when he finds what she has done, are all passages that justify themselves. The philosophy cannot justify them.

Jeffers's work is called by our contemporary critics Greek in its spirit. But incest and murderous love and fires set by maniacs do not make, of themselves, Greek dramas. Jeffers has now the perverse opposite of the Greek mind which sought to show, in its tragedies, the essential order and justice of the universe. In this emotional conviction lies the exultation and serene resignation of the tragedies.

Here is the annihilation of Robinson Jeffers. After a long search for the secret of his failure I come to a very insistent and simple conclusion. An artist performs one office only, no matter what his philosophy or his feeling—he fulfills his reader. Jeffers has this impulse, which, if it were left pure, would make him an enormous figure in our literature. But unhappily for us, another stronger and more ferocious impulse overtakes the first. Underlying all that he writes, Jeffers has more strongly the desire to withhold fulfillment from his reader, to give him pain only, a desire that comes from the same source that compels his preoccupation with cruelty. Jeffers's apologia for having written this poem lies in the prelude. In place of the crucified hawk, he offers himself. "It is necessary for someone to be fastened with nails,/And Jew-beak died in the night. Jew-beak is dead."

This is his attempt to stand in the relation of artist to his people. He offers not healing, but himself . . . at the same time imagining that he has transcended the conceptions of Christianity!

The world is probably not as sick as Jeffers feels it to be. If it were sick enough to accept Jeffers, it could hardly live long enough to do so.

Jeffers Denies Us Twice

H. L. Davis*

The most splendid poetry of my time. Nothing written by this generation can begin to come up with it. Every page—every line, even—is a triumph. I can not praise it more than it deserves. And yet—the poem itself is dead, as lifeless as a page of Euclid.

It moves to an end too determinedly, hammering with feverish energy to drive home to the hilt a truth which was clearly predicated in the first five pages. In that respect, it behaves too much like life, which sometimes overwhelms us with signs, evidences and iterations of a truth that we were entirely ready to agree with in the first place. To create a poem, then, it is necessary to do more than write great poetry; and more than that Jeffers has not done.

The Rev. Dr. Barclay, the chief figure of the book, has outgrown his profession. He confesses that he has been feeding his congregation upon false doctrine; this confession, and a life ensuing of honest doubt and ignorance, would be atonement sufficient for most men to undertake, but not for Dr. Barclay. He has worn authority too long to feel content without it. He gives up imparting false doctrine, only in the ambition of finding the true. He determines to find out the very God in all His secret ways, and considers that he has vacated his authority only until such time as he can claim it by a tenure that will satisfy his own conscience.

The thesis of the book is that no man can find out the very God. No man is strong enough to endure such knowledge. Sanity will give way first. It does give way, and Dr. Barclay plunges to destruction.

The proof is weakened by the reader's perception that Dr. Barclay is, even at the beginning of the book, a feeble egotistical man with bad nerves. The daring of his thought is not courage but desperation, the desperation of a self-distrusting egotism; his destruction is inherent, not in the poem, but in the character that the man had before the poem found him. He is the dupe of even his own learning. Clutching at the profound and terrible under-theme of the Oedipus legend—that he who violates the laws of Nature may fathom her secrets—he commits rape upon his

*From *Poetry* 31 (February 1928): 274–79. Copyrighted by The Modern Poetry Association and reprinted by permission of the Editor of *Poetry*.

daughter, has not got the strength for self-escape or self-annihilation, and dies raving and insane in the mountains; the victim, actually, so far as I am able to judge, of a bad conscience.

But so is everybody else in the poem. There are two women, perverts to Lesbianism, one of whom succeeds in nagging the other into insanity, child-murder and attempted suicide. The outrage of being violated leads Dr. Barclay's daughter into a delirium of hallucinations and to suicide. They have all followed the Oedipean formula; they have all traversed, in one way or another, the laws of Nature, and taken the first step toward a new knowledge, a new law, a new God. But consciousness of having transgressed prevents them from getting any nearer. The consciousness of guilt blinds them to the new perception of truth, and none of them is strong enough—or sensible enough, for that matter —to get rid of it.

"The new wine," the poet warns us, "was too strong . . ." Surely it needed no very hard vintage to destroy these neurotic, hysterical, egomaniacal creatures, cruelly oversexed or overstaled, incapable of even the show of pity or sympathy for anybody but themselves. It may take a tougher breed than humanity makes nowadays to follow Oedipus, but certainly humanity breeds tougher than these, whose weakness must have marked them for destruction long before the beginning of the poem.

I wish that Jeffers had made his poem begin at the beginning of their puniness and unfitness to live in the world. Probably he could not. Every writer must begin a story at the place which suits him best; and this, his beginning, would not have been mine. Stories have actually neither beginning nor end. Every story is like a river; it began flowing with the beginning of the world, and it will not cease till the world comes to an end. I don't doubt in the least that the story of Oedipus is still going on, somewhere, at this very moment.

Jeffers chose to enter this river in this place, and I wish he had explored a little distance upstream.

I have done the story an injustice in telling it. In this poetry it seems inevitable, sombre, swift, menacing. Make no mistake about the poetry; these years have never seen better than this, with its depth and beauty and barbaric splendor. There are no prose passages, there is no flagging, no marking time. Every page—every line of every page—is a triumph.

> 'The April-eyed, the daughter . . .
> And the honey of God,
> Walks like a maiden between the hills and high waters,
> She lays her hand passing on the high rock at Point Sur,
> The petals of her fingers
> Curve on the black rock's head, the lighthouse with lilies
> Covered, the lightkeepers made drunken like bees
> With her hand's fragrance. . . .'

I might have opened the book anywhere, it would be equally beautiful. Every page transfixes the splendor of its incident, and the amazement and terror. Nothing is left half-fused after this lightning, nothing is incompletely grasped, nothing fumbled over. This is poetry as we dream of poetry, the beat and strain of life, the dazzle of inhuman light and the blindness of inhuman darkness. I think of the choruses of Euripides when I read these lines:

> I say that if the mind centers on humanity
> And is not dulled, but remains powerful enough to feel its own and the others, the mind will go mad.
> It is needful to remember the stone and the ocean, without the hills over the house no endurance,
> Without the domed hills and the night. Not for quietness, not peace;
> They are moved in their times. Not for repose; they are more strained than the mind of a man; tortured and twisted
> Layer under layer like tetanus, like the muscles of a mountain bear that has gorged the strychnine
> With the meat bait: but under their dead agonies, under the nightmare pressure, the living mountain
> Dreams exaltation. . . .

If this be any less perfect than the choral poetry of Euripides, I can not see how. I think that it is as perfect, as amply weighted, as moving and as majestic. What it lacks, and what, more noticeably, the poem and the poet himself lacks, is Euripides' humanity, his fierce tenderness, his pity and concern for suffering, for helplessness; and his implacable hatred of cruelty and indifference and injustice, which make the bitterest and most strident of his plays a human passion of accusation against wrong. I can not feel any human passion back of this book's conception. It is a design working out a truth. The details, shocking and hideous and shameful as they appear in the poem, seem to have no purpose except to furnish verisimilitude. They are brutal enough. One must go back to Dante's Ugolino for their equal in lust, for details of hideous and abnormal brutality. But Dante's scene rages with pain over the wilful deformity of his own kind; and Dante could pass from this vengeful cruelty to the deepest and simplest pity—saying to Brunetto Latini in the circle of the perverts, "*non dispetto, ma doglia.*" Not scorn, but sorrow.

Of this, *The Women at Point Sur* has nothing. I can see, in its creation, nothing generous, no greatness of sympathy or indignation, only the will to accomplish a design of accumulated and desperate emotions. It appears to me, in looking back, that Jeffers has given his account of human terror and jealousy and selfishness, vice and foulness and weakness, as having wished to divorce his mind from these and all things human, and see them only as incidents in the procession of planets, no more to be ignored than they, and no more to be pitied. But they *are* to be pitied. The poet is not as the planets are, but human; and to forget that is to be a renegade.

The great poem will be an act of love, neither ignoring nor despising our frailties, but pitying us and them.

We need it.

Cawdor and Other Poems (1928)

A Major Poet

Anne Singleton*

The themes of tragedy, in spite of our timidity, have no enduring substance. They become charming, or insane, or untenable, but they do not remain tragic. The human lamb slain for the passover of the world, the terror of personal death, what are these now but lovely traditional melancholies, aureoled with poetry, their tragedy superseded? The Greek theme, too, the insignificance of man against his doom, has no longer its tragic elevation; it is the routine level upon which our mental life is lived, and it will not give the "catharsis by pity and terror," which Aristotle knew. Tragedy for an adult modern generation does not lie in these themes, and when they are used, as in a play of O'Neill's or a narrative poem of Robinson's, they draw from us the sober recognition that this is indeed the true gait of human affairs, but it is no longer a question of the old experience of catharsis. Tragedy tends to become the mere conceptual opposite of comedy, not an experience at all; and our true bent seems all on the side of Proust's absorbed dexterity with the scalpel, or D. H. Lawrence's romantic obsessions.

Since the publication, some four years ago, of Robinson Jeffers's *Tamar*, we have known what had been withheld before. From first to last Robinson Jeffers turns up with his verse the fresh earth of experienced tragedy, the stuff of reality that *Oedipus Rex* must have had in it when the material it was made of was still alive and compelling in men's minds. He has dealt not with the old gentle themes but with new ones that are well-nigh unbearable reading; with love that mocks its object, with passion for understanding that breaks the mind and degrades the soul, with humanity caught in a net of desire "all matted in one mesh."

He has two passionate themes: one, the hymn to annihilation, to "death the redeemer"; the other the indictment of our needless humanity, "the coal to kindle, the blind mask crying to be slit with eye-holes." The first breaks through in all the poems in flashes of lyric relief and is always the background of his thinking. The second is the foreground theme

*From the *New York Herald Tribune Books*, 23 December 1928, 5. I. H. T. Corporation. Reprinted by permission.

in all his longer poems. He has belabored it, he has driven it home by violence upon violence. His imagination flinches before the indecent intimacy of living, and he has clothed it again and again in the figure of incest; he is repelled by the intrusion of the dead past upon the living present, and he makes of it a scene of defilement.

In *Cawdor* for the first time in his long poems he has laid aside such aids as he has drawn for themes of abnormalities. There are in this poem no variations upon incest or upon perversions. It is the story of the worse than orphaned girl who escapes the forest fire with her burned and blinded father. After she has married the rancher who harbored them, she is inflamed with love for his unawakened and "somewhat earthfast" son. The story does not turn on the consummations of love, but on the passionate acts of death and the mock of the living.

It is not necessary to rank *Cawdor* among Jeffers's other long poems. It is of similar metal, though he has denied himself any material that does not lie to hand in normal living. His necessary preoccupation is still that of *Roan Stallion*, of *Tamar*, of *The Tower Beyond Tragedy*, of *The Women at Point Sur*. What is this preoccupation? It is certainly not that of the wracked soul who has found nothing but horror in the universe. Jeffers has been criticized for his wilful belaboring of violence, but to understand him it is essential to see that it is a chosen violence. For him as for the Rev. Barclay, it is "too easy to be at peace, quieting the mind." Quiet is his first and greatest repudiation. Those who are quiet "die blind, die ignorant"; they are the doomed.

> Tragedy that breaks man's face and a white fire flies out of it; vision that fools him
> Out of his limits, desire that fools him out of his limits, unnatural crime, inhuman science . . .
> These break, these pierce, these deify, praising their God shrilly with fierce voices.

It is the idea back of the fable of Oedipus: he that transgresses the laws of nature shall know of her secrets. But it derives somewhat differently. In Robinson Jeffers for the first time in great literature supreme validity is given to the passionate demand of the creative artist who fears quiet more than pain, more than degradation, who has known the terrible lapses of inspiration and would choose agony rather than quiet. It is this passionate demand that is substituted for any moral principle that divides between good and evil, between praise and contempt. The peculiar violence of Jeffers's treatment arises from this very fact that with him the artist's demand for intensification is the demand of all living, and he embodies this cry for violence in men and women who use it not in any creative activity but in life itself. It turns and rends them. They are burned with the burning house, broken at the foot of the precipice. Nevertheless Jeffers gives to their violence the same interpretation he would give to the violence of the creative artist; here only is there hope, where life "drinks her defeat and devours her famine for food." To understand this identification is to understand what is so often misunderstood—that the pitilessness of Robinson Jeffers's themes is not a scorn of human suffering, a demoniacal aloofness. It is one way of reaching the future, of honoring life: "A torch to burn in with pride, a necessary/Ecstasy in the run of the cold substance,/And scape-goat of the greater world."

It seems to me that here Robinson Jeffers is writing the most powerful, the most challenging poetry of this generation. Poems like "To a Young Artist" in this volume, and some of those printed in the 1928 "Miscellany" and not yet included in his volumes, focus in small compass the incredible strength and sureness of the poet and reach an intensity not touched elsewhere in modern verse. It would be an impertinence to predict where he is going. He has the strength.

Unpacking Hearts with Words

Conrad Aiken*

There is only one thing to be said in favor of the "group review" of books of verse, especially when the group is as miscellaneous as the present one; and that is the fact that nothing can be so well calculated to sharpen anew one's sense of the predicament which any contemporary poet must face. Here are these five poets—Mr. Robinson, Mr. Jeffers, Mr. Coppard, Mr. Sandburg and Mr. MacLeish; and their very dissimilarity, which is striking, suggests, a good deal, that the contemporary poet is in a sense a lost man. Tradition, which in other ages was precise and dictatorial, is now overwhelmingly complex. Which, of all the traditions he inherits, shall our poet obey? Or shall he endeavor to combine several of them, and of the combination to make something new?

The situation is a difficult one, at best; and one is aware of the difficulty when one reads these five volumes of verse. They are all of them good books, very much above the average. But one feels of all of them that they lack that ultimate power and directness and rootedness which seems, unfortunately, to accrue only to those works which are produced at a time when tradition is great and single and even, perhaps, *simple.* That these five poets feel the *need* of some such sustaining certainty and simplicity is at once obvious. . . .

Robinson Jeffers is a remarkable poet: there is no dodging that fact. One may not like him; one may feel him to be uncouth, overstrained, hyperbolic, too laboriously and unintermittently violent; but of his power there can be no question. Is he, too, lost? He has evidently been at pains

*Excerpted from *Bookman* 68 (January 1929): 576–77.

to transplant Sophocles to California; and the effect is a little queer. His consequent grandeurs become at times, unfortunately, a little grandiose; his tragedies lie too close to the horrible; attempting the stark and awful, he too often, like D. H. Lawrence, revels in the merely and rawly abnormal, and with a kind of cruelty; his poems are always bloodshot. But his new poem, *Cawdor*, a kind of nightmare novel in a loose prose-verse (like a semi-prose semi-verse translation from the Greek) is, for all its monstrosities and absurdities and excessive use of symbolism—his wounded eagles and shot lions—a very impressive thing. His people are vivid, psychologically true. If at the outset one feels an extraordinary unreality in the whole affair, disbelieves in these farmer folk who talk like Clytemnestra at one moment and like a Henry James or Dostoevski character the next, one soon finds oneself being swept off one's feet by the sheer force of Mr. Jeffers' creative power. He seems to be developing something of Dostoevski's ability to take one bodily into an unreal world so unified and consistent and apprehensible that one ends by believing it against one's will. That is a rare kind of power: if only Mr. Jeffers can hold himself down a little, be a shade less drastically and humorlessly melodramatic, one feels that he might give us something pretty astonishing. Even so, *Cawdor* is a fine thing, despite its bad lapses. He is a poet to be watched enviously by his fellows.

The Problem of Tragedy

Morton Dauwen Zabel*

The theme of Robinson Jeffers' new poem is the tragedy of a woman who meets the passion and selfish pride of men on their own terms, but finds herself the victim of an unimagined lust whose end comes only with the hideous defeat of those who caused her own humiliation. Even this curt summary is sufficient to indicate that *Cawdor* shares with *Tamar*, *Roan Stallion*, and *The Women at Point Sur* those properties of tragic violence and broad dramatic conflict which we have come to regard as this poet's particular marks. The sensitiveness to all the forces of ancient terror, the infinite pathos of human blindness and vanity, and the strange unerring ways of biological and psychological life—these came out in that first obscure volume which gave us, five years ago, a new and remarkable writer. Since then it has become customary to think of Mr. Jeffers as the only one of our contemporary artists who has plunged bravely into the darkest waters of experience and found there the incalculable tides and currents which the Greeks tried to fathom. The comparison with Euripides has been inevitable, not only because of the subject-matter of

*From *Poetry* 33 (March 1929): 336–40. Copyrighted by the Modern Poetry Association and reprinted by permission of the Editor of *Poetry*.

these narratives, but also because of their style. And critics have even found occasion to point out the essential dissimilarity of Mr. Jeffers' work to that of the Greeks: its lack of real penetration, its barren spirit, its dearth of the pity which an instinct for scientific curiosity has denied him. Meanwhile Mr. Jeffers continues to write, probably quite uninfluenced by the mandates of his readers and eager to complete a body of work which he outlined long ago and determined to see to its end.

It is not necessary to deny his work the truth and beauty which it unquestionably has. Any individual reader may fail to discover here a genuine reality, but that after all remains the failure of the individual reader. When work shows, as this does, ringing eloquence combined with a passionate search for honor, we are quite safe in crediting the author with some of the final attributes of genius. His shortcomings are to be credited largely to an age which has disestablished many of the relationships and laws whereby it was possible for former generations to think of life in terms of noble pity and grief. The very factors which make it possible for Mr. Jeffers to stand apart from our huge cities, our political warfare and our industrial vanity allow him to indulge in a kind of oracular aloofness. The disclosures of science have armed him with a seer-like omnipotence from which he looks down on the swarming efforts of man. He is not one of the struggling millions, like Sandburg or our other city poets. He is no road-side humanitarian, like Frost. Therefore he scorns to extend the hand of compassion to his creatures; he allows them to murder, to blind themselves, to wound and mutilate their bodies, and to break their fearful hearts.

When, in the course of his mounting drama, he stops to comment, it is with an almost disinterested candor:

> The nerves of man after they die dream dimly
> And dwindle into their peace; they are not very passionate,
> And what they had was mostly spent while they lived.
> They are sieves for leaking desire; they have many pleasures
> And conversations; their dreams too are like that.

Or, translating science into a more fantastic imagery, he speaks with the calm demeanor of a laboratory worker:

> In their deaths they dream a moment, the unspent chemistry
> Of life resolving its powers; some in the cold star-gleam,
> Some in the cooling darkness in the crushed skull.
> But shine and shade were indifferent to them, their dreams
> Determined by temperatures, access of air,
> Wetness or drying, as the work of the autolytic
> Enzymes of the last hunger hasted or failed.

The mistake behind this lies in the fact that, instead of writing poetry wholly in the spirit of modern reason and logic, he has endeavored to combine these factors with antique dramaturgy. His obsession for heroic violence and the grand passion of the Greeks furnishes him with wild and massive themes, and the comments of science seem very weak and puny in the midst of them. He wrote one masterpiece, *The Tower Beyond Tragedy.* The lesson in singleness of motive there presented has not served him very faithfully.

But *Cawdor* has passages of magnificence not often found in poetry today. Some of the early pictures of the Pacific coast and the redwood forests, the sweeping fires and gaunt ranges, are unforgettable. Where the ocean beats on the rocks three people hunt for sea-food:

> They went to the waste of the ebb under the cliff,
> Stone wilderness furred with dishevelled weed, but under each round
> black-shouldered stone universes
> Of color and life, scarlet and green sea-lichens, violet and rose anemones,
> wave-purple urchins,
> Red starfish, tentacle-rayed pomegranate-color sun-disks, shelled worms
> tuft-headed with astonishing
> Flower-spray, pools of live crystal, quick eels plunged in the crevices. . . .

And, since this is a narrative poem, it must be said that few others of our time can compare with it for technical skill. The interest is consistent, the movement certain, and the shaping coherent. The characters of Fera Martial and Cawdor suffer because they are charged with too much purpose and too futile a passion; but the girl Michal and the inviolate brother Hood are alive with sympathy, and the minor figures have much variety and picturesque charm. Certain details are worked out with a sure touch. At one point Fera goes dizzy:

> She felt
> Her knees failing, and a sharp languor
> Melt through her body; she saw the candle-flame (she had set the candle
> on the little table) circling
> In a short orbit, and Cawdor's face waver, strange heavy face with the
> drooping brows and confused eyes. . . .

And many incidents are amazingly sharp in definition.

There are shorter poems in this book, notably a fine elegy on George Sterling, which aid in showing Mr. Jeffers' complete mastery of his instrument. His line may often be regular blank-verse, but it can swell into a full diapason of great power.

Dear Judas and Other Poems (1929)

Poet or Prophet?

Rolfe Humphries*

Once mysticism takes full possession of him, you are likely to have a spoiled artist on your hands. Not that the mystic experience is without value—it expands and clears the vision, exalts the sense; but the value is also the danger. Where everything is seen as one, it is difficult for anything to be either omitted or created. Your mystic artist sees himself as one with Nature, and that is very good for his vision of Nature; he sees himself as one with God, and that is just too bad for his vision of man.

Such considerations are applicable to the work of Robinson Jeffers, whose latest book, *Dear Judas,* is undoubtedly the most spectacular event of the poetic year. "Mystic" has been written of Mr. Jeffers, by his admiring friends, as a term of high praise, without careful inquiry into its critical value. This is, of course, natural, for the strength of Mr. Jeffers hits you between the eyes. No one can deny his tremendous power, his unique manner, the compulsive force of his narratives, his accurate, sensuous, poetic vision of the lonely acres about his home. His weaknesses come from the same source as his strength and they are almost equally formidable—a laxity of language; a proclivity for talking symbol, not sense; a scant artistic ruthlessness, particularly in knowing what to leave out; a romanticism gone somewhat rank; an inability to project character, or too loose an ability to project himself.

Two long poems make up most of his new book. One, writes the author, "is a species of passion play, called *Dear Judas.* It seems to me to present, in a somewhat new dramatic form, new and probable explanations of the mystical characters and acts of its protagonists." Such a play as might be staged in semi-darkness, one imagines, with the face of Lazarus blue against emptiness; and the trouble is that it seems to be felt in semi-darkness, too. Blacking out background, Mr. Jeffers denies himself the use of that skill which is his chief excellence, and neither ideas nor characters fully emerge from the pall that hangs over Jerusalem.

A scrap or two of random evidence indicate that the author cares less

*Reprinted from the *New Republic* 61 (15 January 1930): 228–29.

for *Dear Judas* than for *The Loving Shepherdess.* The second poem is indeed more readable than the first, more impressive, more pathetic, more substantial; there is an extraordinary vividness about the scene in which the action occurs. In the light from that landscape, so pervading detail with reality, only steady scrutiny discovers what the running glance is likely never to see—that the characters who come and go are not real at all, are probably not meant to be. Like most of his kind, Mr. Jeffers loves Nature more than he loves humanity; people he can suffer only as creations of his own, projections of himself; or he sets symbols stalking in human guise. Impose such persons on very Californian hills, and unity is violated. But Mr. Jeffers is no respecter of unities. Even in seeing Nature, he looks at a thing the Greek way, and the next minute, without shifting his gaze, the Celtic way also. His sense of unity is so peculiar to himself and so rich that it beggars the classical conventions.

The loving shepherdess, Clare Walker, is a sort of female Jesus, "a saint . . . going up to a natural martyrdom, aureoled with such embellishments as the mind of the time permits." She is sweeter than Tamar, California, Fera, the women at Point Sur, but she is really very much like them. They are all doom-bent, mad in Scorpio; all of them have something wrong with their secrets. They are martyrs not only to the compulsion of their own nature, but also to the need of their creator's philosophy; they seem designed, like caryatids, to support its burden. This philosophy, implicit always in the longer narratives, is explicit and recurrent in the lyrics:

> Mourning the broken balance, the hopeless prostration of the earth
> Under men's hands and their minds,
> The beautiful places killed like rabbits to make a city,
> The spreading fungus, the slime-threads
> And spores; my own coast's obscene future: I remember the farther
> Future, and the last man dying
> Without succession under the confident eyes of the stars.
> It was only a moment's accident,
> The race that plagued us; the world resumes the old lonely immortal
> Splendor; from here I can even
> Perceive that that snuffed candle had something . . . a fantastic virtue,
> A faint and unshapely pathos . . .
> So death will flatter them at last: what, even the bald ape's by-shot
> Was moderately admirable?

This vision of the world is not poetic but prophetic, and we are easily excited by the prophets. "The poet does not aim to excite," writes Mr. T. S. Eliot "—that is not even a test of his success—but to set something down." One poem like *Tamar*, and you may believe that Mr. Jeffers has set down something prodigious: two, three such poems, five, seven—the emotional mechanism is betrayed by its own fluency; he has set down only himself. Prophets are like that, a whole show in themselves; they do not have to be—and never are—good dramatists. No great dramatic writer can let himself run in the prophet's groove; nor can he lack the leaven of humor, the salt of wit. A lyric writer may; as lyrist, Mr. Jeffers has often excellently fulfilled the poet's aim.

The lyric poems have never, in fact, received their due attention; unfortunately, they have been introduced in scattered fashion and at a point when the reader's emotional faculties, exhausted by the longer narratives, have been unable to focus on them. Perhaps no serious obscurity or backwardness in understanding the poet has arisen from these difficulties; nevertheless, a regrouping suggests very illuminating possibilities—suppose, for example, that all the California stories were bound in a volume, or that we might have his collected lyrics. *Flagons and Apples* (1912), and *Californians* (1916) are worth reading in any attempt to comprehend the poet's work as a whole; the obvious deduction is that he has grown more in stature than any poet of our day, perhaps than any poet ever. This conclusion is almost incredible, and an alternative presents itself, less obvious, less welcome, but certainly rather arresting. Is it possible that the bad poet of 1916 became, after a decade's silence, not a good poet at all, but simply a bad prose writer with a good trick? Let us examine a specimen or two, from "The Loving Shepherdess," chosen at random and without malice, and set them down as prose:

> "I'll leave you alone if you like, you promise to stay by the fire and sleep." "O, I couldn't, truly. My mind's throwing all its wrecks on the shore and I can't sleep. That was a shipwreck that drove us wandering. I remember all things. Your name's Onorio Vasquez: I wish you'd been my brother." He smiled and touched her cold hand. "For then," she said, "we could talk old troubles asleep: I hadn't thought, thought for a long while, tonight I can't stop my thought. But we all must die?" "Spread out your hands to the fire, warm yourself, Clare." "No, no," she answered, her teeth chattering. "I'm hot."
>
> The sky had blackened, and the wind raised a dust when they came up the road from the closed quiet of the wood, the sun was up behind the hill but not down yet. Clare passed the lichen-plated abandoned cabin that Vasquez had wished her to use, because there was not a blade of pasture about it, nothing but the shafted jealousy and foodless possession of the great redwoods. She saw the gray bed of the little Sur like a dry bone through its winter willows, and on the left, in the sudden sea-opening V of the canyon, the sun streaming through a cloud, the lank striped ocean, and an arched film of sand blown from a dune at the stream's foot. The road ahead went over a bridge and up the bare hill in lightning zigzags; a small black bead came down the lightning flashing at the turns in the strained light, a motor car driven fast. Clare urged her flock into the ditch by the road, but the car turned this side the bridge and glided down a steep driveway.

Is it pertinent to ask whether the reader can restore these lines to their original form, whether he can distinguish in them the original rhythm as it beat in Mr. Jeffers' mind? He may be somewhat baffled and amazed if he tries, and then looks up the answers (pp. 90, 72); he must, in honesty, ask himself the basis of this division of lines, whether the measure goes with sense or breath, and how it has transmuted such writing—if it has—to precious stuff.

Perhaps we do not see the forest for the trees. Or is it possible that what we see is not really a forest at all, but just Birnam Wood coming along to Dunsinane? That would be, *pro tempore,* a more startling phenomenon, although of less perennial importance.

A Critic and Four Poets

Theodore Morrison*

All these are men of excellent capacity, but still men. A figure of an altogether different stature has been waiting in the background. Robinson Jeffers has much in common with the great story-tellers, and something in common with the masters of poetic drama. His power seems at times to be almost without limit—the strong, swift compression of his phrases, his rapid, condensed command of narration.

Great tragedy is the province of Mr. Jeffers, but he has committed some aberrations in the government of his realm. He is as nearly without reticences as a writer can well be. I feel that his rough assaults on traditional modesty are often entirely natural and justified. They have a function in the story he is telling, and Mr. Jeffers is simply not even faintly prudish. But at times his disregard of the usual rules of restraint is not really needed, and then the detail in question might better be left out. And the trouble goes deeper. In some of the poems for which Mr. Jeffers is best known—*Roan Stallion* and *Tamar,* for example—the material as a whole is at fault. Incest is a favorite and not very successful subject. I am not sure how far some of his most violent scenes are intended for symbolism, and how far some of his failures may be due to imperfect mastery of it. In any case, what the reader finds is horror so extreme that it falls into the grotesque, and misses its object by excess.

But read Jeffers at his best, as he may be seen in *The Tower Beyond Tragedy* and in the principal poems contained in his new book. In *The Tower Beyond Tragedy* he deserts his favorite scene, California, for ancient Greece, and writes a poetic drama on the return of Agamemnon to Mycenae, his murder by Clytemnestra, and the vengeance of Orestes. It

*Excerpted from a review of four poets in the *Bookshelf,* an insert of the *Atlantic Monthly* 145 (February 1930): 24, 26, 28. Reprinted by permission of Anne Morrison, for the estate of Theodore Morrison.

is magnificent. No one has guessed the depth, the height, the power of contemporary poetry until he has listened to the Cassandra of Robinson Jeffers, and the voice of the murdered king crying through her. In this poem the music of Jeffers is at its best. I do not feel that he always makes the form of his work count as form. His usual lines are long, irregular, and unrhymed. True, they are often strongly rhythmic, and not as loose as the vagabond sentences of Whitman. But their length usually forbids the recognition of typical units of rhythm, on which the form of poetry so much depends. In *The Tower Beyond Tragedy,* however, Jeffers succeeds in combining freedom from the usual measures with the distinct and unmistakable presence of poetry. The lines are like a pack of hounds in full cry—noble music indeed to the ears of any reader wearily dissatisfied with the "diminutive lyrics" to which so many magazines and volumes of the day are limited. One thinks of Shakespeare's envious phrase, in the sonnets, for his rival: "The proud full sail of his great verse."

The Tower Beyond Tragedy may be read in *Roan Stallion, Tamar and Other Poems.* Jeffers's new book, *Dear Judas,* is in his best strain. The title poem is a pseudo-drama on the Passion. What other profane writer has dreamt such a Christ, such a Judas, such a Mary, let alone setting them down in the glory of such poetry? "The Loving Shepherdess" is a story of today, terrible and harrowing, but full of poetic beauty and power. Who would have his bowels of compassion wrung, let him read this. Other poems cry for mention, but I must leave the reader to explore Jeffers for himself.

Robinson Jeffers

Yvor Winters*

It is difficult to write of Mr. Jeffers' latest book without discussing his former volumes; after his first collection he deals chiefly with one theme in all of his poems; and all of his works illustrate a single problem, a spiritual malady of considerable significance. Mr. Jeffers is theologically a kind of monist; he envisages, as did Wordsworth, Nature as Deity; but his Nature is the Nature of the physics textbook and not of the rambling botanist—Mr. Jeffers seems to have taken the terminology of modern physics more literally than it is meant by its creators. Nature, or God, is thus a kind of self-sufficient mechanism, of which man is an offshoot, but from which man is cut off by his humanity (just what gave rise to this humanity, which is absolutely severed from all connection with God, is left for others to decide): there is consequently no mode of communication between the consciousness of man and the mode of existence of God; God

*From *Poetry* 35 (February 1930): 279–86. Copyrighted by the Modern Poetry Association and reprinted by permission of the Editor of *Poetry* and Janet Lewis Winters.

is praised adequately only by the screaming demons that make up the atom. Man, if he accepts this dilemma as necessary, is able to choose between two modes of action: he may renounce God and rely on his humanity, or he may renounce his humanity and rely on God.

Mr. Jeffers preaches the second choice: union with God, oblivion, the complete extinction of one's humanity, is the only good he is able to discover; and life, as such, is "incest," an insidious and destructive evil. So much, says Mr. Jeffers by implication, for Greek and Christian ethics. Now the mysticism of, say, San Juan de la Cruz offers at least the semblance of a spiritual, a human, discipline as a preliminary to union with Divinity; but for Mr. Jeffers a simple and mechanical device lies always ready; namely, suicide, a device to which he has not resorted.

In refusing to take this logical step, however, Mr. Jeffers illustrates one of a very interesting series of romantic compromises. The romantic of the ecstatic-pantheist type denies life, yet goes on living; nearly all romantics decry the intellect and philosophy, yet they offer justifications (necessarily foggy and fragmentary) of their attitude; they deride literary "technique" (the mastery of, and development of the sensitivity to, relationships between words, so that these relationships may extend almost illimitably the vocabulary) yet they write (of necessity, carelessly, with small efficiency). Not all romantics are guilty of all of these confusions, nor, doubtless is Mr. Jeffers; but all of these confusions are essentially romantic—they are very natural developments of moral monism. And Mr. Jeffers, having decried human life as such, and having denied the worth of the rules of the game, endeavors to write narrative and dramatic poems—poems, in other words, dealing with people who are playing the game. Jesus, the hero of *Dear Judas*, speaking apparently for Mr. Jeffers, says that the secret reason for the doctrine of forgiveness is that all men are driven by the mechanism-God to act as they do, that they are entirely helpless; yet he adds in the next breath that this secret must be guarded, for if it were given out, men would run amuck, would get out of hand—*they would begin acting differently.*

The Women at Point Sur is a perfect laboratory of Mr. Jeffers' philosophy. Barclay, an insane divine, preaches Mr. Jeffers' religion, and his disciples, acting upon it, become emotional mechanisms, lewd and twitching conglomerations of plexi, their humanity annulled. Human experience, in these circumstances, having necessarily and according to the doctrine no meaning, there can be and is no necessary sequence of events: every act is equivalent to every other; every act is at the peak of hysteria; most of the incidents could be shuffled around into varying sequences without violating anything save, perhaps, Mr. Jeffers' private sense of their relative intensity. Since the poem is his, of course, such a private sense is legitimate enough; the point is that this is not a narrative, nor a dramatic, but a lyrical criterion. A successful lyrical poem of one hundred and seventy-five pages is unlikely, for the essence of lyrical expression is concentration; but it is at least theoretically possible. The difficulty is that the lyric achieves its effect by the generalization of emotion (that is, by the separation of the emotion from the personal history that gives rise to it in actual concrete experience) and by the concentration of expression. Narrative can survive in a measure without concentration, or intensity of detail, provided the narrative logic is detailed and compelling, as in the case of Balzac, though it is only wise to add that this occurs most often in prose. Now Mr. Jeffers, as I have pointed out, has abandoned narrative logic with the theory of ethics, and he has never achieved, in addition, a close and masterly style. His writing is loose, turgid, and careless; like most anti-intellectualists, he relies on his feelings alone and has no standard of criticism for them outside of themselves. There are occasional good flashes in his poems, and to these I shall return later, but they are very few, are very limited in their range of feeling and in their subject matter, and they are very far between. Mr. Jeffers has no remaining method of sustaining his lyric, then, other than the employment of an accidental (i.e., non-narrative) chain of anecdotes (i.e., details that are lyrically impure); his philosophical doctrine and his artistic dilemma alike decree that these shall be anecdotes of hysteria. By this method Mr. Jeffers continually *lays claim* to a high pitch of emotion which has no narrative support (that is, support of the inevitable accumulation of experience), nor lyrical support (that is, support of the intense perception of pure, or transferable, emotion), which has, in short, no support at all, and which is therefore simply unmastered and self-inflicted hysteria.

Cawdor alone of Mr. Jeffers' poems contains a plot that in its rough outlines might be sound, and *Cawdor* likewise contains his best poetry; the poem as a whole, and in spite of the confused treatment of the woman, is moving, and the lines describing the seals at dawn are fine, as are the two or three last lines of the apotheosis of the eagle. Most of the preceding material in the latter passage, however, like most of the material in the sections that give Mr. Jeffers' notions of the post-mortem experience of man, are turgid, repetitious, arbitrary, and unconvincing. The plot itself is blurred for lack of stylistic finish (that is, for lack of ability on the part of the poet to see every detail of sense and movement incisively down to the last preposition, the last comma, as every detail *is* seen in Racine or Shakespeare); and it remains again a fair question whether a moral monist *can* arrive at any clear conclusions about the values of a course of action, since he denies the existence of any conceivable standard of values within the strict limits of human life as such. In *The Tower Beyond Tragedy* Mr. Jeffers takes a ready-made plot, the Clytemnestra-Orestes situation, which is particularly strong dramatically, because Orestes is forced to choose between two sins, the murder of his mother and the refusal to avenge his father. But at the very last moment, in Mr. Jeffers' version, Orestes is converted to Mr. Jeffers' religion and goes off explaining (to Electra, who has just tried to seduce him) that though men may think he is fleeing before the furies he is really just drifting up to the mountains to meditate on the stars; and the preceding action is, of course, rendered morally and emotionally meaningless.

In the latest volume, the title poem *Dear Judas,* is a kind of dilution of "The Women at Point Sur," with Jesus as Barclay, and with a less detailed background. Mr. Jeffers' mouthpiece and hero, Jesus, is little short of revolting as he whips reflexively from didactic passion to malice, self-justification, and vengeance. The poem shares the structural principles, or lack of them, of *The Woman at Point Sur,* and it has no quotable lines, save, possibly, the last three, which are, however, heavy with dross. *The Loving Shepherdess,* the other long poem of the present volume, deals with a girl who knows herself doomed to die at a certain time in childbirth, and who wanders over the countryside caring for a small and diminishing flock of sheep in an anguish of devotion. The events here again are anecdotal and reversible, and the emotion is lyrical or nothing. The theme had two possibilities: the poet could have immersed the girl in a dream of approaching death, or he could have immersed her in the sentimental pathos of the immediate situation. There are moments when he seems to be trying for the former effect, but his perceptions are not fine enough and the mass of anecdotal detail is too heavy; the poem succeeds in being no more than a very Wordsworthian embodiment of a kind of maudlin humanitarianism—which is a curious but not an unexpected outcome of Mr. Jeffers' sentimental misanthropy. The heroine is turned cruelly from door to door, and the sheep fall one by one before the reader's eyes, the doors and the sheep constituting the bulk of the anecdotal material; till finally the girl dies in a ditch in an impossible effort to give birth to her child.

The short poems in the book deal with themes that Mr. Jeffers has handled better before. He has written here and there impressive lines descriptive of the sea and its rocks, and of dying birds of prey. "Hurt Hawks II," in the *Cawdor* volume, is the most perfect short poem and is quite fine; there are excellent lines scattered through other pieces. These poems are, however, limited both in paraphrasable content and in experiential implication: they glorify brute nature and annihilation and are numb to the intricacies of human feeling; they share in the latter respect the limitations of all mystical poetry. Mr. Jeffers' insistence on another of his favorite lyrical themes, his own aloofness, is becoming, by dint of repetition, almost embarrassing; one has the constant feeling that he is trying to bully the reader into accepting him at his own evaluation.

Self-repetition has been the inevitable effect of anti-intellectualist doctrine on all of its supporters. If life is valued, explored, subdivided, and defined, poetic themes are infinite in number; if life is denied, the only theme is the rather sterile and monotonous one of the denial. Similarly, those poets who flee from form, which is infinitely variable, since every form is a definite and an individual thing, can achieve only the uniformity of chaos; and those individuals who endeavor to escape morality, which is personal form and controlled direction, can, in the very nature of things, achieve nothing save the uniformity of mechanism. One might classify Mr. Jeffers as a "great failure" if one meant by the phrase that he had wasted unusual talents; but not if one meant that he had failed in a major effort, for his aims are badly thought-out and are essentially trivial.

Dear Judas

F. W. Dupee*

Neither of the two long narratives in this volume will greatly advance the reputation of the poet. After *Cawdor*, with its wonderful eloquence, its indications, however germinal, of the ability to project character, they are a sad shock and disappointment. To approach them first from the formal side, they represent, I believe, a diminution of poetic skill. In the past, notably in *Cawdor*, the prelude of *The Women at Point Sur*, *The Tower Beyond Tragedy*, and many of the shorter lyrics, we have encountered a poetic craftsman of high talent; a verbal richness and ingenuity, unfortunately not always controlled; a language, original, varied, heavily charged with thought; and above all an abundance of superb metaphor. The prelude of "The Women at Point Sur" is among the highest achievements of modern poetry: here the stiff elements of former techniques, from the Elizabethan line to Imagism, are involved in a fluid synthesis. One is conscious of the predominance of no single method. The style is not experimental. Though original and personal, it is also final. More remarkable still, the poet, though writing of disintegration and spiritual desiccation, is, himself, integrated at the time of writing. Unlike T. S. Eliot in *The Waste Land*, he does not permit the subversive nature of his content to influence his form.

The rest of Jeffers ranges itself on a scale of which the Prelude is the peak. Much of *Cawdor* is near that peak, especially those passages which describe the posthumous experiences of Martial, Hood, and the eagle. Many, very many, of the shorter poems have equal value. In *The Tower Beyond Tragedy*, which as a story is vastly strained and unreal, the mere sorcery of language and imagery almost seduces us into acceptance.

In *Dear Judas*, the first of the two long poems in this new volume, even this sorcery is lacking. The writing is by no means bald, but its texture is comparatively thin. In *The Loving Shepherdess*, the second narrative, there is more richness, but there are also long prosaic, almost barren passages. It is not that Jeffers has attained to a simplicity of theme which

*From *Miscellany* 1 (March 1930): 34–36. Reprinted by permission of Barbara H. Dupee.

will bear this simple treatment. In both poems there is material of such nature as to require the most vivid presentation to make it even temporarily plausible. In *Dear Judas*, the passion story is submitted to an unconventional, very Jeffersian interpretation. After two thousand years the main protagonists of the event—Jesus, Judas, and Mary—are said to survive, but only as symbols of three passions which, Jeffers assures us, are not eternal, are, to be sure, fading. They return to the vicinity of Jerusalem and re-enact the tragedy, reinterpreting its main motives in the light of their disillusionment. Considered simply as a story, *Dear Judas* has this disadvantage over the version of St. Matthew: that Jesus, Judas, and Mary are, as Jeffers himself says, "nearly unfleshed of time." They are mere symbols, and as they move about among the events of the narrative they do not reverberate as human beings, but give out a hollow sound. Mary, as Night the Mother, has a dual function. Hers is the womb which gives birth to humanity and then, at the end of life, provides the dark refuge of annihilation. As such, she sees human activity, even the enterprises of prophets, as so much expended breath. She says of Jesus: "The surest-caught fish twists in the net and babbles to the others, / The cords cutting his gills, *I have come to save you.*" Jesus is the fanatical and deluded prophet, mad for power over the people, conscious of his height above men, and somewhat giddily appalled by it. Judas, on the contrary, as the symbol of pity, expends his sympathies upon men and animals and is condemned for it by his master. Recognizing that Jesus is bent upon martyrdom, he betrays him only that he may save his life. Thus we see that the original blood of the narrative, in which Christ and Judas conflicted as individuals and the symbolism (if there was any) was that of a mortal war between good and evil, is replaced by a thinner fluid in which the protagonists cease, not only to be individuals, but even to be adversative symbols. *Dear Judas* is the first notable poetic attempt to reinterpret the Passion from the monistic, relativist point of view.

The action of *The Loving Shepherdess*, however, is contemporaneous and local. The scene is in California among the familiar redwoods, cypresses, rocks, and ocean headlands. The story is not, of course, realistic, but, like Jeffers' other narratives, it is magnified into a kind of myth. The young heroine of the poem, Clare Walker, is pregnant with the child of a tragic union. Learning that, through biological causes, she will not survive the birth, she devotes herself to tending a flock of sheep, an action which illustrates her possessive love for mankind.

These poems represent, therefore, a development in the thinking of the poet, but a development which is not logically satisfactory. Hitherto in Jeffers' world there has been no place for pity or love. There have been only contempt and lust. In that world, which is an extension of the Nietzschean one, there are two orders of beings: on the one hand the People, "the active little bodies, the coupling bodies, the misty brainfuls of perplexed passion," and on the other hand the Prophets, who are distinguished from the People not by a superior ability to force their will on circumstances, but by the gift of envisaging the sad plight of humanity. (The term Prophet is not Jeffers' term and may be misleading, since these gifted individuals are not preachers, are, indeed, often inactive.) Into this world Jeffers has now projected the element of pity and possessive love. In *Dear Judas* we have seen the element condemned. In the other poem it is shown to be inefficient but none the less glorious. Exactly what is to be the agency of this new motive, it is difficult to see. Since it is inefficient, it appears to be merely an intrusion upon the stony logic of Jeffers' world order. We may make this *logical* criticism of the new development, and at the same time entertain in our minds a crawling suspicion that the preoccupation with pity is a mere attitude, a buskin borrowed from Dostoevsky to increase the poet's stature as a thinker and to widen the range of his emotional effects, as Shelley adopted Platonism and Byron the role of a social outcast.

But whether this novelty is a piece of undigested wisdom or merely a pose, it has not greatly affected the nature of Jeffers' poetry. The familiar symbols and ideas recur in both narratives. The prophet's consciousness of his position is transferred to the experience of Jesus: "I feel [he says] my immeasurable height above men. / My heart is lonely." And the glorified sexual symbol is transferred to Mary: "Oh garden that the glory from my body haunted, / The shining that came forth from between my thighs . . . / Is gone." The symbol of the wounded bird (usually hawk or eagle) turns up in a reference to Peter:

Peter has flung a stone and
has broken the hawk's wing.
The trustful hawk that perched in the fig-tree: now it will never again
rejoice in the blowing air
And blue spaces, but trail pain till it starves.

And there are re-statements of other familiar themes: the longing for annihilation and the association of that condition with darkness and night, the admiration for the happy unconsciousness of animals. Thus the old vessels are transferred to a new use, but they are informed with no new liquid. Is it because of too frequent repetition that these figures strike us here as banal, even sentimental, or merely because they are here not well expressed?

Mr. Rolfe Humphries has indicated (in an excellent critique in the *New Republic* for January 15) another rooted similarity between the earlier poems and these more recent ones. Clare Walker, he says, like Fera, Tamar, California and other women of Jeffers' creation, is "doom-bent, mad in Scorpio." These heroines are not converted to a tragic view of life by the events of the story. From the outset they are mad with disillusionment, fiercely fatalistic, prepared for the worst of fates. From a purely artistic point of view, this method contrasts unfavorably with the classic one. In Greek plays, for instance, though the sense of general trouble is abroad from the start, the central figures enter upon the action with a favorable view of the world and a belief in the efficacy of their own wills. With the single and striking exception of *Hamlet,* the order of nature—conviction by experience—is likewise followed in Shakespeare. In that play, to be sure, the conviction of pessimism is implicit in Hamlet's first soliloquy; implicit, indeed, in the cryptic bitterness of the first asides.

The disadvantage of this method is, of course, that the possibility of tragic growth is denied. In "Hamlet," the action may continually uncover new facets of the prince's genius; it may deepen but it cannot alter his initial convictions. Thus the profoundly dramatic element of change is excluded from the play. *The Loving Shepherdess* might have centered, to better advantage, around the events which led to Clare's "sainthood." As it is, the poem is really an epilogue, and, so far as the main character is concerned, it is static.

There is another and more immediate disadvantage of the method criticized above. Nearly everyone, I suppose, is conscious of unreality and immense strain upon entering Jeffers' dramatic world. The people have neither our sympathy nor our understanding. They talk in despairing figures of a savage world of lust and human mean-ness, which is not the world of the ordinary, normal individual. If there is any truth in that stricture of Aristotle's which states that in tragedy the spectator must be able to identify himself with the feelings of the protagonist, to imagine himself in the protagonist's shoes, then it is most necessary that the characters shall enter upon the action with an attitude towards life which is that of the normal being.

But the trouble is, of course, that Jeffers' philosophical attitude will not permit him to compromise, even with his art. That is a great shame for the future of his poetry. For in general, successful narrative or dramatic poetry demands of the poet an attitude towards humanity so well assimilated that he can function freely as an artist, applying himself to what is his legitimate interest: the *ethos* and *psyche* of individuals. But Jeffers' pessimism is not a belief, it is an obsession, representing itself to his mind in a few major symbols which are in themselves obsessions, blinding him to those individual differences of soul out of which the fire and conflict of literature are generated.

Descent to the Dead: Poems Written in Ireland and Great Britain (1931)

Jeffers Writes His Testament in New Poems

Horace Gregory*

In this book of sixteen short, elegiac poems, Robinson Jeffers has written his little testament. Here, if anywhere, is to be found his epitaph, which reads: "I am not dead. I have only become inhuman . . ."

A few lines further on he says:

> I wander in the air,
> Being mostly gas and water, and flow in the ocean;
> Touch you and Asia
> At the same moment: have a hand in the sunrises
> And the glow of this grass.

The identification with natural phenomena is complete; humanity is left far behind him. Being a true Romantic Jeffers returns to the pantheism of the early nineteenth century—but with a difference, for he has traveled through the nightmare of civilization to be saved only by the most dangerous of all panaceas, the delusion of grandeur.

Since this latest volume of poems raises the question of personal salvation, it might be well to summarize the contents of an early and very nearly forgotten book of Jeffers's called *Californians.* For those who protest that the now familiar attitudes struck in *Tamar, Cawdor* and *The Tower Beyond Tragedy* are morbid and distasteful, I recommend this early Jeffers item. In this volume a number of conventional verse forms are neatly tricked out in a manner approved by droves of successful magazine and newspaper versifiers. Fully half of the book is written in praise of California's climate—then, suddenly, the spirit of the book changes. There is a quick, hot-headed, unmotivated revolt against the lyrical sweetness that introduced the volume. The book closes with the usual note of Romantic disillusionment. The poet is unpretentious, innoxious, and, as I have hinted before, could not be singled out from a hundred others who write in a polite but bewildered fashion for women's magazines.

*From the *New York Evening Post,* 31 December 1931, 9. Reprinted with permission of New York Post Co., Inc.

Jeffers as a minor poet was a desperate failure. Whatever happened in the years between writing *Californians* and *Tamar* convinced him that he could make no compromises with his gifts as a poet or with a flat statement of his own omnipotence. His own introversion and frustration as a lyric poet in the Romantic tradition became transfigured into a sense of universal destruction and decay. The only escape for Jeffers lay along a road toward super-inhumanity. Very likely he would agree with Spengler and follow his conviction that all of Western civilization is more than ripe for burial.

And now we have his *Descent to the Dead,* poems written in Great Britain and Ireland. He has gone to Celtic Britain to look at the graves of his ancestors, to remember that they are now ghosts in the wind and names to be heard in half-forgotten legends. His speech at the grave of Ossian is characteristic:

> I also make a remembered name;
> And I shall return home to the granite stones
> On my cliff over the greatest ocean
> To be blind ashes under the butts of the stones.

The grand manner that often faltered in the progress of many earlier poems is assumed with natural dignity.

It is perhaps unnecessary to say that Jeffers's particular despair over the fate of humanity is admirably suited to the subject of his elegies. He has grown too large and has become too secure in the practice of his medium to reduce the quality of his emotions into terms of sentimentality. The mood that he approaches here is not at all unlike that found at the source of T. S. Eliot's *Waste Land.*

Although Jeffers explicitly denies all political and economic motives behind the poems that he has written for this volume, he is by no means the isolated, accidental genius that he imagines himself to be. The problem of the frustrated Romantic poet may be found in the best of contemporary literature in English and is stressed in no uncertain terms by the fate of Stephen Dedalus in *Ulysses.* Jeffers's elegies fall into the main stream of the literature that is being written today. His dream of grandeur so far as his work is concerned has become a reality. His elegies are among the best examples of Romantic poetry written by an American, and it is entirely possible that his boast of immortality will be justified by future generations of readers who will not fail to recognize his name.

Round about Parnassus

William Rose Benét*

The first edition of *Descent to the Dead*, by Robinson Jeffers, which comes to me from Random House, one of five hundred copies numbered and signed by the author, was designed by A. G. Hoffman and printed by Printype, Inc. It is a beautiful book. But unlike most beautifully printed books nowadays the poetry it contains is actually distinguished. The language is beautiful, and robust even though the mood induced has been a dwelling on death, in the midst of cairns and dolmens and ringed circles of great stones. The poems were written in Ireland and Great Britain on the occasion of Mr. Jeffers's recent trip thither. He identifies himself with Ireland through his forefathers. He is impressed by the living quality of the great dead. He moves in the presence of mighty ghosts. They overcome for him, temporarily at least, all faith in the present living world where men seem shadows walking, a midge-dance "of gutted and multiplied echoes of life in the latter sun." Death and life are both beautiful but death is a resolution of the discords of life, and a thing beyond and above even any earthly immortality. It is better to rest beneath the ageless stones, to be dust. Yet the dead of an age of blood and battle retain strange life:

> I hear like a hum in the ground the Boyne running through the aging
> Fields forever, and one of our great blue spiral-cut stones
> Settle in the dark a hair's breadth under the burden of the hill.
> "We hear from cairn to cromlech all over Ireland the dead
> Whisper and conspire, and whinnies of laughter tinkle in the raths.
> The living dream but the dead are awake."

Struck out of these pages is one wonderful phrase for the barrows near Finvoy, County Antrim,—"bee-bright necropolis." Flashing out of the reveries are two vividly terrible pictures, Mary Byrnes killing her lover on Shane O'Neill's cairn; Father O'Donnel, the old priest, spitting on his Christ before an altar in Donegal, "because the tortured torturer is too long dying; because the strain in the wounded minds of men / Leaves them no peace."

That last is a remarkable and unforgettable presentation. While the description of the ghosts seen in England is impressive the most truly impressive of the English poems is "Subjected Earth." It is the last poem. "Shakespeare's Grave" is a fine poem, too, having Shakespeare speak of his "passionate ruins," and, at the end, " 'Oh, a thousand years / Will hardly leach,' he thought, 'this dust of that fire.' "

Such is an indication of the movement of the verse, of its predominating tone. Jeffers, come as he says from "the west of the world, where

*Excerpted from a review of two poets in the *Saturday Review of Literature* 8 (16 January 1932): 461. Reprinted by permission.

hardly / Anything has died yet," feels the overpowering burden of mortality in what we call older lands. And yet his mood does not seem to us altogether new. He is in love with rock, with monumental silence, and if not precisely in love with death his only way of seeing life is in terms of the colossal cruelty of nature and the mad drama of human passions or the twisted futility of human endeavor. One must have a rather strong stomach for life not to be too heavily depressed by his view of life. It is one view. I recently read *Cawdor* for the first time, and it seemed to us characteristic of this poet that only the caged eagle in it begot in the poem a superb lyrical passage descriptive of the flight of its spirit after death. The dead kings of Ireland appeal to him as the dead eagle appealed, dead things of ravage, men of blood. The cruelty of nature deeply attracts him. It is, in fact, his obsession. This and the uncontrolled passions of humanity certainly still make, as they have always made, for the most powerful dramatic poetry. The story of *Macbeth* is a wonderfully imagined primitive story of murder. The "tragedy of blood" is a commonplace as the basis of the greatest Elizabethan drama. Cawdor, at the end of that poem, slashes sight from his own eyes, having killed his son. The Greeks derived great drama from incest and physical violence. As a dramatic poet, Jeffers moves in the most primitive tradition.

So far as his rhythmic utterance goes, the feeling still persists in me that Jeffers's manner has for the most part been too loose and prolix. Given a short section of any Jeffers poem I think I could recognize his authorship without having any other indication that he had written it. But I am not sure. There are passages so intensely imbued with his own individuality that one could not mistake them for the work of anyone else. There is often essential form. And, as often, to me, there is not. It is not a question of his notably long line, nor a question of the absence of strict metrical form as distinguished from inherent rhythm. One wrestles with a Proteus so far as his style is concerned. This constitutes my doubt about the man as a great poet, for he certainly possesses certain qualities of greatness. We have to judge him by higher standards than we apply to most poets. The range of his pondering and the power of his language necessitate that. This handful of present poems is but an "aside" compared with the main body of his work, but it has led me into these speculations. Whatever may be the truth he is one of the most striking poets of our period.

On the Theme of Time

Eda Lou Walton*

Robinson Jeffers is one of the poets today who is totally preoccupied with the theme of time. It is as if the human vision had been stretched suddenly, as if the eye of man were no longer on his own age save as that age is one hour in a continuous flow of time. T. S. Eliot, Archibald MacLeish, Hart Crane, Yvor Winters, and, in a more completely disillusioned way, William Butler Yeats are all obsessed, driven out of themselves, driven into a desire for oblivion by this intensified and modern awareness of infinity. And once this obsession overpowers the poet, he cannot write anything without feeling the necessity of divorcing himself from any strictly personal theme. Love, hate, passion, ennui—all become relative to the knowledge of these emotions manifest in the writings of poets of all periods. The eye focuses on a point, discovers that the point is the circumference of the world, in fact, the circumference of all worlds. Such an attack upon a poetic subject, such an angle of vision suddenly spreading out explain much of the imagery in modern poetry.

When Robinson Jeffers, therefore, turns to write elegies, he writes them not in terms of the duration of a personal grief, not in the intimate imagery of such a grief, but in terms of time. He writes them on the perishing of peoples, on the annihilation of races, on history ever continuous and seemingly discontinuous. In this new book, *Descent to the Dead*, he has returned to the land of his own ancestors, to Ireland, to England. These are dead lands; they have known more of time, as he sees it, than has his own Pacific Coast. They prove to him conclusively the paradox with which Eliot likewise has been concerned, that the dead are more living than are the "living dead."

The dead live through their histories, through their remembered expression in any art form, through the epochs they have brought into being; the living are dead because one must see them through the wrong end of the telescope, one is among them, one analyzes each deadly daily task, each petty liberty. In this new collection of lyrics Jeffers attempts to answer the question, What is death? It is life in the minds of those who follow after you, life only in memory, but memory is, therefore, more living, more enduring than life itself. And for one such memory, wrapped round the name of a great person, generations of men die; such is the theory of selection, of the right of the fittest to survival. The superman, then, with whom Jeffers has long been concerned, is he who endures past time as it is normally measured. He endures past human emotion (the briefest of all brevities), he becomes inhuman while he lives, and after he dies he is remembered as having surpassed humanity's dictum. Such a man gives him-

*From the *Nation* 134 (3 February 1932): 146–147. Reprinted by permission of The Nation Company, Inc.

self in life to fury, to intensity like that of nature in great storm; after he dies, he is remembered for his frenzy.

So this new collection of elegies, written in rhythms closely approximating the quantitative Greek, written in statements sometimes closely approximating the simplicity and directness of prose, but escaping the prosaic because so condensed, so vehement, is the logical conclusion of Jeffers's theme of desire for annihilation: he believes it necessary to escape the bonds of humanity (through violence), and then to be reunited with a larger measure of time, nature. Mountains endure beyond our sight; the body reabsorbed into dust has a boundlessness past that of life. This is a kind of pantheism, but Jeffers's own kind. Beauty in nature is achieved through spanning a greater compass of years than puny man may span. Jeffers's feeling for nature is like that of the ancient Britons. Although his ancestry is, in part, Celtic, Jeffers does not feel nature as gentle. He is much more like the early Scandinavians in his feeling for the waves and winds. He is terrified and entranced. If Jeffers had lived in a period when people believed in monsters he would have created appalling monsters to personify natural forces. Instead, since he has a scientific outlook, he presents the idea of natural law as terrific and ruthless. Human tenderness is, therefore, a mere protective fiction; nature alone illustrates what life really means.

Jeffers as a lyric poet is, let me repeat, never personal. In his lyrics, elegiac, philosophical, didactic, he is pronouncing a creed molded and confirmed by the thought of the twentieth century. He is a romantic turned nihilist. His lyrics are the direct vehicle of his vision; in them he allows himself none of the romantic grandeur of the narratives, got through presenting unintellectual characters and their actions. In his lyrics, he is an intellectual—romantic, bitter, frustrated, and confused—a mystic in his most intense moods, but intellectually opposed to mysticism, a man who seeks a philosophical system and can formulate none. There is, for him, no "tower beyond tragedy," no moment of peace. He has no clear idea of unity. Nature is greater than man, therefore more important. Death is an extended fretfulness and not really perfect annihilation. And there is no peace. Man's one hunger is for oblivion, and the only possible oblivion would be a total destruction of earth—something which the mind cannot quite grasp.

There is one other point concerning technique; Robinson Jeffers is, in his narratives, often very faulty, very unpoetic in the turn of a single line or group of lines. There are passages in the long poems which are in very bad taste. If they escape the censor it is because of the dramatic force of the narrative. Jeffers can tell a story (despite his symbolism, despite his obsessions); he understands his characters and presents a well-motivated tale. He has a perfect sense of human drama. This is a tremendous power in a narrative poet. But only in his lyrics does he show his command of the poetic line, his precise sense of language, and this in a rhythm which is almost alien to our tongue, which is so dangerously close to prose that only Jeffers with his knowledge of Greek poetry can keep it from becoming prose.

Thurso's Landing and Other Poems (1932)

Harrowed Marrow

Anonymous[*]

Life, a hawk hanging in California's stainless sky, stares down on Life, a ground-squirrel crouching on California's sun-bleached desert hills. When the squirrel begins to tremble, when the trembling reaches the marrow of his consciousness, the hawk swoops. After stripping off the flesh, he cracks the bones, sucks the trembling conscious marrow out. Fed with consciousness, his essential bread, the hawk returns to the stainless sky, hangs waiting for the ground-squirrel's son, their sons, their sons. . . .

Reave Thurso, with his mother and lamed brother Mark, lives on the coastal farm left by his father who killed himself when he could not make it pay. His limestone quarry buildings lie in decay; only a rusty cable, stretched across the canyon over the farm, hums in the air in memory of him.

Thurso's wife, Helen, fears him more than she loves him, hates his destructive will that is irreversible as the tide. After a deer-killing she runs off with Thurso's friend, Rick Armstrong, and hides successfully for a year. When Thurso tracks her down she goes off with him quickly, to save a meeting between him and her lover. On the way home Thurso pretends to break down the car, waits in the desert for Armstrong's pursuit. But Armstrong does not pursue; all Thurso can kill is a lizard that rambles by.

Home again, Helen finds it more dreadful than ever. Thurso's mother hates her, watches her like a hawk. Between lust for Helen and visions of his father's ghost, Mark begins to go mad. To remove all trace of his father's memory, Thurso cuts down the humming cable, is cut down himself. Hopelessly crippled, in ceaseless agony, he hangs on to suffering and life. Helen, who hated Thurso for his irreversible will, now loves him for it. In mercy she tries to put him out of his torment, but he will not allow her. After his crazed brother hangs himself, Thurso gets Helen to cart him, sodden with pain, up to a sea promontory. There, in a quarry shed, she surprises him with kisses, cuts his throat. When the old mother comes up the hill she finds Helen poisoned, dying. She has eaten the con-

[*]From *Time*, 4 April 1932, 63–64.

traceptive pills she used to prevent more life. The old mother, too tough herself for any hawk's beak to tear, is left squatting on her sorrows as on a pile of cracked and pithless bones. . . .

Such is the theme, such the characters, of a new poem by Robinson Jeffers, whom a considerable public now considers the most impressive poet the U. S. has yet produced.

Eyrie

Hard by the Pacific surf-line at Carmel, California, stands a tower of grey Santa Lucia granite, sea-worn boulders rolled up from the shore and heaved into place by Poet Jeffers for his own perch. For several years the stones rose in their courses; as they began to invade the upper air, a hawk dropped down to haunt them. Now Hawk Tower stands 30 feet high; in its turreted top is a socket to hold a flag pole to flaunt a flag, though neither hawks nor Poet Jeffers favor flapping flags.

The building of the tower was urged by Poet Jeffers' wife, who thought the exercise would be good for her husband. The building has proved useful to the whole family, who have there their "silent rooms." To its two-room base, Garth Sherwood and Donnan Call, the Jeffers' twin sons, resort in rainy weather. On the floor above, Mrs. Jeffers, who is devoted to music, Irish folk-songs in particular, has installed a small organ. Poet Jeffers, to whom all music is "just noise," occupies, with a table and a chair, the tiny room above. Here in the mornings, when his slow pulse beats only 40 times a minute, he slowly writes his poems; in the afternoons, when his pulse speeds up to 60, he plants trees, rolls stones.

The family eat and sleep in the house nearby, built also of sea boulders, but shaped after an old Tudor barn in Surrey which Mrs. Jeffers once admired. In the one-room attic the family sleep; downstairs they live their quiet family life. They have no telephone, no electric lights, no servants, but they entertain a few friends now and then. Poet Jeffers "chose the bed down-stairs by the sea-window for a good death-bed . . . when the patient daemon behind the screen of sea-rock and sky thumps with his staff, and calls thrice: 'Come, Jeffers.' "

Poet Jeffers, though gentle (he has never killed an animal) is not shy; though not shy he is not sociable, seeks neither the companionship of old friends nor acquaintanceship with new. Towards local Californians, as toward the human species as a whole, he is reserved, cold.

Most local Californians reciprocate his attitude. The most notable exception was California's poet, the late George Sterling, who doffed his poetical crown to Poet Jeffers, wrote a hero-worshipping study of him. In spite of this he remains to most Californians more of a cloudy stranger gone native than a sunny native son.

Nest

Poet Jeffers' birthplace was Pittsburgh, in 1887. From North Ireland had come his paternal grandfather. His father, an LL.D. learned in Latin, Greek, Hebrew, Arabic, had married an orphan 23 years his junior. John Robinson Jeffers was the first fruit; the second, Hamilton Jeffers, now engaged in astronomical work at Lick Observatory, came seven years later.

John Robinson, at 5, toured Europe with his parents, under his father's tutelage. From 12 to 15 he went to school at Vevey, Lausanne, Geneva, Zurich, Leipzig. At 16 he entered the University of Western Pennsylvania, but when his family moved to Pasadena he switched to Occidental College, Los Angeles, took his bachelor degree. He first met Una Call, whose second husband he was later to become, while he was a post-graduate student at the University of Southern California.

In 1907 he accompanied his family again to Europe, entered the University of Zurich, but soon left to study medicine at the University of Southern California. Thence he went to Seattle and, to get some outdoor work, entered the forestry department of the University of Washington. At 25 he received a legacy from an uncle. Independent, he went to live at Hermosa Beach, passed his time swimming and writing verse. In 1913 he married Una Call Kuster.

The Jeffers' intention to live in Europe was thwarted by the War. Looking for a place to live they came on the spot where Hawk Tower and Tor House now stand: "When the stagecoach topped the hill . . . and we looked down through pines and sea-fogs on Carmel Bay, it was evident that we had come without knowing it to our inevitable place."

Wings

His wanderings now over, Poet Jeffers devoted himself to following his mind's rising, widening gyres. He had already written much poetry, published one book. At 14 he had won a *Youth's Companion* poetry prize. A conventional book of love-poems, *Flagons and Apples* (1912), he followed four years later with *Californians.* In its most notable poem, "Invocation," he addressed the westward-shining evening star that had led his ancestors out of Asia, across Europe, the Atlantic, America, to leave him, a solitary poet, stranded on "the verge extreme, and shoal/Of sand that ends the west." Balked by the Pacific Ocean, Poet Jeffers, unless he were to retrace his father's steps, had only three directions left to go: down, up, in. At different times he has taken all three.

For eight years he published nothing. He explained to Journalist James Rorty, who came across him while editing, with Poet George Sterling, an anthology of native California poetry, that he did not think anybody would be interested. *Tamar and Other Poems* (1924) had just been published in New York by an obscure printer named Boyle. The plates were offered free by Printer Boyle to at least two large publishers, who declined to print the poem because of its incestuous theme. Through the efforts of James Rorty and friends, the Boyle edition received a fanfare of reviewers' praise. In 1925 Liveright brought out *Tamar* in its edition of *Roan Stallion, Tamar and Other Poems.* In the latter volume Poet Jeffers generalized his theme:

> Humanity is the start of the race; I say
> Humanity is the mold to break away from, the crust to break through, the coal to break into fire,
> The atom to be split.
> Tragedy that breaks man's face and a white fire flies out of it; vision that fools him
> Out of his limits, desire that fools him out of his limits, unnatural crime, inhuman science,
> Slit eyes in the mask; wild loves that leap over the walls of nature, the wild fence-vaulter science,
> Useless intelligence of far stars, dim knowledge of the spinning demons that make an atom,
> These break, these pierce, these deify. . . .

The visions, the desires that fool man out of his limits lead Poet Jeffers' tragic heroes and heroines into dark and terrifying ways. *Tamar, The Tower Beyond Tragedy, The Women at Point Sur* all tell incestuous tales. *Roan Stallion* tells of a woman's love for a horse. Though critics, with few exceptions, have extolled the splendor and intensity of Poet Jeffers' works, some women think that he spoils his poems with such outrageous themes. Even his wife complained. "Robin," said she after he had finished *Roan Stallion*, "when will you quit forbidden themes?" Robin answered with an enigmatic smile. To him, there is nothing in his writings either "surprising or subversive, but the mere common sense of our predicament as passionate bits of earth and water." To dignify men's passions, men's predicaments, he had merely motivated his tragedies with themes already given classic sanction by the Greeks. A brief excursion into Christian mythology in *Dear Judas*, apparently taken from sense of duty, did not much advance his thought; neither did *Descent to the Dead*, a compilation of 16 poems written in Ireland and Great Britain on a trip with his wife and twins about three years ago, during which Poet Jeffers spent much of his time looking at graves.

"The soil that I dig up here [wrote Jeffers of *Cawdor and Other Poems*] to plant trees or lay foundation stones, is full of Indian leavings, sea-shells and flint scrapers. . . . Not only generations but races too drizzle away so fast, one wonders the more urgently what it is for. . . ." Poet Jeffers has already shown how, against the desert western American landscape, the characters of his imagination, impelled by Greekish lusts, drizzle themselves away. In *Thurso's Landing* he writes his most native American, least Greekish tragedy, leaving sexual perversion almost entirely out. Its terrors are more Amerindian than Greek—the terrors of a diminishing race under Nature's relentlessly observant, semi-conscious eye. The outlines of the American continent and of its troubled inhabitants grow colder and clearer under Poet Jeffers' western-starry light.

The coast hills at Sovranes Creek:
No trees, but dark scant pasture drawn thin
Over rock shaped like flame;
The old ocean at the land's foot, the vast
Gray extension beyond the long white violence;
A herd of cows and the bull
Far distant, hardly apparent up the dark slope;
And the gray air haunted with hawks:
This place is the noblest thing I have ever seen.
        No imaginable
Human presence here could do anything
But dilute the lonely self-watchful passion.

A Transient Sickness

Granville Hicks*

The problems of suffering and death and of the ultimate extinction of humanity will, so far as one can see, be problems in any society; but the extent to which they occupy men's minds, as well as the attitudes men take toward them, may, as history shows, vary with changes in the social structure. No one can doubt the depth of Robinson Jeffers's despair, but it is, as Newton Arvin once pointed out in the *New Freeman*, a strange fact that, whenever Jeffers ventures to make a specific indictment of the civilization he hates, he makes it in terms very similar to those in which other men express, not a cosmic despair, but a recognition of the destruction that must be done before a better society can be created. In this book, for example, there is a poem on Edison:

A great toy-maker, light-bringer, patient
Finder of powers that were promptly applied to foolish and mean
Purposes; a man full of benevolence,
Eager for knowledge, has dropped his tools and forgotten contrivance.
Why must the careful gifts of good men
Narrow the lives and erode the souls of people, as trader's
Whiskey unravels a run of savages?

There are at least two answers to the question Jeffers asks; he has seen only one of them. A man of his caliber could, obviously, be satisfied with no easy solution. Unable in the years when his creative powers were

*From the *Nation* 134 (13 April 1932): 433–34. Reprinted by permission of The Nation Company, Inc.

taking shape to find any purpose in whose service they might be employed, he concluded that "civilization is a transient sickness." To express that conviction he has used in his poems the most violent symbols he could invent. Of human nature he here says:

> It is rather ignoble in
> its quiet times, mean in its pleasures,
> Slavish in the mass; but at stricken moments it can
> shine feebly[1] against the dark magnificence of
> things.

As a matter of fact, human nature does not shine feebly in Jeffers's poems. It flames in terrible heroism. *Thurso's Landing* is perhaps the most human poem he has written, in the sense that its characters act from comprehensible motives. It is the story of Reave Thurso's determination, senselessly cruel in the small affairs of life but wholly majestic when matched against the agony and the certainty of death. It moves swiftly, in lines terser and firmer than those the poet has hitherto composed, sweeping forward on the wings of an imagery even nobler than that we have known.

There is, one cannot deny, a kind of validity in this and all of Jeffers's poems; such power was not born of self-deceit. But the validity is there, not because his vision is inevitably true, but because it is a possible truth. He sees only the way of death, and there is a possibility that men may take the way of death. But men are not likely to go that way without struggle. Even Jeffers struggles, though he does not wish to. There is a parable of the real Jeffers in his own Margrave, who tries to examine his heart-beat while he thinks of his approaching hanging, but whose scientific objectivity yields to his fear of death. In Jeffers it is his passion for life that overcomes the calmness with which he endeavors to contemplate the annihilation of the race. But that passion serves only to lend the vision of annihilation power and beauty. If that passion had been, at the outset, directed into other channels, what might it not have accomplished? Helen says of Reave Thurso: "he was like a king in some ways, and if he had found any great thing to do/He might have done greatly." That, one feels, might be Robinson Jeffers's epitaph.

Note

1. Ed. note: Hicks misquotes Jeffers here; "feebly" should read "terribly."

Five Notable Poets

Louis Untermeyer*

Thurso's Landing continues the strain of transplanted Greek tragedy which Robinson Jeffers announced in *Tamar* and amplified in *Cawdor* and in *The Women at Point Sur.* The setting is the author's Californian coast, a background fierce and melodramatic as the events it overshadows; the *dramatis personae* are nakedly—and a little too insistently—symbols of tortured humanity, "all compelled, all unhappy, all helpless." The main characters are Reave Thurso, his wife Helen, his brother Mark. Helen hates Reave for his cold strength and wantonly betrays him; she despises Mark for his weak tenderness and hastens his disintegration. Passions turn upon themselves and rend their possessors, motives twist about until Reave, ruthless in action, is struck down and crippled by his own overactivity. Mark goes mad and hangs himself. In a finale of relentless expiation Helen stabs the suffering Reave to death and poisons herself on the promontory. Only the old mother, a grim chorus, remains. This *résumé* gives no hint of the propulsion of Jeffers's narrative nor the power of his long but rapid line. The title-poem extends to one hundred and twenty-four crowded pages, and there is no passage that fails to move the reader with the strangeness and shock of a shattering experience. The shorter poems, no less characteristic in condensed force, play a set of variations about the favorite *leitmotiv.* Whether long or short, the tales and lyrics centering about incest, wholesale murder, erotomania, or a building up of nameless, numberless brutalities, elaborate a single theme. The idea—I might almost say the *idée fixe*—which runs through Jeffers's six volumes might be rendered as follows: Life is horrible. Love, as we know it, is inverted and hence incestuous; not one self-adoring man in a million expresses outward-going passion. Death is the beautiful capricious savior, "the gay child with the gypsy eyes." Civilization is a transient sickness. Were the world free of this botch of humanity, this walking disease of consciousness, it would be a cleaner place, one in which the noble, impersonal elements would be at home. In a few thousand years this may well happen, and life will no longer be a torture for the living. Meanwhile our nature, "ignoble in its quiet times, mean in its pleasures,/Slavish in the mass" can, in its "stricken moments," occasionally "shine terribly against the dark magnificence of things." Meanwhile we can learn from hawks and headlands; we can learn to bear; we can endure. Sometimes the philosophy is implicit in the action of Jeffers's characters; sometimes it is explicit, and the poet steps out of the drama to say:

> No life
> Ought to be thought important in the weave of the world, whatever it may show of courage or endured pain.

*Excerpted from a review of five poets in the *Yale Review* 21 (June 1932): 815–17.

> It owns no other manner of shining but to bear pain; for pleasure is too
> little, our inhuman God is too great, thought is too lost.

The flaws in this philosophy are obvious. Jeffers's torn creatures exist only in states of unremitting tension; for them the world is all raw extremes, never alleviated by a moment's humor or a temperate impulse. Never in this country has literature been so charged with violence; compared with Jeffers's work, O'Neill's plays are reasonably calm and Faulkner's fictions are coolly mechanical. In his complete voidance of the kindly or the casual, Jeffers reveals his distrust of normal life. Though the actual tower he built on Point Lobos with his own hands is made of granite, it is no less a tower of ivory. His concern with elemental forces and phantasmagoria is a way of release, release from a world of daily adjustments. Such an evasion is too simple to satisfy; as Hugh I'Anson Fausset wrote in another connection, "it is easier to exploit the possibilities of mental death than the demands of creative life." In an effort to escape these exactions of the ordinary, Jeffers is, like Lawrence, always serious and sometimes hysterical. Like Lawrence, he writes partly with his mind, partly with his nerves; and like Poe, that most pitiful of escapists, he is forever fascinated with death.

But between Jeffers the philosopher and Jeffers the poet there is a significant dichotomy. The philosophy is negative, repetitious, dismal; the poetry, even when bitterest, is positive as any creative expression must be; it is varied in movement and color, it vibrates with a reckless fecundity. It is like nothing else of which we are proud to boast; it is continually breaking through its own pattern to dangerous and unfathomed depths. This is not a work to be enjoyed without sacrificing that sense of ease dear to the casual reader; I am not sure that, in the common sense, it can be "enjoyed" at all. But here is an undeviating, full-throated poetry, remarkable in sheer drive and harrowing drama, a poetry we may never love but one we cannot forget.

Poets and Others

Yvor Winters*

In the spring of 1930 I published in *Poetry* a review of Mr. Jeffers' *Dear Judas*, in which I summarized the chief weaknesses of his narrative poetry. The same weaknesses persist in *Thurso's Landing*, though in a milder form. The doctrinaire hysteria of the earlier narratives is seldom to be found here. There is an attempt at some sort of coherent narrative, but the result is merely dogged and soggy melodrama. Mr. Jeffers' verse

*From a review of nine poets in *Hound & Horn* 5 (July–September 1932): 681–84. Reprinted by permission of Janet Lewis Winters.

continues to miss the virtues of prose and verse alike: it is capable neither of the fullness and modulation of fine prose nor of the concentration and modulation of fine verse. There is an endless, violent monotony of movement, wholly uninteresting and insensitive, that may have a hypnotic effect upon a good many readers, much as does the jolting of a railroad coach over a bad roadbed:

> After twenty miles he turned
> The carburetor-connection, slyly regarding
> His seat-mate, she fogged with misery observed nothing.
> The engine went lame. "What's the matter?" he said, turning
> The carburetor-connection. . . .

And again:

> Against the black horror of death
> All living miseries looked sweet; in a moment of aimless
> Wild anguish she was unable not to cry out. . . .

For brute clumsiness and emptiness such writing can hardly be equalled, and the second passage is a mosaic of stereotypes. Both passages are typical. The book is composed almost wholly of trash.

Give Your Heart to the Hawks and Other Poems (1933)

North of Hollywood

Henry Seidel Canby[*]

Robinson Jeffers lives on that Pacific Coast which for good and for ill has so powerfully stirred the American imagination; he draws his themes from a territory of the imagination (a region of strong and often morbid sensation) which lies nearer to California than to any other mundane state; indeed he is one of those poets, and they are not the least important, whose work is an emanation from an environment definitely geographical as well as spiritual, and an interpretation of Nature in a way which Wordsworth and Emerson would have understood. His poetry, which is certainly major at its best, stands apart from cults and schools. It is as untroubled by the intellectualisms of the metaphysical school as the mist-wreathed, sun-baked slopes of the California foothills. The passion for perfection of the imagist, and also his reticence before the common passions of humanity, are unknown to it; like California, it is made up of masses where fineness of detail is lost in the sensationalism of violent contrast. But it escapes even less than the metaphysics of T. S. Eliot from the current implications of this troubled period. Indeed, like so many of the best novels of our time, its uncritical inclusiveness makes it a better register of the Zeitgeist than work more withdrawn into the inner rooms of the scholar's or the esthete's mind.

Now Jeffers has been known as a poet of cruelty and horror, who has celebrated in dramatic narrative, sensational to the point of melodrama, the harsh incoherences between man's expectancy and his fate. The inhumanity of his monotonously beautiful coast seemed to weigh upon him until, ignoring its cities and bungalows, he peopled the empty canyons of its wilderness with figures in which perverted passions broke through suppressions into blood and fire. His rather loose verse took on aspects of grandeur as it lifted the mountains and the sea to a plane of wild imagination, then too often broke into sensationalism as the passions and despairs of his homely people were unloosed, like hopeless souls of sinners in some old illuminated manuscript, writhing toward the eternal pit.

[*]From the *Saturday Review of Literature* 10 (7 October 1933): 162. Reprinted by permission.

His cruelty, his almost brutal pessimism, has been in close accord with the spirit of the newer American novelists, although the difference in style, and especially in subject matter, has obscured the resemblance. The readers who rushed for Hemingway or Faulkner have hesitated before the poet's lift out of realism into a super-world as heroic as a Wagner drama. But relative neglect does not imply lesser significance.

Jeffers's new book is called *Give Your Heart to the Hawks and Other Poems.* The poet, he says in "Triad," is one whose affair is "to awake dangerous images and call the hawks." Like science he feeds the future, he serves God, "who is very beautiful, but hardly a friend of humanity." How often when writers of our cheerful race (Poe, Melville, O'Neill) look into the depths they find God to be no friend of humanity! The God of Jeffers approves of stoicism. His title poem, a battle of souls in a mist of blood, differs from the relentless poems of his past in that stoicism wins through at the end, when the genial optimism of our progressive period and the laissez-faire of conventional act and orthodox religion have all been defeated. That poem begins on what might be called the 1929 levels of familiar experience. "Under the vast calm vaulting glory of the afterglow," a drunken party is under way on a wild and lovely California beach. It mounts into vulgar horseplay and sexual desire, while undercurrents of finer emotions sweep through the protagonists, hot contraband liquor not sufficing to quench the consciousness of the "enormous peace of the sea," and the cruel beauty of the cliffs overhanging. Then in a release from inhibitions, retarded action breaks out of the subconscious where it has long been willed. There is adultery, murder—a brother kills a brother, and a guilty wife begins a long struggle to save her guilty husband from moral disintegration.

Now, as after the easy self-indulgences of the twenties, the characters in this story face realities they had ignored. Life drops from the happy commonplace into horrid depths; the old human struggle, familiar in starker eras, begins again.

Give your heart to the hawks, says the young wife caught in casual adultery, to her husband who has killed his brother, the courts will only free your body, conquer your own remorses, and trust nature which is beautiful and of which perversions, like you and me, are only a part. The hawks of nature feed the future, thus serving God, and for that you must endure. When deep passions are stirred, the easy compounding with error which serves Hollywood and the bungalows is a way to destroy the soul.

Tortured by inarticulate remorse, driven by her will, the husband tries to rely on a self which in the easy days has never met spiritual emergencies. He fights against nature, he fights literally against the hawks which carry his wife's symbolism. The poem sways between a majestic beauty of encompassing landscape where the décor is a vital part of a human story (in this how often do Americans fail!), and a battle of minds, made morbidly concrete in bloody circumstances, where the brute creature lifted by his wife's will toward self-reliance smashes and kills as he slips back toward convention, superstition, self-pity, and mere despair. She loses him, of course; in the moment of his yielding he kills himself because he cannot "peel off" his humanness, rise to her belief that all human feelings, repentance, and blood thirst too, are not very important in so vast a world. Her will and the unborn child she has forced from him remain. The poem ends, unlike Jeffers, in a stoic triumph for those who are free of a world that believed God cared for its pleasure—for those "more hawk than human."

And it is recorded here not only for its current moral significance but for the extraordinary beauty of its descriptive verse, its skillful blending of the familiar and exalted, which suits the changed temper of a new day that is repelled by mere heroics yet craves a lift above realism, and for the singularity of sadistic cruelty, spiritual torture, revealed and resolved in a culture which has given us gold, oranges, sentimental movies, the open-air life—and now this. But it is recorded particularly for its moral significance, since here is an American poet who, while Hollywood danced and Los Angeles sold real estate below him and San Francisco played the market above, like some morbid Hebrew prophet saw visions of blood and disaster on his mountains, and now that the iron has crushed the soul of so many pleasant illusions, seems perversely to have felt the strength of will, the depth of energy, behind the aimless scurry of American life, and has made a woman the symbol of the anti-defeatism of a race that, even if God is no friend of humanity, will accept the rigors of nature, seeing its grandeurs, and fight on toward a future.

Is this too metaphysical an interpretation of a poem of adultery, murder, and the fruits of remorse? Murder has supplied the trivial reading of Americans for a decade now; we murder more freely than other races; violence is in our blood, mixed with benevolence and a restless energy; here is a murder story (like Browning's) intended to hold the mirror up to nature—the inhuman nature of the hills, the too human nature beneath the superficialities of the American scene. Malicious critics will say that Jeffers and O'Neill should sit telling old tales together with a pool of blood between them. But good-natured people go to excess when they feel deeply. In spite of its morbidity, and perhaps because of it, here is a poem that troubles the water as if there passed by some angel of judgment.

A Poet at Odds with His Own Civilization

Eda Lou Walton*

For Jeffers the universe is a mechanism with one intense desire to recreate by going back to the source of life. His male characters are symbolic of creative thought. His female characters are symbolic of the blind earth desire toward the source of life. Incest, one of his themes, is the symbol of the return to the source of life, to earth, to Pantheistic godhood. Any act of violence is a break with humanity which must be shucked off if man would understand the god of Nature. The only relation of any value is that between man and the universe. For the rest, the universe is in continuous change, man's relationships with his fellow beings are always altering. Pause and peace happen only when, at some moment, man feels himself identified with the universe, with Nature. And Nature, most beautiful when most violent, can be sought as peaceful only between terrific upheavals, only in those rare hours of quiet after storm. Just as violence in Nature is followed by calm and beauty so is violence in human action succeeded by consummate certainty and peace. Tranquility cannot be desired for its own sake, nor as continuous. It is to be found only after passion is spent.

Students of Jeffers's poetry know all this. The narratives in this new volume (which includes a reprint of the poems in *Descent to the Dead*) merely reaffirm it. *Give Your Heart to the Hawks* is the story of a man, who, having murdered his brother, is not allowed to give himself over to the judgment by the people, but must judge himself. Thus, having shaken off the code of humanity by murder, he is forbidden to reenter the human world. He must give his heart to the hawks, birds of freedom, for meat, rather than to men. In order to be able to acquaint himself with his own act, he commits cruelty after cruelty, violence becomes necessary to him. He has broken the mold of humanity. But as usual in Jeffers, this superman struggling for his own peace cannot obtain perfect unity with the violence and sudden peace of Nature. He goes mad, he kills himself. *Resurrection*, the second long narrative, is the tale of how a dead soldier, unsatisfied in lust, returns, after years of struggle through death back to life, to possess his wife, now remarried and hating him. The symbols here are clear. Through death we come to life. The unsatisfied passions cannot die. Beauty can be born only from the union between life and death. Necrophilism is made symbolic of the passionate desire of the dead toward rebirth. "I think now that there's nothing can keep you quiet if you *want* enough," writes the poet. The third narrative, *At the Fall of an Age*, is again a story using the idea of necrophilism. Helen of Troy, the unperishable, is taken in lust by the dead Achilles. Companioned by the dead soldiers she

*From the *New York Herald Tribune Books*, 8 October 1933, 6. I. H. T. Corporation. Reprinted by permission.

seeks out her old friend, Polyxo. And Polyxo hangs Helen for revenge. Polyxo would end beauty. Helen, hanged, is more beautiful than ever, her body is the symbol of beauty new born, of the coming of a new age.

These stories fit the general scheme of Jeffers's philosophy. Symbol after symbol employed in this volume is identified with a symbol in an earlier poem. The crucified hawk, the Christ symbol, is here again. The prophetic Spanish-Indian, Onorio, tells of visions that indicate how man may become superman by washing away his sense of sin. Every plot indicates Jeffers's immersion in his own particular kind of Pantheism, his belief that Nature is the only expression of God, that man is too puny, too caught in the crowd usually, to find this God, that he finds Deity only in terrific passion and succeeding peace, then loses Him in returning to humanity.

But Jeffers is, for all of his fixed scheme of belief, being forced into argument. He is having difficulty now in adjusting his romantic philosophy to the events of this age. The poet has always hated the industrial scene. Machines, cities, communal and leveled life are his abhorrence. As a Pantheist, he would have man seek the hills, live alone, somewhat primitively, and in close contact with the mountains and the sea. As a Pantheist, he is, of course, a violent individualist. He would deliver man from serfdom, apparently, by some kind of a turning back of the hands of time. Despite his knowledge of science, Jeffers hates the historical results of man's inventiveness. Man among men is an ant, a sheep, one of the herd. Only by self-isolation can he find greatness; only by super-human violence and passion can he declare himself god-like. He must, therefore, get away from industrial cities, he must be beyond the mean laws and customs of society, he must seek his own personal salvation through a denial of human values and an individual communion with the more violent aspects of Nature. All this is, of course, a kind of Byronism, certainly romanticism and dated.

To the leveling influence of this age, Jeffers answers and must continue to answer as follows: Both Marxism and Fascism demean man whose greatness is in individualism.

> Science, that makes wheels turn, cities grow,
> Moribund people live on, playthings increase,
> But has fallen from hope to confusion at her own business
> Of understanding the nature of things;—new Russia,
> That stood a moment at dreadful cost half free,
> Beholding the open, all the glades of the world
> On both sides of the trap, and resolutely
> Walked into the trap that has Europe and America;—
> The poet, who wishes not to play games with words,
> His affair being to awake dangerous images
> And call the hawks;—they all feed the future, they serve God,
> Who is very beautiful, but hardly a friend of humanity.

Industrial society is the enemy of individualism. Men live in it because they have not the intensity, the passion to seek the Pantheistic God. To Jeffers's idea of the god, they answer that it is a "sterile enormous splendor" with no pity. Men cannot understand that human pity is weakness. This "inhuman God" is, however, "beautiful and too secure to want worshippers." If, therefore, men cannot stand by themselves, they "must hang on Marx or Christ, or mere Progress." They must be sheep when they should be leaders.

The ants are good creatures, there is nothing to be heroic about.
But the time is not a strong prison either.
A little scraping the walls of dishonest contractor's-concrete
Through a shower of chips and sand makes freedom.
Shake the dust from your hair. This mountain sea-coast is real,
For it reaches out far into past and future;
It is part of the great and timeless excellence of things.

Since, however, most men *are* ants and this industrial society seems to have come to stay, Jeffers's prophecy of freedom for men can apply only to such few men as may be able to live in isolation. Only these men may, through the poet's own brand of mysticism, find peace. They may be able to find quiet and perfect isolation.

Knowing all the while that civilization and the other evils
That make humanity ridiculous, remain
Beautiful in the whole fabric, excesses that balance each other
Like the paired wings of a flying bird.
Misery and riches, civilization and squalid savagery,
Mass war and the odor of unmanly peace.

Most men, however, moving with the age, will find in Jeffers no message and no solace. The poet, intrenched in his personal religion, will be more and more a voice in the wilderness, crying out to no purpose whatsoever.

Robinson Jeffers

James Rorty*

Because Robinson Jeffers has struggled so determinedly to organize and use what would appear to be the greatest natural and acquired equipment of any contemporary poet, each new book of his becomes for the reader—he now has a world audience—an obligation to participate in that struggle. We need great poetry very much, and there has seemed to be a better chance of getting it from Jeffers than from anybody else.

*From the *Nation* 137 (20 December 1933): 712–13. Reprinted by permission of The Nation Company, Inc.

One brings to that renewed struggle needs, demands, and hopes bred out of the bewilderment, suffering, and struggle of the contemporary world, and one finds—what? That still, in some curious way, this struggle is irrelevant to the poet's own needs and purposes; that the world struggle is not a part of him nor he of it; that the drive of his art is becoming, if anything, increasingly tangential to the need of a world which has seized upon and is using for what it is worth almost every considerable poetic talent of his generation. Not that Jeffers is unaware of this need. He is profoundly, almost pathologically sensitive. But this sensitiveness is checked and distorted by an almost pathologically powerful will. Not the will of life, but the will of the poet, be done. Because he is a great and utterly serious artist, we feel that his struggle is ours. But unless our struggle becomes also his, we cannot always go on feeling this. In the end, Jeffers's attempt to break through, or rather to secede from, the human status must bring its penalties, not merely in the alienation of his audience but in the loss of power, for the power is not really in the artist but in the life struggle which he expresses.

As craftsmanship, *Give Your Heart to the Hawks* is in many respects one of Jeffers's ablest performances. But one starts unconvinced, for the tragedy is frailly premised on drunkenness and chance, and one ends, as too often in Jeffers's terrible stories, racked but unsatisfied. The title poem is rich with profound insights and contains much beautiful writing. But Jeffers has painted the same canvas, or similar canvases, before, and the characters are much too similar to characters in earlier dramas. We are entitled to ask more than this of Jeffers. More, too, than the shallow, half-true comment he gives us in the brief poem entitled "Intellectuals:"

> Is it so hard for men to stand by themselves,
> They must hang on Marx or Christ, or mere Progress? . . .
> Yourself, if you had not encountered and loved
> Our unkindly all but inhuman God,
> Who is very beautiful and too secure to want worshippers,
> And includes indeed the sheep with the wolves,
> You too might have been looking about for a church.

It is no accident that the moment this greatly gifted artist, this finely disciplined and informed mind, attempts to breathe in and then breathe out the contemporary social air, he sounds frail and inept. The explanation, probably, lies somewhere in the life experience sketched in some detail for the first time in Dr. Powell's *An Introduction to Robinson Jeffers*, which is an intelligent, workman-like study entirely worthy of reissue by an American publisher.

Jeffers is the son of a Calvinist theologian who appears to have had some private means. He read Greek fluently at five; was forced as a child to study nature, the Bible, and the classics; rebelled against his father. He spent three formative years in European boarding-schools reading

Swinburne, Shelley, and Nietzsche. At fifteen he could "think," says Dr. Powell, in Italian, French, German, Latin, and Greek, as well as in English. He was mentally precocious, physically strong, and excelled in studies ranging from theology to geology. To this equipment he added a year of medical school in Los Angeles, followed by zoology, silviculture, and law at the University of Washington in 1913. That year he married, went to Carmel, and except for two brief and comparatively recent trips to Ireland and to New Mexico has stayed there ever since, writing poetry.

The points to note in this summary are the precocity, the Calvinistic inheritance, the extraordinary range of reading and study, and the exemption from the economic struggle made possible by a small income. Doubtless, as a tremendously superior and very sensitive youth, the life he encountered laid an early emotional basis, which his erudition could amply confirm, for his later misanthropy. He did not "break out of" the human status. He never fully entered into it. His life quite evidently has been wholly that of the student and scholar.

The product of that extraordinarily isolated life, organized and disciplined by a powerful mind and will, has been a rich yield of poetic literature, nothing less and nothing more. What is missing is life. D. H. Lawrence hated people too, with a somewhat similar kind of inverted Messianic love. But Lawrence experienced the economic struggle—life as well as literature—and he gave us more, I think, than Jeffers has yet given us.

Jeffers has been called bitter, harsh, inhuman. It would be more just to say that he is all too human; that his alterations of sadism and masochism are the evidence of a still untempered softness. Otherwise, why this running off into partial and arbitrary fables? That way gives us literature, magnificent part-saying, to use Whitman's phrase, but not quite the ultimately erect and liberating gesture of human tragedy; not new life, not the renewing synthesis for which the fevered and disintegrating body of the age is crying.

The Dilemma of Robinson Jeffers

John Gould Fletcher*

No American poet now living has been more fortunate in his appearance than Robinson Jeffers. His first book of any consequence arrived on the scene just when all the early talk and discussion concerning the "New Poetry" was rapidly dying down. The talk and discussion had left secure the reputation of Robinson, Frost, Lindsay, possibly Sandburg; it had made the Imagists talked about but not followed; but now a new group of

*From *Poetry* 43 (March 1934): 338–42. Copyrighted by the Modern Poetry Association and reprinted by permission of the Editor of *Poetry*.

post-war radicals were to arrive on the scene, to resuscitate Pound and to proclaim Eliot and to produce an intensely intellectual, critical, metaphysical type of poetry that was to leave no other reputations intact except those which by temperament and direction were closely allied to their aims.

Against this current, as against every current, Mr. Jeffers stands and has stood aloof. One cannot rank him in the Eliot camp, along with Ransom and Tate. His version of Greece, compared with that of H. D., is like a great stone group of Titans and Centaurs as against a water-color drawing. He shows nothing of Sandburg's or Lindsay's folk-mysticism, or of the New England school's somewhat wearisome self-analysis. He has followed no forbears, unless it be the pathetically irresponsible George Sterling. And he has no really valid descendants. It is this aloofness, apart altogether from his extremely high skill in versification, that has granted to him his unique position.

And yet, if one examines this man closely, one may find certain features that are not unfamiliar. His misanthropy, his feeling that man is an unfortunate accident, gaining dignity only from sheer conflict with the gods, what is that but a bringing up-to-date of early nineteenth-century Byronism? His inhuman anti-human God, though derived probably from Nietzsche, what is that again but the mask of a Calvinism akin also to that of Byron? His isolation on the Pacific Coast, combined with the pride he quite obviously (and justly) feels as a spokesman of his community, what is that, too, but a new version of the familiar Byronic exile? And his patient rebuilding-up of Greece on the shores of the Pacific; what is that, too, but a romanticist's conception? This is not the Greece of Homer or Plato, but of Kleist and Hölderlin.

One may say of him therefore that though he will be always a valuable, an important poet, he will never achieve that apparently inevitable fusion of earthly and eternal interests which is what the world demands from its great poets. Of the qualities that go to make up a supreme poet: a Homer, a Shakespeare, a Milton, an Aeschylus, or a Goethe, he possesses only *some*. He is able to take lives of people of the present day and to relate them to a scheme of eternal (albeit in his case definitely nonhuman) values in a way no American poet has yet done. He is able also at will to summon up values from a great pagan past and to use them as a means of criticizing and condemning our shallow present-day. He is also (and perhaps this is his highest distinction) deaf to the parrot-cries of the communists that there can be no poetry that does not deliberately and shamelessly serve an obvious social purpose, and exalt one class above another. All this is greatly to his credit.

But when, some years ago, he tried to reembody the figure of Christ into a poem, the result was flat failure. He made Jesus merely another romantic and Byronic superman, with the usual Nietzschean contempt for mere humanity, a reading which is both grotesque and absurd. And his work since then has shown certain significant changes in direction. He still prefers to write about characters which are warped, thwarted, distorted mentally or morally, and hence inferior to their creator. But he has striven recently to imbue his conception of them with a little less fatalism and more sympathy. This is especially true in regard to his women characters. This tendency, already noticeable in *The Faithful Shepherdess* [sic], is even more apparent in the title-poem of the present collection.

The story is unusually simple; a modernized version of the Cain and Abel story. Fayne Frazer, married to Lance, is falling in love with his brother Michael, when Lance, seeing their dalliance, throws his brother from a cliff. To the crowd coming Lance wishes to tell all, but is forbidden by Fayne, who says that he had better "give his heart to the hawks for a snatch of meat" than let mankind control it—thereby obviously following Jeffers' own philosophy. She makes it appear that the fall from the cliff was an accident, but Lance becomes a haunted man, spending his time in killing hawks, injuring himself, and doing other half-insane and horrible things. Finally, in the hope of curing him, and under a fortune–teller's guidance, Fayne and he ride out to a spot in the mountains where there is said to be a spring surrounded by laurel. Just as they reach it, Lance throws himself from a cliff, leaving Fayne with his child in her womb to perhaps redeem the future.

Now it is obvious that of all these figures, it is chiefly to Lance that Mr. Jeffers wishes to attract our attention. Through the slaying of his brother—a slaying perfectly motivated by Fayne's attentions to Michael—he becomes the figure upon whom the chief Nemesis of the inhuman powers which, according to the poet's own philosophy, govern human affairs, is bound to fall. His heroism should therefore be shown in his long struggle with these powers. Jeffers, on the contrary, makes him nothing but a poor half-witted creature, with no definite purpose in his actions or thought. It is only Fayne, the much sinning and yet much forgiving, who holds our attention from first to last. She may be ignorant, stupid, the voice of a blind maternal instinct; but by her patience, her forgiveness, even by her double-dealing, she brings to naught Mr. Jeffers' own anti-human philosophy.

The difficulty, therefore, with Mr. Jeffers' position as a poet seems fairly easy to state. He is equipped for his task both as regards technique and philosophy. And as, unlike Mr. Eliot and the rest, he has never for a moment questioned that the poet has still a function to fulfill even at the present day, he has given us a great number of interesting poems. But his poems tend to get less and less interesting as he is obliged, by the tenets of his own inhuman creed, to make use in every poem of characters with strong streaks of neurotic obsession; or else to write pompous and inflated absurdity, as he does in the other long poem, *Resurrection,* of the present volume. This is his dilemma, and it is likely to operate to the total destruction of his poetry, unless he can soon find a new set of characters, a new background and outlook to go on. But to do so means the abandonment of most of the fatalistic aloofness which has already made him what he is. What he will do in this quandary, remains to be seen.

Solstice and Other Poems (1935)

Three New Books of Poetry

Percy Hutchison*

Those who have come to find in the startling poetic genius of Robinson Jeffers something not akin either to the elder poets or to the general run of poetry turned out today will not be disappointed in this new collection. True, it is a little more scattering than is usual with this Californian. Usually his major piece occupies approximately two-thirds of his book. *Solstice* uses up not more than a third of the present volume, with another third given to an epic drama the title of which is *At the Birth of an Age*, perhaps the most nearly philosophical thing Mr. Jeffers has yet done, that is, if it is conceivable that this thundering narrator of tragic tales could ever turn philosopher.

Solstice is in the true Jeffers manner. Simple, as the fundamental story of every one of his previous excursions has been, the story is briefly this: Madrone Bothwell, mother of two young children, has been divorced by her husband for the lovers she has had. In taking to herself lovers, Madrone had considered herself amply justified, but the law has been on the side of the husband, and has awarded him the children. Bothwell comes out to the lonely ranch on the night of the great Solstice wind to claim the boy and the girl. Madrone slays the two children and kills herself.

Thus barely told the summary is melodramatic enough to suit the most avid. But the melodrama of the tale is the least of Mr. Jeffers's concerns. His sole interest is the emotional conflict, which goes on within the breast of the mother. And in handling this sort of thing, allowing, of course, for a three-century change into modernism, perhaps even Freudianism, Jeffers is truly Elizabethan. Following his surcharged lines one is now exalted, now whirled into the depths of hell, as with Webster himself. Yet one must not be misled. Webster was for law and order; Jeffers is for neither order nor law. And which is right? There is the rub. And that is why this Coast iconoclast so piques one today. Plunging to the roots of things, as Jeffers does, he may be right. But when the law says that

*Excerpted from the *New York Times Book Review*, 20 October 1935, 28.

Madrone is not a competent mother, may not the law be right? A reader must follow the tumbling, smashing, driving lines of the poet and decide for himself. And, by the way of parenthesis, it should be stated that Jeffers is not to be appreciated, if, indeed, understood, until read aloud. His rhythms are for the ear, not for the eye. Take lines like these for an example:

> And the rain stinted. Madrone went down from the house between the
> night and the half-light and saw the gray breath
> Of the hot spring drift north, against the stone-hard darkness and body of
> the sea.

The verse of Robinson Jeffers is like that of Whitman. It must be conned, and aloud, again and again.

In the poem *At the Birth of an Age* Mr. Jeffers has gone to Norse and Teutonic mythology and tradition for a starting point. Gudrun, widow of Sigurd, who had been murdered by Gunnar and Hoegni, has lured them to the camp of Attila the Hun, whom she has subsequently married in order that they shall be killed.

But Jeffers goes beyond the ancient stories; his poem is an exploration of what was merely explicit in the time-hoary tale. Gudrun kills herself. In a note, written, Mr. Jeffers states, while the poem was in process, he saw a moral for the present age: "The theme of self-contradiction and self-frustration, in Gudrun's nature, intends to express a characteristic quality of this culture-age. . . . Its civilization is the greatest, but also the most bewildered and self-contradictory . . . that has ever existed." The minor poems of the book—they are but a handful—may be neglected. Robinson Jeffers has never been impressive in his short pieces. But in *At the Birth of an Age* we have a new conception of this arresting poet, a new Jeffers who has plunged deeper than heretofore. Whether, as time goes on, he will bring to the surface pearls of greater price, or only more iridescent shells, time alone will tell.

About Poetry and Poets

Ruth Lechlitner*

With Wagnerian thunder, Robinson Jeffers in the opening narrative poem of this volume, *At the Birth of an Age*, carries on the *Nibelungenlied* with the story of Gudrun who, having betrayed her three brothers to the Hun Attila, kills herself. But Jeffers doesn't allow his noble heroine any peace in the immediate hereafter: she has accepted "Christianity," hence her spirit must suffer for her sins. She meets and converses with Prometheus, the "hanged god," who sings Jeffers' theme–song: "With-

*From the *New Republic* 85 (8 January 1936): 262–63. Reprinted by permission.

out the pain, no knowledge of peace, nothing. Without the peace, no value in the pain."

This part of the poem, for all its confusing symbolism, rises to those dramatic heights which Jeffers, with his superb command of form, so often achieves. His Grecian chorus of Promethean singers, however, in passages such as the following, voice the poet's indictment of modern civilization:

—And who is to lead us in that day?
The gnomes of the chaste machines?—Not they.
—What, the scared rich?
—Snow: the sword.
—Into the ditch.
—Man has no nobler lord.
—Now the age points to the pit, all our vocation
Is to teach babes to jump.—Oh sterile
Process of Caesars, all the barren Caesars.

Jeffers tries to explain the whole poem's symbolism in an introductory note. Christianity, he says, has built a great, but contradictory civilization: it has caused a tension between civilization's two poles: western blood and superimposed orientalism. Further, he states, as the Christian *faith* becomes extinct, the Christian *ethic*—i.e., philanthropy, socialism, communism, etc.—gets stronger. All of which means, according to Mr. Jeffers, that because of the ascending Christian ethic, our civilization is on the downward path.

Solstice, the book's title-poem, is just another Jeffersian Carmelodrama. The short concluding lyrics, with their symbols of Rock (which some might interpret as ivory tower) and Hawk (emblem of Caesar) are more revealing. In "Shine, Republic," Jeffers says that America was "born to love freedom," but that freedom requires "blood for its fuel." Hence, America: "you will hood it like a kept hawk, you will perch it on the wrist of Caesar." This has the Jeffersian prophetic note. Not that he desires fascism, or communism either—oh no. Just plain annihilation of humankind (followed by peace) will do Mr. Jeffers nicely. Provided, I gather, that he can sit alone in his stone tower, surrounded by California scenery, while the whole disgusting business is going on, and dash off a last dramatic poem or two before Peace gathers him to her bosom.

Jeffers on the Age

Robert Penn Warren*

It is not probable that *Solstice and Other Poems* will do much to alter the reputation of Robinson Jeffers, for this collection brings nothing new.

*From *Poetry* 49 (February 1937): 279–82. Copyrighted by the Modern Poetry Association and reprinted by permission of the Editor of *Poetry* and Robert Penn Warren.

It is hard to say what kind of newness we expect when we pick up another volume by an established poet whose work we have read in the past. To expect something new need not brand one as light-minded and frivolous, even though the appetite for novelty, once out of hand and without center, is a dangerous thing for poets and readers of poetry, and accounts perhaps for the fickleness of the public, the hysteria of reviewers, and the random experimentation of the poets themselves. Needless to say, when we pick up that recent book of the established poet, we expect something not new; we expect some characteristic turn of mind, a development of faculties with which we are already acquainted, a flavor of the old idiom—on the whole, a continuity of some kind, for we do not like to feel that the poet in his new self has betrayed the poet in his old self more glibly and irresponsibly than we would do so. If the new self has betrayed the old self too readily, we are inclined to suspect that the poet never did mean what he said, that he is merely a clever eclectic, and that we were deluded in our former estimate; if the poet's experience of his poetry was meaningless, perhaps ours was meaningless too, and we ourselves should reconsider. But we also demand in the new book something new, a new formulation of the old qualities, perhaps, but that at least, and a somewhat lively sense of potential variety in experience. We do not like to feel that, though we can predict the beginnings, we can predict the ends. If not new concepts, we want at least new percepts to keep us awake and to feed the understanding by their just relations to, and embodiments of, the old concepts.

The present book contains a great deal of self-imitation. The title poem, *Solstice,* is like nothing so much as an ether dream Jeffers might have about some of his own poetry. The stereotypes of situation and language are here without the interest that was now and then achieved in *Tamar, Roan Stallion,* or *The Women at Point Sur.* In relation to the better of the earlier narratives the present one is repetition without direction. Waiving any question of the basic theme and impulse in the work of Jeffers, one might say that the only probable escape from this vice of self-imitation would be by a process of emphasizing and exploring the aspect of special character instead of the aspect of the general symbol on which Jeffers' poetry is so largely based. For these symbols have themselves been stereotyped. Our interest in the symbolic force of these narratives might be refreshed if we could be made to apprehend more intimately the persons as persons. All of this merely goes to say that Jeffers is often deficient in the dramatic sense; and this deficiency is more than of trifling importance in a writer who sets out to be a dramatic and narrative poet. The figures, gigantic, terrifying, and parabolical, are often on the verge of sinking back, again to be undifferentiated, into the general and often vague matrix of emotion from which they are shaped.

At the Birth of an Age, a much more interesting poem than *Solstice,* suffers less from this situation. The strictly dramatic part of the poem gives the story of Gudrun's self-conflict in relation to her brothers, Gunnar, Hoegni, and Carling, who are finally killed, not because she clearly wills her revenge for the death of Sigurd, but because she stands in vacillation after they have been lured to the camp of Attila's Horde. After Gudrun herself is dead, and the action proper is complete, the spirit of Gudrun, various choruses of spirits and voices, and the Hanged God, moralize the meaning of the preceding events and of life in general. The poet has assisted in pointing the rather inadequate communication coming from the spirit world by providing an introductory note on the meaning of the poem:

> The theme of self-contradiction and self-frustration, in Gudrun's nature, intends to express a characteristic quality of this culture-age, which I think should be called the Christian age, for it is conditioned by Christianity, and—except for a few centuries' lag—concurrent with it. Its civilization is the greatest, but also the most bewildered and self-contradictory, the least integrated, in some phases the most ignoble, that has ever existed. All these qualities, together with the characteristic restlessness of the age, its energy, its extremes of hope and fear, its passion for discovery, I think are bred from the tension between its two poles, of Western blood and superimposed Oriental religion. . . . This tension is really the soul of the age, which will begin to die when it ceases.

The first half of the poem has some of the most effective dramatic writing in Jeffers' work, and some of the most sharply visualized scenes. The action, as action, is given a real psychological focus in Gudrun. But the idea in the introductory note is not satisfactorily assimilated into the action—is not really dramatized—and the rhetorical fury of the last half, with occasional bursts of moving phrase, scarcely welds the materials of the poem into a whole.

On the whole, the short poems in the present volume compare less favorably with earlier pieces of the same nature than does *At the Birth of an Age* with previous long pieces. Jeffers has done several extremely effective short pieces, but the short poem usually shows him at his most turgid and feeble. When the support of a narrative interest is withdrawn, as in the short poems, Jeffers is ordinarily unable to achieve the concentration of interest in detail that gives the short poem its power. His short poems tend to be fragmentary comments, gnomic utterances without adequate context.

Such Counsels You Gave to Me and Other Poems (1937)

No Escape

Louis Untermeyer*

Robinson Jeffers is a poet whose utterance is so definite in its premises and so downright in its conclusions that the reader is compelled to take sides and appraise him not as a poet, but as a preacher, a force, an influence. Since his themes are, for the most part, tortured, and his conclusions are (from the human standpoint) almost negative, if not nihilistic, the number of Jeffers's readers will be limited to the hard few. These few thousand will treasure every statement in his latest volume, a volume that is packed with the strange combination—or is it a contradiction?—of revery and violence which has marked all the author's volumes since *Tamar* and *Roan Stallion*.

In essence, the philosophy of Such Counsels You Gave to Me is not so much a statement as an annotated restatement. Jeffers says what he has said again and again: humanity is debased; its civilization is degenerate; its increasingly huge centers are hideous; its machines are unholy; it is not fit to inhabit this once-clean earth. Love cheats the flesh, bewilders the mind, and betrays the spirit. Even death is dubious and no sure release, since annihilation is impossible in a universe where there is "no cave of peace, no night of quietness, no escape but change."

Death and the futile wish for escape are the main theme of the new volume; the poet's contempt for the average man and his reverence for abstract truth are the subsidiary motifs. In one poem he acknowledges, for the first time, his mission: "To be truth-bound, the neutral/Detested by all the dreaming factions, is my errand here."

The title poem is, like so many of Jeffers's longer poems, an adaptation of an old tale. But where most of the others were modernizations of myths and legends, this is an expansion of a ballad, the well known "Edward, Edward." The sixty pages are as emotional as they are modern, as passionate as they are perverse, as original in utterance as they are familiar in subject. Once again Jeffers employs an unhappy family relationship to evoke a sense of personal tragedy against a background of

*From the *Saturday Review of Literature* 16 (9 October 1937): 11. Reprinted by permission.

universal terror. The twenty-two other poems are less imposing, but they are scarcely less interesting. The shorter quasi-lyrics celebrate strength, the consolation of transient beauty, the solidity of sea-granite, and the will to endure against the horrors of new ways to give pain, new slaveries. Such elements do not make pretty verses, but they make impressive monoliths of poetry.

California Hybrid

Anonymous*

Poets want to take truth by the hand; prophets want to get truth by the tail. A hybrid of poet and prophet is tomahawk-faced Robinson Jeffers, almost as much famed in the U.S. for doing his writing in a stone tower, built by himself, overlooking California's Carmel Bay, as for his violent free-verse narratives and black-diamond lyrics in *Tamar, Roan Stallion, The Women at Point Sur, Cawdor,* et al.

Jeffers' latest book, *Such Counsels You Gave to Me,* is predominantly in his prophetic vein. Its title-poem is a fast-moving narrative of a student's sick return from pre-medical school to the farm of his swinish father and mother. In an atmosphere supercharged with nervous prostration, sadism, fornication, drunkenness, adultery and lack of funds the young student, at his mother's instigation, poisons his father. Maternal incest and suicide are thereafter overwhelmingly indicated, but Author Jeffers finally prescribes his hero's self-sacrificial surrender to the Law to put his story out of its misery. From the residue of ideological wreckage readers may salvage some souvenirs of sense by recalling that incest, in Jeffersian prophecy, symbolizes "racial introversion: man regarding man exclusively—founding his values, desires, a picture of the universe, all on his own humanity."

Few such symbological catch-alls confuse the book's shorter poems. They are mostly straightforward recordings of what Poet-Prophet Jeffers sees and feels when he looks around him in A.D. 1937. Samples:

> The age darkens, Europe mixes her cups of death, all the little Caesars fidget on their thrones,
> The old wound opens its clotted mouth to ask for new wounds. Men will fight through; men have tough hearts . . .
>
> I see far fires and dim degradation
> Under the war-planes and neither Christ nor Lenin will save you.
> I see the March rain walk on the mountain, sombre and lovely on the green mountain. . . .

*From *Time,* 18 October 1937, 86–87.

> I wish you could find the secure value,
> The all-heal I found . . .
> The splendor of inhuman things. . . .

Occasionally Poet Jeffers presents splendid glimpses, not of inhuman, but of nonhuman things:

> Perhaps their wildness will never die from these mountains.
> The eagle still dawns over the ridges like a dark sun . . .

Such glimpses, however, are few and cursory. The book as a whole reveals no new juxtaposition of the parts of Jeffers' hybrid nature, but rather a wearied division between them—with the aging prophet still hell-bent on emitting clouds of sulphur and smoke, and the poet simultaneously becoming more and more corner-loving and mealy-eyed.

Landscape with Jeffers

Louise Bogan*

The hero of Mr. Jeffers's latest set-piece of human savagery walks off the stage acting in an unusual way for a Jeffers character. He is moved, because of pity, to a moral decision. He chooses to shoulder another's punishment, after considering the advantages of suicide and escape. Previously he has acted in the usual Jeffersian manner: abetted his mother's incestuous passion for himself and stood by at his father's murder. He then turns over in his mind the question of whether anything is anything. Is there any crime, any innocence, any binding "human taboo"? Finally he decides that modern man has certain duties ("life is not rational"), and that retribution is one of them. So he turns away from union with the "clean" California wind and the "sane" California mountains, and chooses to expiate, not his own guilt, but his mother's.

All this is very fine, or would be in a character less queerly constituted than this young man is sure to be. Jeffers decides, at one point in the action, that human taboos can be transcended. God must have gone beyond human taboos. He is rather confused, however, on the stand that both ancient and modern man have taken concerning taboos. And he cannot, try as he will, in this case, force his characters to go beyond them. The mother-son incest theme proves too much for him. Classically and primitively, this breach of taboo brings down automatic punishment on even the unwitting transgressor. The wrath of the gods winds up, as Cocteau has expressed the process, like an infernal machine and fells the culprits. Oedipus actually marries Jocasta, in ignorance. A plague falls upon Thebes. In modern and romantic tragedy the incest-tainted hero,

*From the *Nation* 145 (23 October 1937): 442. Reprinted by permission of The Nation Company, Inc.

like Hamlet, is usually stricken with inaction. The hero in Jeffers's poem walks open-eyed into the beginning of an incestuous relationship with his mother. But at the last moment he sheers off. He talks as though he were capable of anything. In point of fact he is capable of nothing but a great many obscurely expressed wrong reasons for his traditional stirrings of conscience. And he arouses little sympathy in the reader. For he and his mother—who, like most of Jeffers's women, *is* capable of anything—seem not so much puzzled and depraved as simple-minded. And, perhaps unfortunately, in the humanity Jeffers professes to despise, the moral struggles of idiots somehow do not count.

The romantic poet should not continue, over a long period, to excoriate the humanity of which he is a member. The satirist can manage analysis and defamation of the human race. He stands outside. The romantic is involved in the action. The more he strives to identify himself with clean and mindless nature, the more he must degrade his characters and increase the enormity of their crimes. Meanwhile, his own importance increases by leaps and bounds. He is soon no longer content to be chorus, commentator, or prophet. He tends toward the state of God Himself. Jeffers says:

> I the last living man
> That sees the real earth and skies,
> Actual life and real death.
> The others are all prophets and believers
> Delirious with fevers of faith.

and again:

> "To be truth-bound, the neutral
> Detested by all the dreaming factions, is my errand here."

Notions of this inflated kind now frequently appear everywhere in Jeffers. His lyrics, the forms he has many times successfully filled with his intense emotion and remarkable descriptions of natural beauty, are now vitiated by pronouncements. It is a pity that his mixed, parochial, and rather Presbyterian disgusts must thus gain headway. A man who has, from the beginning, turned away from the arts, "sports and gallantries, the stage, the antics of dancers," as childish nonsense, must at length grow peevish, even surrounded by noble landscapes. "Bitter earnestness," for the dramatic poet, can be a faculty which cuts both ways.

"In very truth, the man who can see all creatures in himself, himself in all creatures, knows no sorrow." Such a man is also protected against ultimate confusion and obsession. Jeffers's great talents, allowed some humble relation to the race, which, whatever its faults, can at least laugh and change, might have escaped the limits that now increasingly distort them.

Poet's Page

Muriel Rukeyser*

Jeffers has taken the large inward theme on which his finest work rests, and in his latest book has done an incest-tragedy in the meanings which he has specialized: guilt, ambition, conquest of tabu, conquest of nature and civilization into a unique assertion. But in the title poem the story is truncated, the return is to infancy, not to birth, the act is not committed. The son, in a knot of college chemistry and family, goes home after failing a mid-term exam. His father, presented throughout with a beast-image ("the powerful coarse-fibered man, an inch less tall / and twice as broad, sunburnt and wind-bitten, dark-haired, / and the eyes paler blue, like the eyes of domestic swine, Howard thought, the white ones") stands as a quite ordinary business man, refusing to repair his son by giving him thirty dollars a month. The mother, the Jeffers woman again, is the clew: beautiful, powerful, frustrated (the *Main Street* frustration gone west), she has the Jeffers-woman consciousness of superiority to her husband, and plays off her son continually against him. This time, the child is near breakdown from exhaustion, the lost hope that he may finish college, excitement over progress in chemical research, and the load of guilt and suspicion placed on him by his love for his mother. The story is a filled-in and up-to-date version of the bare magnificent ballad from which the title comes. The variations depend on the bottle of KCN, the atmosphere of an outer world full of threats and war, the showing of the mother's breasts as climax, and the frightening and vivid scenes with the son's *Doppelgänger*, seen white and merging on the hills at the beginning and the end. The hallucination walks beside him after the murder, after the mother's love has been offered and refused; and the son decides to stand trial.

The second half of the book shuttles between description which has already sealed the Carmel coast and the country behind it as Jeffers' country, recognizable in the sea, the tangled shore, the colors of hills and passes, the one hawk always hanging in the air—all this which has made him a great place-poet, and defined a meaning for his district—between such description and rabid attacks on man's beliefs, attempts and struggles not to acquiesce. Integrity, he repeats, truth, loneliness. But they appear in attacks so mixed and meaningless, so half-true in their insistence, that, reading these shorter poems, one is tempted to accept only the half that rests on emotion for quality or place, setting aside every mental step. But it is impossible to treat an important poet as a submental type, even when he has thrown all the names in one bag, and spills out for condemnation Spain, China, Russia, Germany, Power, Lenin, Caesar, Humanity. The mess of ideas is shocking. Jeffers has, powerfully, hatred of violent will; but he has even more strongly what Joseph Conrad called the "desire for finality," a

*From the *New Republic* 93 (29 December 1937): 234. Reprinted by permission.

superstition, a religion, a blood-need for climax that urges him, fearing a stupid and brutal crowd, to bury the race; and, fearing imperfect love, into its extremities. And this makes tragic poetry, great wishes for perfection, choked demands for peace—and, for solution, total destruction (Jeffers is totalitarian, too) or a walk in the hills ("I wish you could find the secure value, the all-heal I found") and an end like this:

> rich unplanned life on earth
> After the foreign wars and the civil wars, the border wars
> And the barbarians: music and religion, honor and mirth
> Renewed life's lost enchantments. But if life even
> Had perished utterly, Oh perfect loveliness of earth and heaven.

The Selected Poetry of Robinson Jeffers (1938)

Nine and Two

Anonymous*

Robinson Jeffers, California's unofficial laureate, this month published his *Selected Poetry.* In its foreword he stated his poetic creed. He declared that "poetry must concern itself with (relatively) permanent things." His work at its best does give an impression of the emptiness of the American continent, an emptiness which the continent fills with (relatively) permanent things like forests, mountains, rivers and 130 million people, and which Jeffers, for the most part, fills with mythological personages, semi-scientific platitudes, nonpoetical intensities, and—for the pay-off—mental exhaustion.

> The poet as well
> Builds his monument mockingly . . .
> Yet stones have stood for a thousand years, and pained thoughts found
> The honey of peace in old poems.

Because his words are impersonally grandiose instead of personally grand, Robinson Jeffers, who in another place and another time might have been a prophet, is here and now a vasty poetaster.

Tragedy or Violence?

Dudley Fitts†

Mr. Jeffers anticipates objections to his work in a very interesting poem, "Self-Criticism in February." It is in the form of interior dialogue, too long to quote here; but in it he raises the following points: (a) his poetry has a disproportionate tendency towards violence; (b) the characters of his fictions are too often "ghosts and demons and people like phantoms . . . praying for destruction"; (c) he is without an "ideal," he has never sung "That God is love, or perhaps that social Justice will soon prevail." In

*Excerpted from a review of eleven poets in *Time*, 26 December 1938, 41–44. Reprinted by permission from *Time.*

†From the *Saturday Review of Literature* 19 (22 April 1939): 19. Reprinted by permission.

answer to (a) he observes that our time is founded on violence, "pointed for more massive violence"; to (b), "Alas, it is not unusual in life"; and to (c) he says, echoing Nietzsche, "I can tell lies in prose." The answers seem conclusive; but as one turns to them again and again during the reading of these poems, one's doubts about them increase.

The long narrative poems provoke the most doubt. Our time is "founded on violence," the poet reflects the time. But does he? Surely there is violence enough: incest, bestiality, imbecility, arson, murder, suicide, all nakedly set down with the vehemence of a latter-day Kyd. But the violence exists (or a lack of art makes it seem to exist) for its own sake. It is meaningless beyond itself. Well, so is the violence of our time: I am thinking, for instance, of the aerial bombing of child refugees in Catalonia clamoring at the French border. It would seem, then, that reflection is not enough; that reflection is not true. It is not true, because it lacks philosophy. (A large word; but I mean the opposite of the nihilistic disgust that is Mr. Jeffers's attitude towards his people.) And from this too-true-to-be-true violence a disconcerting quality emerges: mirth.

"Look on the tragic loading of this bed." What is it that keeps the corpse-strewn finales of *Othello,* of *Hamlet,* of *Lear* from being Grand Guignol and funny? The tragic passion, the affirmative attitude towards human suffering. In *Thurso's Landing, Give Your Heart to the Hawks,* and *Tamar* there is only the suffering, and the attitude towards it is destructive. A short poem of this nature may succeed, and, indeed, Mr. Jeffers's short poems are generally his best ones; but disgust and horror cannot successfully be sustained for so long as this poet would sustain them. By the time Helen Thurso cuts Reave's throat with his own hunting-knife and then proceeds to kill herself, oh very lingeringly, with abortion-tablets (whatever they may be), there has been so much visceral outrage, so much public drinking of blood, that the temptation to laugh is almost overpowering. And it is not an hysterical laughter.

Two of these long poems are valid, although their validity may be the fortuitous result of their being placed in this Californian Chamber of 'Orrors. *The Tower Beyond Tragedy* is the myth of Agamemnon's death; and while Mr. Jeffers insists on the incestuous Elektra-Orestes theme with a gusto that would probably astonish Sophocles, the remoteness of the myth, the grandeur adhering to it, and the magnificent rhetoric of many of Clytemnestra's speeches combine to make a powerful poem. Observe, in this case, that the poet's attitude was largely determined by tradition. The other success is *The Loving Shepherdess,* a parable of self-sacrificing love. Here the pastoral quality is so beautifully managed that one forgets the essential absurdity of the heroine in her philanthropic quest. The myth atmosphere is again in control: *credo quia absurdum.*

Mr. Jeffers's great virtues are the ability to tell a story and to sustain tremendous rhythms for long periods. His curious verse-form, a development of Whitman's is perfectly suited to narrative. In his descriptions of scenery he is always effective. What he lacks is restraint (yes, let's admit that Nature is unrestrained) and, above all things, humor. One does not mean by "humor" a sense of fun, but a sense of balance, of design, of (let us brave the answer to Objection A) proportion. Some day someone is going to laugh right out in meeting.

Robinson Jeffers

Sherman Conrad*

The first reaction to this volume is one of astonishment at its mere size; it runs to 615 packed pages. And in his preface Jeffers says that this is only half of his published work. Most of his maturer work is here, however: *Tamar, Roan Stallion, The Tower Beyond Tragedy, The Loving Shepherdess, Thurso's Landing, Give Your Heart to the Hawks, Descent to the Dead, At the Birth of an Age*, in their entirety; passages from *Cawdor* and *The Women at Point Sur*; 100 short pieces, 4 of which are new. *Dear Judas* and *Such Counsels You Gave to Me* are omitted. But seen in collection, even these uniquely notable works bulk out of all proportion to the residual impression of them that memory has accumulated during the last fifteen years. After re-experiencing them in this book, that superficial first feeling of bulkiness is seen to have the deepest implications and provides as good a basis as any for making a short, useful statement about Jeffers's achievement as poet.

In his foreword Jeffers tells of his recognition, in an experimental period before 1920, that "poetry must reclaim substance and sense . . . physical and psychological reality." His cause was common here with others in the so-called Anglo-American movement in poetry—Pound, Eliot, the anti-Georgians. Like them he sensed that "poetry would find its old freedom" through a renewed traffic with prose, in that shifting borderland where the two exchange vigors. Jeffers, however, rejected "modern" French and English poetry as "thoroughly defeatist" and "was led to write narrative poetry." His capitulation to the methods of prose appears now to have been too complete. *La poésie*, like *la vérité*, exists only *dans les nuances*. That unaccountable solace and ecstasy that are poetry's special bounty are nowhere in these 600-odd pages bestowed. There is an occasional intuition of such an approach—as always, when image intensifies in brilliance and definition—but it always misses, diluted into mere language, deflected into diagrammatic idea. His plays are no more theater-poetry than Hugo's; his narratives are poetically as diffuse as "The Lady of the Lake."

Having asserted Jeffers's lack of poetry in that pureness which the

*From the *Nation* 148 (3 June 1939): 651–52. Reprinted by permission of The Nation Company, Inc.

true poet reveals, it is immediately necessary to define another sense in which his writing attains to the condition of poetry. For it does; the experience of it is valid and undeniable. Whitman is a convenient comparison. What gives life to the work of such writers—and in practice it is useless to distinguish such *life* from poetry—is the vividness of the man's personality as put on the page. (Whitman does, of course, very signally achieve true, created image at times, as in "Out of the Cradle.") Jeffers's poetic impact for his contemporaries comes from the intensity of his personal point of view. Nietzsche's phrase, "The poets lie too much," was a formative one for him he says. He has told his truth at all times; the short first-person lyrics are no different in this from the narratives. His truth is that particularly contemporary segment of truth that has lent importance to the work of Faulkner, O'Neill, and, among lesser talents, James Cain.

The only legitimate criticism of this kind of poetry lies in the plain fact that few if any writers have enough in their personalities to keep themselves or their readers going. Whitman is one of the few who was wide and deep enough, beneath the ballyhoo loving enough, to keep most of the actually prosy bulk of his work inspirited with poetry. But, "I am cold and undiscriminating," Jeffers says. Una Jeffers, his wife, "has been my nerves, eyes, sympathies." He sees life intensely, but through a pinhole: pin point of a hawk's eye, might be his own phrase. As a single image of horror, Tamar Cauldwell or Clytemnestra rivets and purges us with terror, if not with pity. The repetition of this same spectacle in poem after poem results in something as grotesque and boring as a sideshow of freaks. In a collection of these works, such as this book, Jeffers's crippling limitations are completely revealed.

Jeffers's position is not an easy one. He has found no truth more finally acceptable than Spengler's cyclical decline of cultures, and behind that the final exhaustion of the universe resulting from the second law of thermodynamics. Thus he has been unable to believe in the worth of anything with whole seriousness. From this deficiency, this lack of Yeats's "fighting-mad" violence, comes the sprawling enervation and the very small satisfaction to be had from his poetry. He has loved neither art nor life enough. But here criticism must halt. For in the deepest sense Jeffers obviates human values, and criticism has no others.

Sources of Violence

Delmore Schwartz*

The present volume is beautifully printed, contains a handsome photograph of Jeffers, and is furnished with a very interesting and dignified

*From "The Enigma of Robinson Jeffers," in *Poetry* 55 (October 1939), part 1: 30–38.

foreword by the author. Although only half of his poetry is here and the important poem called *The Women at Point Sur* is omitted, evidently because "it is the least liked and the least understood" of his poems, nevertheless this selection presents a sufficient span of writing in its six hundred pages to give any reader a just conception of what Jeffers has done. Above all, this selection invites a brief consideration and judgment of Jeffers' work as a whole, especially with regard to its sources.

At least one source is the scientific picture of the universe which was popular and "advanced" thought until a few short years ago. The versions of the implications of 19th-century science afforded by writers like Haeckel and Huxley seemed to create a picture of the world in which there was no room for most human values. The world was a wound-up machine or a whirling mass of chemical elements which stretched out without end and without purpose. No Deity assured justice or love or immortality, but the infinite emptiness reported by astronomy and the survival of the fittest of Darwinism seemed to comprise a definite and indubitable answer to human effort and belief. This is the world-view which has been the basis, in part, of the work of many other and quite different authors. It is to be found in the novels of Theodore Dreiser, in the plays of Bernard Shaw, in the criticism of H. L. Mencken (who suggests Nietzsche as an early and much more serious example), in the early philosophical writing of Bertrand Russell, in the poetry of Archibald MacLeish, and Joseph Wood Krutch's *The Modern Temper*, where it is explicitly announced that such things as love and tragedy and all other specifically human values are not possible to modern man. Russell suggests I. A. Richards, whose "sincerity ritual" to test the genuineness of a poem operates in part by envisaging the meaninglessness of the universe in the above sense, and Krutch suggests some of the best poems of Mark Van Doren, where the emptiness of the sky is the literal theme.

When Jeffers says in his foreword and in a number of his poems that he wishes to avoid lies, what he means by lies are all beliefs which would somehow deny or ameliorate this world-view. When he speaks repeatedly of stars, atoms, energy, rocks, science, and the power of Nature, it is the Nature of 19th-century science which he has in mind and which obsesses him. For Wordsworth, but a hundred years before, Nature was an image of the highest values; for Jeffers it has become merely a huge background which proffers only one delight, annihilation, and which makes human beings seem to him puny and disgusting beasts whose history is the tiniest cosmic incident.

But Jeffers' disgust with human beings seems to have another and less intellectual source. The poems he has written about Woodrow Wilson and Clemenceau and the brutality of modern warfare suggest that the source of his obsession with human violence was the World War. Here again parallels plead to be mentioned, as if an age were an organic entity, for one remembers that other writers who came to young manhood during the war, William Faulkner, Eugene O'Neill, Ernest Hemingway, have been similarly obsessed with violence, cruelty, rape, murder, and destruction. The California coast which serves as a background for Jeffers, and to which he came, he says, by pure accident, provides a third dominant element. "The strange, introverted, and storm-twisted beauty of Point Lobos," as Jeffers' stage-set for his narrative poems, is merely another example of how birds, or perhaps one should say, hawks, of a feather flock together.

The world-picture of 19th-century science, the World War, and Jeffers' portion of the Pacific Coast are not, however, merely sources of his work, but actually, with little disguise, the substance of his poems. Of these three elements, the cosmology in question has definitely been discarded with the radical progress of science and scientific thought, and with the recognition that some of the supposed implications of 19th-century science were only the emotions of those who had lost their childhood faith or been dismayed by the bigness of the universe, as if bigness were an especially significant aspect. The World War too turns out not to have been either merely a display of human brutality or the crusade of an idealist, as Jeffers seems to take it to be when he writes of Wilson; but something quite different. And as for Point Lobos, one may very well question whether it can be accepted as a more accurate exhibit of Nature than Wordsworth's Lake Country, the state of Connecticut, or the city of New York. Such a question is to be raised only when the poet takes his landscape as being of universal significance.

The point involved is one of truth, the truth not of ultimate beliefs, but given facts. The poetry of Jeffers represents for the most part a response to the particular facts just mentioned. But if the facts are poorly envisaged, how adequate can the response be? Stated in terms of ideas, Jeffers' response is an ideology. Stated in terms of the emotions, his response is hysterical. Human beings are often brutal, Nature is sometimes violent, and life is indeed a mystery, but to respond as Jeffers does by rejecting humanity and saluting the peace of death is to come to a conclusion which is not only barren, a result which pleases Jeffers, but also false, and thus in the end without interest and without value.

This falsity has various consequences which define it precisely. There is no need to raise the usual and banal objections, to argue like a schoolboy over whether or not Jeffers is self-contradictory in denying human freedom and presenting characters who choose their actions, or to urge the contradiction of writing poetry which will only be read by the species which is being rejected, or to howl with facile radicalism that this tragic attitude is made possible by an income. It would be simple for the admirer of Jeffers to answer each of these accusations. But what cannot be adequately defended are the consequences in the poetry itself, both in the lyrics where we are presumably to get a representation of emotion and in the narrative poems where we ought to be getting a representation of human action.

The narrative poems constitute the major part of Jeffers' work and it is upon them that the weight of untruth is most unfortunate. In *The Tower Beyond Tragedy,* for example, the alternatives presented to the hero are: either incest or a complete rupture with humanity. One needs no knowledge of the Agamemnon story to know that this is not a genuine tragic dilemma, either for Orestes or for any other human being. And again in *Roan Stallion,* the two alternatives presented to the heroine, either sexual intercourse with a drunken and brutish husband or with a horse, are not mutually exhaustive of all possible choices, and the dénouement is not made more plausible when the stallion kills the man, in obedience to nothing but the doctrinal requirements of the poet. What happens in both stories and throughout the narrative writing is not only not true of human life even at its most monstrous—such untruth might conceivably be justified as an extreme use of symbols—but the untruth is essentially a matter of the contexts provided by the poet, the situations which he has furnished for his characters. Orestes' choice is unjustified by the character he has been given and the life which confronts him, and the heroine of "Roan Stallion" is untrue in the same literal sense, both characters being compelled to their acts by nothing but the emotion of the poet, an emotion utterly removed from their lives and differently motivated.

The same lack is present in the lyrics, and as in the narratives it was a narrative lack, so in the lyrics what is absent betrays itself in lyrical terms. The following poem, "Science," is worth quoting as an example to justify this judgment and also as a typical statement of doctrine:

> Man, introverted man, having crossed
> In passage and but a little with the nature of things this latter century
> Has begot giants; but being taken up
> Like a maniac with self-love and inward conflicts cannot manage his
> hybrids.
> Being used to deal with edgeless dreams,
> Now he's bred knives on nature turns them also inward: they have thirsty
> points though.
> His mind forbodes his own destruction;
> Actaeon who saw the goddess naked among leaves and his hounds tore him.
> A little knowledge, a pebble from the shingle,
> A drop from the oceans: who would have dreamed this infinitely little too
> much?

What is to be noted here is the number of shifts the poet finds necessary in order to state the observation which concerns him. The machines of science which man cannot manage are named as giants, hybrids, knives. The knowledge of science which makes possible these machines is successively compared to a vision of Diana, a pebble, and a drop of water. The classical allusion to Actaeon's vision of the goddess is also in abrupt disjunction with the previous metaphor, man as a dreamer who has bred knives and as an introvert who has begotten giants. There is no rule or law which makes it impossible for a poet to go from one metaphor to another even in a very short poem, but such a transit can only be justified if it accomplishes some expressive purpose. Here the shifts, however, weaken each metaphor, preventing the reader from getting a clear picture of a thing, process or condition, by means of which to grasp the notion and the emotion in question. Actaeon's vision of Diana is plainly not at all symmetrical with man as a begetter of dangerous giants. And the reason for this disorder is the desire of the poet to state an emotion about modern industrialism or armament in terms of the belief—too general to be meaningful—that knowledge is a dangerous thing for man. If the emotion were justified by a fact, then the fact would provide the emotion with adequate lyrical terms. But, to repeat, since the fact was imperfectly envisaged and the poet saw modern industrialism merely as an instance of incestuous brutality (man is introverted, self-loving, and thus incestuous for Jeffers), the emotion could not command the metaphors which would make it consistent and vivid upon the page.

The argument may seem theoretical and had better be made more evident and more lucid by comparison. Lear upon the heath with Kent and the fool represents a vision of the cruelty of the human heart which is in every sense more appalling than any equivalent desolation to be found in Jeffers. And yet the difference in literary terms is immense. The poet has managed to adhere to the formal burden of the play and of blank verse, he has provided a suitable individuation for the main characters, and he has not found it necessary to resort to continuous physical violence in order to present the emotion he feels about the human heart. A further point to be made, probably by the open-eyed optimist, is that Kent, the faithful friend, does accompany Lear upon the heath, and Cordelia does balance the cruelty of Goneril and Regan at the plausible ratio of two-to-one. One could scarcely consider *King Lear* a play in which it is affirmed that God's in His heaven and all's well with the world. Nor could one conceivably affirm that the poet was engaged in telling comforting lies about the human species. But the play is nevertheless a representation of life which can stand as a measure of what one means by the whole truth when one is confronted by such writers as Jeffers. Two other relevant touchstones may be mentioned in passing, *Moby Dick*, in which there is a similar regard for Nature, and the writing of Pascal in which the astronomical diminution of man is considered in its implication as to man's importance in the universe.

The mention of Shakespeare, however, may suggest a fundamental difficulty with the critical method which is being used. If the poet is examined by his ability to present the truth, and if many of his formal defects are attributed to emotions which spring from a distorted view of particular facts, then what is one to say when a ghost or witch appears in Shakespeare, or when in some respect the poet's substance is a response to beliefs about the world which the reader does not find acceptable? The problem of belief in poetry makes its inevitable re-appearance, like an unwanted cat. Without wishing to raise the whole subject, the answer here seems fairly plain. The predicament of Hamlet does not depend in the least upon the actuality of ghosts (a question about which there is no need to be dogmatic), and in general, most great poetry does not depend upon the truth of its philosophical beliefs, although it requires them as a structure and a framework. But in Jeffers the beliefs about the world and the consequent emotions are the substance of the poetry, and the observations of land and sea and the narrative characters are merely the means, which reverses the relationship. In the *Inferno*, the Christian system helps to make possible a vision of human beings; in Jeffers, the human beings are there to make possible a vision of Jeffers' ideas of the world. Hence the literary critic is pressed to judge the ideas and the emotion which they occasion. It might also seem that Jeffers is being taken too literally, that his avowed rejection of humanity is "really" a subliminal disguise; and his hatred of cities might be understood as a social reaction. But in Jeffers, as opposed to other poets, it is impossible to make such a translation without ceasing to be a literary critic and becoming biographer, psychoanalyst, or sociologist. The substance of the poetry is his emotion about humanity and the wide world. The poet's business is to *see*, by means of words, and we can only judge him by what he presents as seen.

One is permitted to adopt any belief, attitude, or emotion that especially pleases one. But when one begins to act upon belief or emotion, and in particular when one begins to write poetry, a million more considerations, in addition to the few already mentioned, intrude of necessity. When one attempts to write narrative poems about human beings, the obligation of a sufficient knowledge of human beings intervenes, the necessity of a definite measure of rhythm descends upon one, and literature as an organic tradition enters upon the scene. Jeffers undoubtedly has a keen sense for the landscape and seascape he writes about and he is by no means without a knowledge of human beings. But on the basis of detesting humanity, the natural tendency is to turn away from a strict view of human beings as they actually are and to regard a concern with literature, *technically*, as being at best unnecessary, at worst a hindrance. The result is that the characters Jeffers writes about tend to become repetitive abstractions, and the long line of Jeffers' verse is corrupted repeatedly by the most gauche inconsistencies of rhythm. The causal sequence seems indubitable. The poet has decided that the emotion he feels is strong enough to justify any manipulation of characters; and the breaches of consistency in his rhythm appear to him to be merely a "literary" or formal matter:

> I say
> Humanity is the mould to break away from, the crust to break through,
>   the coal to break into fire,
> The atom to be split . . .

and the poet is breaking away from literature as well as humanity in his poems, which we are asked to accept as literature, and in which we are presumably presented with humanity.

Be Angry at the Sun and Other Poems (1941)

The Day Is a Poem

Stanley Kunitz*

Looking back in his flight, Robinson Jeffers sees the world turning to salt, as he had prophesied in his long crying of violence and doom. Mixed with his horror is a pardonable trace of pride, such as might become a vehement old warlock who, after interminable conjurings, suddenly produces a fell spirit from his kettle of bones and excrement.

> Well: the day is a poem: but too much
> Like one of Jeffers's, crusted with blood and barbaric omens,
> Painful to excess, inhuman as a hawk's cry.

With this stricken world, dyed in the "noble, rich glowing color of blood," Jeffers can be friend: it is the familiar world of his imagination. Now that he begins to retrace his footsteps, it may be pertinent to inquire why he left us in the first place and to what fellowship he may return.

The picture of Jeffers as avatar, stone-breasted and prehistorical, living in majestic isolation with a gang of clacking Furies for company, has been one of the formidable illusions of twentieth-century poetry. To have created that illusion is in itself a triumph. Actually, like the early nineteenth-century Romantic poets, he has been wielding his bright sword against the industrial revolution and the rise of scientific materialism. Since the time was late and the fight seemed lost, he could only renounce the civilization that had suffered itself to be tainted. All this disaffection, carried to the extreme of nihilism, stems from an overpowering disgust with "the immense vulgarities of misapplied science and decaying Christianity." What Taine said of Byron may be said, with equal appropriateness, of Jeffers: "Inevitably imprisoned within himself, he could see nothing but himself; if he must come to other existences, it is that they may reply to him; and through this pretended epic he persisted in his eternal monologue."

Continuing his "pretended epic," Jeffers opens this volume with a

*From *Poetry* 49 (December 1941):148–54. Copyrighted by The Modern Poetry Association and reprinted by permission of the Editor of *Poetry* and by permission of the author.

long narrative poem entitled *Mara,* which does no more than restate, with a new cast of incestuous phantoms, the allegory he has been writing for some twenty years. With practiced hand he flicks his long whip-like lines; the rhythms are beautifully controlled; the story leaps from one explosion of emotion to another; if at times the language turns tasteless and gauche, particularly in expressions of sentiment, at other times it redeems itself effortlessly, as when "the artery sprayed like a firehose," or "the slow flies vultured the table." But nowhere does it match his best writing, when the language turns all to light, as in saying of a man's dying, "It is only someone dropping a mask. / A little personality lost, and the wild / Beauty of the world resumed." That is from another and better poem in this book.

Mara itself is only a mask, and when it is dropped, a monumental ennui stares out at us. Here are "a cancerous old man, a jealous wife . . . , and a little young hot adulteress between her two men," one of whom is her husband, the other his brother. It is old stuff to Jeffers; he is bored writing it, and, what is worse, we are permitted to sense his boredom, his feeling that he has spun too many myths out of himself, that they have turned on him and are devouring him. He wants a living symbol who can project his sense of tragic destiny; who can enact on the world's stage the grandiose drama of Romantic irony and Romantic despair; into whom he can pour the disastrous vials of his spirit. Into the midst of "Mara," as though he had been waiting restlessly in the wings all the time, bursts, if only for a moment to take his bow, the Person for whom Jeffers has been waiting, the genius of his dire prophecies. We do not actually see him; our only contact with him is through his voice, his passionate high bark heard on the radio, bringing "scorn and dog wrath" from the pits of Europe, as the war starts and an old man wearily handles his pain.

Bruce Ferguson, the protagonist of *Mara,* who hangs himself "by a horse-hair hackamore under a beam in the barn," may be the last of an ill-starred dynasty beginning with Tamar Cauldwell from Lobos. For better or worse, Jeffers has found his flesh-and-blood Manfred. In *The Bowl of Blood*, a 27-page masque following *Mara,* he introduces, for the first time in English poetry, Hitler as hero.

The scene of *The Bowl of Blood*—a magnificent accomplishment, by all odds the most important poem in the book—is a desolate cabin on the Schleswig shore of the North Sea. Attended by three maskers, a fishwife with a gift for prophecy leans over a basin of blood. Hitler has come to her for consultation. Out of her trance appear first the visions of Frederick the Great and Napoleon, enacted by the maskers. Reminding the Leader of how they failed, these apparitions serve only to agitate him: "This is my Gethsemane night, Christ's agony in the garden: only to great artists / Come these dark hours."

At last appears the spirit of his friend Ernst Friedenau, a young German soldier of 1917. The seance takes a turn for the better. The British, it is predicted, will be "howked out" of Norway. Holland and Flanders will submit. France will fall within sixty days. But Friedenau gives one emphatic warning: "Strike not England too soon . . . Strike in September; or if later, better."

This is false advice. Why is it given?

"Because a prompt invasion would catch England in anguish and end the war this year; which is not intended. The war must grind on, and grind small. It must not end when France falls, nor when England is beaten. It must not end when the ends of the earth are drawn in. God is less humane than Hitler, and has larger views."

The tragedy must be played out, "down into dreary revolution and despair, exhaustion and shabby horrors and squalid slavery," down to the death of "the boys without blemish," down to the finish of Europe.

At the close of the masque the medium, struggling to regain consciousness, upsets the basin of blood at Hitler's feet. He cries out in horror, pays her "the usual small fee," and leaves the cabin. "Watch this man, half conscious of the future, / Pass to his tragic destiny."

Jeffers' work has always had the force and the torment of great art. This poem contains, in addition, virtues for which he had not consistently prepared us: beauty of form; imagination of a high order; a style economical, just, bone-clean. Of the quality of the writing I need say only that it is maintained not far below the level of this passage:

> Listen: power is a great hollow spirit
> That needs a center.
> It chooses one man almost at random
> And clouds him and clots around him and it possesses him.
> Listen: the man does not have power,
> Power has the man.

Yes, the masque is undoubtedly a success—I am even tempted to call it the greatest masque since *Comus*—but when Jeffers takes, as it were, the somnambulant Leader's arm and conducts him sympathetically from the scene, I cannot help experiencing a curious shiver of apprehension, not so much for what he has here done with Hitler as for what Hitler may do to him. What is the nature of the impulse that led Jeffers to treat Hitler as a tragic figure, instead of as the ubiquitous Beast of Berchtesgaden? Rationalizing, one may say that Hitler is to Jeffers what Lucifer was to Milton, and one would rest content with that analogy if only it were possible to regard politics as a fiction. To my mind, Hitler is Jeffers' hero not because Jeffers condones the fascist program but because Hitler is the instrument of that destruction of civilization, that obliteration of humankind, which Jeffers has long invoked as both necessary and good. Violence is all. It is the recurrent theme of the lyrics that close this book:

It is not bad. Let them play.
Let the guns bark and the bombing-plane
Speak his prodigious blasphemies.
It is not bad, it is high time,
Stark violence is still the sire of all the world's values.

Jeffers' myth of himself is that he stands beyond moral judgment, so far removed from the hot human struggle that he is like Fawn Ferguson bathing in the mountain stream and watching, without a tremor, as a cream-colored car far down the mountain crashes through the bridge-rails and goes pitching down the canyon. "There was nothing to do about it at this distance."

Jeffers stood "at this distance" when he wrote *The Bowl of Blood.* His dilemma is that as he approaches the contemporary scene in other poems, written on a lower level of the imagination, his symbols of violence and his death-wish for our civilization assume inevitably a political coloring. The nature of that coloring may be deduced from his observations on our world at war.

Roosevelt and Hitler are one to him, "the two hands of the destroyer." Germany and England are one to him. What does it matter? "If England goes down and Germany up / The stronger dog will still be on top, / All in the turning of time." "Beware of taking sides," he warns.

I am willing to grant that the integrity of Jeffers' life has been such that he could support a view so extreme, but only if his position were in fact as extreme, as out-of-the-world as he supposes. Then he would be invulnerable, and what he says could be construed as the kind of high foolishness discerned by Blake: "If a fool would persist in his folly, he would be wise."

In order to elucidate Jeffers' world-views I have had to over-simplify his position. Actually, in this book he is not a consistent thinker: frequently he does not think at all; what I wish to stress is that in becoming a topical poet he has forfeited the detachment on which he prides himself. He *does* take sides, sometimes contradictory sides. England he praises—"bleeding, at bay, magnificent, at last a lion"—when he is not dispassionately watching her go under; Russia he sneers at; Finland he eulogizes—"the best nation in Europe." To "the dupes that talk democracy" he is unkind, for he is one who, like the old boar of the mountains, believes in tusks. He projects a vision of "armed imperial America," powerful, guilty, doomed, and this albeit with qualms he celebrates in the manner of Henry Luce proclaiming the American Century. Doctor of doom, with the works of Spengler in his bag, he prescribes, for the mass he despises, mass-suicide.

Perhaps a certain confusion has developed in Jeffers' mind between the non-human and the in-human. His pursuit of the one endowed him with a ferocity and grandeur of spirit that made him a legend in his time, as if he summed up, in a gesture of unappeasable nihilism, man's distaste for his own corruptibility. Now that he returns to the historical scene, it must be as one of us in a world of moral obligations and human values. For him to abnegate these responsibilities would be to range himself on the side of the destroyers. It is a critical moment in his career.

Lonely Eminence

R. Ellis Roberts*

With the possible exception of Robert Frost, Robinson Jeffers is to a European the most American of contemporary poets. He is in the tradition of Thoreau, of Melville, of Whitman—men who never rejected or imitated European thought and way of life, though they may, at times, claim to transcend it by virtue of a hopeful Americanism. I know that many critics will boggle at the association of Jeffers and hope; but that is only because hope has been too easily confused with a facile optimism, even with the vulgar acceptance of the advertiser's motto "Boost, don't knock!"

Jeffers is no booster for human nature—nor was Jonathan Edwards, nor was, fundamentally, Abraham Lincoln. That one looks for analogues to Jeffers among men who were not poets is evidence of his lonely eminence as a poet. In this new volume, which contains some of his finest and most prophetic work, I am reminded of no other poetry except the later Yeats, another lonely and undeceived poet of our day. When I say "undeceived" I mean Jeffers is never a slave to the popular cant of the market-place or the literary salon. I think he is sometimes self-deceived. When he writes in "Battle":

> It would be better for men
> To be few and live far apart, where none could infect another; then slowly
> the sanity of field and mountain
> And the cold ocean and glittering stars might enter their minds.

I question immediately, Why think valley and mountain, the heavens or the unpredictable ocean to be saner than man's soul? Is the Amazon or the Mississippi less turbulent and tormented than the difficult, intimate flow of the blood to and from the heart? Does not the blood of man control and color his vision of the natural world? But a poet has a right to his own philosophy, and Robinson Jeffers is, since Lucretius, the greatest poet to accept, in certain moods, a theory of pantheism; though often his

*From the *Saturday Review of Literature* 25 (25 April 1942): 8. Reprinted by permission.

view of nature, though it is starker, is not far from the more personal theory of Wordsworth.

The most remarkable work in this book is *The Bowl of Blood.* It is a masque of Hitler, and shows him consulting a witch who foretells the future, summoning for him the spirits of Frederick the Great, of Napoleon, and of a friend who was killed in the last war. It is a tense, taut piece of work, packed with imaginative understanding and a rare quality of vision. In it, as in so many of these poems, Jeffers's profound pity for humanity is nobly, sternly expressed. The core of it can perhaps be found in the second Masker's answer to the question "How can one man gather all power? How does a man dare?"

> Listen: power is a great hollow spirit
> That needs a center.
> It chooses one man almost at random
> And clouds him and clots around him and it possesses him.
> Listen: the man does not have power.
> Power has the man.

In this Robinson Jeffers comes very near the traditional Catholic doctrine of possession; and in another poem, "Nerves," he asks

> Or is it that we really feel
> A gathering in the air of something that hates
> Humanity; and in that storm-light see
> Ourselves with too much pity and the others too clearly?

Robinson Jeffers has always felt that sinister, envious, encompassing power; and who dare say now, looking at the history of our time, that his vision has been too terrible?

I must not leave this book without calling attention to the tender, pitiful poems in it. They have a dignity and a grave beauty he has never exceeded—the personal "For Una," the lovely memorial for a bull-dog, the poignant beauty of "Two Christmas Cards." No one from the island can read without emotion the first of these with its nostalgic and hopeful refrain:

> Lichen and stone the gables
> Of Kelmscott watch the young Thames:
> England dies in the storm,
> Dies to survive, and form
> Another and another
> Of the veils under veils of the vanished Englands.

The long narrative poem *Mara* has much of his old skill as a story-teller—here he has no rival except John Masefield—but it has not quite the force or the pace he can give to a story; and there is uncertainty as well as subtlety in his handling of the "deceived and jealous man." The whole book will confirm any intelligent reader that here is one of the few major poets now writing in English, a man who has his narrowness and his obliquities but who is fit to sit down, as Yeats desired to sit, with "Landor and John Donne," for he has clung, as they, obstinately to his creed: "Yet I believe truth is more beautiful / Than all the lies, and God than all false gods."

Spring Is Far Off

Benjamin Miller*

A certain class of critics will unduly corroborate the poet's wish "to lament the obsession with contemporary history that pins many of these pieces to the calendar, like butterflies to cardboard." But perhaps many more of his readers will take hold of the poet's further word regarding these verses: "Yet it is right that a man's views be expressed, though the poetry suffer for it. Poetry should represent the whole mind; if part of the mind is occupied unhappily, so much the worse. And no use postponing the poetry to a time when these storms may have passed, for I think we have but seen a beginning of them; the calm to look for is the calm at the whirlwind's heart."

In this his ninth major volume Mr. Jeffers has written what will in all probability stand as the strongest and most profound verses to come out of this war. With extraordinary sensibility to poetic tragedy and with the paradoxical strength of a passionate disinterestedness, he allows the monstrous decay and violence of these times to speak themselves out, and refuses to have any part in them except to "christen each poem, in dutiful hope of burning off at least the top layer of the time's uncleanness."

The religious aesthetic which has always been the unfailing resource and distinction of the Jeffersian philosophy expresses itself in the manner and spirit of great poetic drama, that is, in the full-blown maturity of the tragic sense of life. The result is the paradox of all critical religious experience. Man is redeemed not *from* the tragic context but *within* it.

The Jeffersian temper is aligned with the radical prophetism of the Hebrew tradition and with the tragic-religious awareness of the Greek dramatists. Man is hurled against the universe and against his history, but the impact generates no spark of mock heroics. The tragic enlightenment compels the poet to move within the structure of a profound hopelessness. Yet the roots of his solitary religious attachment are in the same moment driven profoundly Godward. "Yet I believe that truth is more beautiful than all the lies, and God than all the false gods." There is strength to protest "the immense vulgarities" of our time, to know our God "by his high superfluousness,"

*Reprinted from the *Christian Century* 49 (3 June 1942): 729.

> the great humaneness at the heart of things,
> The extravagant kindness, the fountain
> Humanity can understand, and would flow likewise
> If power and desire were perch-mates.

Mr. Jeffers concludes the long dramatic narrative, *Mara*, with this poet's homily:

> This pallid comet announces more than kings' deaths.
> To tail it with purer color I add
> That the mountains are alive. They crouch like great cats watching
> Our comic and mouse-hole tragedies, or lift high over them
> Peaks like sacred torches, pale-flaming rock.
> The old blue dragon breathes at their feet, the eternal flames
> Burn in the sky. The spirit that flickers and hurts in humanity
> Shines brighter from better lamps; but from all shines.
> Look to it: prepare for the long winter: spring is far off.

Writing from the depths of our enormous corruption, Mr. Jeffers still finds it possible "to present contemporary things in the shape of eternity." In *The Bowl of Blood* the Second Masker despairs of the possibility. "If it were possible, it would please no one. The present is always a crisis; people want a partisan cry, not judgment. No long views, for God's sake." And our other poets have chosen to fashion partisan cries, not judgment.

Mr. Jeffers' mystical-religious integrity and his redemptive awareness of the wholeness of life and things have not been altered from volume to volume. His message is the one breath of the organ blown through many reeds: *Love the more beautiful God, and not man apart from that.* What many of Mr. Jeffers' critics have marked for "nostalgic solitariness" is seen to be the tragic solitariness of religious strength and courage. Whatever his name or sign, the great tragic poet assumes increased stature in the day when our common awareness is of the evil thing, "too dark to understand."

Mr. Jeffers reminds us that this is the hour of masses and masters, and that, "come peace or war, the process of Europe and America becomes a long process of deterioration." We have bound the body of our people together, made peace in the state and maintained power upon lies and the clever instruments of our ingenuity.

> Thus the great wave of a civilization
> Loses its forming soul, falls apart and founders . . .
> Then we must leave it to the humble and the ignorant
> To invent the frame of faith that will form the future.

Medea: Freely Adapted from the "Medea" of Euripides (1946)

California Euripides

Donald A. Stauffer*

Robinson Jeffers has shown the impress of Greek tragedy ever since his earliest works. In his latest slim volume he has joined the long line of Greek dramatists among poets who write in English. None of them except Milton in his *Samson Agonistes* has managed simultaneously to imitate and to create with complete success. Jeffers' *Medea* is more intense than Arnold's *Merope,* more controlled than Swinburne's *Atalanta in Calydon,* more conventional in subject than Eliot's *Murder in the Cathedral,* less straining after modern theories than O'Neill's *Mourning Becomes Electra.*

And yet somehow this *Medea* falls short of any of them, even Arnold's *Merope,* which is not such a corpse as people keep repeating. Jeffers is caught on the horns of a minotaur. He cannot decide whether to be a Greek dramatist or Robinson Jeffers. In this two-act drama he is not very good at being either. The style is disappointing. His lack of technical regularity, characteristic throughout his work, stands him in poor stead when he essays Doric discipline. It is as if Walt Whitman were playing at being Sophocles. Instead of effects of purity and simplicity Jeffers often falls into flatness and looseness: "He said he would." "You are right, friends." "She doesn't know what she is saying." "Poor soul, it hasn't helped this one much." "What? No! I told you. The day is today, Medea, this day. And the hour is now."

These do not sound like scraps from high poetic tragedy. And though some of these samples are picked at random from the remarks of minor figures or from the chorus of Corinthian women, the play rarely rises even in climactic moments. When Medea first meditates a fiend's destruction of her rival Creusa, she says, trembling: "Ah . . . It's enough. / Something might happen. / It is . . . likely that . . . something might happen."

A row of dots is not an adequate literary expression of deep hatred and submerged jealousy, nor do irregular lines with occasional capitalizations at the left constitute poetry. Jason throughout is given the

*From the *New York Times Book Review,* 21 April 1946, 7. Copyright 1946 by The New York Times Company. Reprinted by permission.

stature of a telegraph messenger boy; his portrait is hardly that of a first-class prig.

The nadir of bathos is reached after Jason threatens to take away Medea's children by force. Medea retorts: "Try it, you!" The long, loose lines of Jeffers' earlier volumes have been no help in this present attempt at bare compression. Nor does the play achieve form and variety through choric interludes between episodes. Jeffers does not use the chorus formally. Instead, the chorus speaks when it has a mind to, like a crowd in the bleachers, and in equally desultory fashion.

On the other hand, the imitative mode of Greek Tragedy—this play follows fairly closely Euripides' *Medea* in plot, though it collapses the reasonable and intensifies the frenetic—forbids Jeffers to be himself except for brief flashes. The bleak, spacious landscapes and the pitiless animality that he can do so well are only glimpsed. The vultures, stallions, wolves and dogs in this play are his trademarks and additions. The subject fits his gifts, and by sheer concentration on the flaming passion and cruel pride of Medea, alone, far off from Asia among the foreigners, he has created a figure of terror and hatred. She will not die as a pigeon or a lamb. " '—No, like some yellow-eyed beast that has killed its hunters let me lie down / On the hounds' bodies and the broken spears.' " She only is realized: the children are almost mute sacrifices to her hatred against a Jason that lives vitally merely in her mind or memory. All the rest, with the possible exception of the Nurse, are voices.

The properties are more alive—Euripides' burning poisonous crown and golden robe—and the most intense passage describes sadistically the destruction of her rival Creusa and of Creon. But this is an orgasm of vengeance, and the play flickers and smolders out to a sullen end in which pity has never been aroused, nor fear purged. We have watched the "woman of the stone forehead and hate-filled eyes." We have seen with the chorus,

> the black end,
> The end of great love, and God save me from it:
> The unburied horror, the unbridled hatred,
> The vultures tearing a corpse:
> God keep me clean of those evil beaks.

We have found a few nearly perfect phrases—the "starlike faces" of the children, or "Salt-scoured bones on the shore / At home in Colchis."

The play might act well, for with proper lighting and an ambitious actress it could explode uncompromising horror in the heart. But it is neither a great tragedy nor a good poem. It is a melodrama that falls between two styles.

In the ancient, pottery colors of brick and black and in the decorative motifs, the handsome exterior of this volume evokes the Greek more easily than what the volume contains.

At the Theatre

Brooks Atkinson*

If Medea does not entirely understand every aspect of her whirling character, she would do well to consult Judith Anderson. For Miss Anderson understands the character more thoroughly than Medea, Euripides or the scholars, and it would be useless now for anyone else to attempt the part. Using a new text by Robinson Jeffers, she set a landmark in the theatre at the National last evening, where she gave a burning performance in a savage part.

Mr. Jeffers' "free adaptation," as it is called, spares the supernatural bogeymen of the classical Greek drama and gets on briskly with the terrifying story of a woman obsessed with revenge. His verse is modern; his words are sharp and vivid, and his text does not worship gods that are dead.

Since Miss Anderson is a modern, the Jeffers text suits her perfectly and releases a torrent of acting incomparable for passion and scope. Miss Anderson's Medea is mad with the fury of a woman of rare stature. She is barbaric by inheritance, but she has heroic strength and vibrant perceptions. Animal-like in her physical reactions, she plots the doom of her enemies with the intelligence of a priestess of black magic—at once obscene and inspired. Between those two poles she fills the evening with fire, horror, rage and character. Although Miss Anderson has left some memorable marks on great women in the theatre, Medea has summoned all her powers as an actress. Now everyone realizes that she has been destined for Medea from the start.

The general performance and the production are all of a piece. As the nurse, Florence Reed is giving an eminent performance that conveys the weariness and apprehensions of a devoted servant who does not quarrel with fate. John Gielgud's Jason is a lucid, solemn egotist well expressed in terms of the theatre. As Creon, Albert Hecht has the commanding voice and the imperiousness of a working monarch. The chorus of women, which has been refreshingly arranged in Mr. Gielgud's unhackneyed direction, is well acted by Grace Mills, Kathryn Grill and Leone Wilson. The parts of the two young sons are disarmingly represented in the guileless acting of Gene Lee and Peter Moss. Hugh Franklin as Aegeus and Don McHenry as the Tutor give agreeable performances, innocent of the stuffiness peculiar to most classical productions.

Ben Edwards' setting of the doorway to a Greek house is no more than pedestrian designing, although Peggy Clark has lighted it dramatically, and Castillo has dressed the characters well. Your correspondent could do very well without the conventional theatrical effects—the lightning and the surf especially, for, unlike the acting, they derive from the old-fashioned theatre of rant and ham.

*From the *New York Times*, 21 October 1947, 27.

Out of respect for Miss Anderson's magnificent acting in this incarnadined drama, they ought to be locked up in the lumber room. For she has freed Medea from all the old traditions as if the character had just been created. Perhaps that is exactly what has happened. Perhaps Medea was never fully created until Miss Anderson breathed immortal fire into it last evening.

Medea

Kappo Phelan*

It is necessary to say at once that Robinson Jeffers's "free adaptation" of Euripides has resulted in an astonishing collaboration: a great performance. If the advance promotion stories are true, and Judith Anderson did indeed solicit the poet for his version of the "barbarian bride," he has, reversibly, solicited from her a most stern accomplishment. I think the result is monumental. And I think it should rather be described than analyzed. The script itself has been in print for more than a year now and has been worried by far firmer scholars than I shall ever be; the nibbling, useless problem of adaptations has only too recently taken space in this column; sometimes it seems to me impossible for an eager critic ever to reach performance at all. But in this instance I find there is only one *reflection* which I feel should be recorded: and this will be that the truly Euripidean compassion of the Chorus (the Corinthian women) seems somehow miraculously to be justified, even extended, by Miss Anderson's attack. I am unsure whether to deal this to writing or playing, but the distinction is not important. Alien, awful, alone, this Medea is dark, sinuous, preying, fawning, shrieking, and incessant. It is possible to say she is also pitiable? Yes. Violating every possible archetypal ethic, is it possible to say she is still a woman? Yes. This is a sheer line and is maintained. Add to it in a scene, whose necessarily bright air, massive architecture, and harbor view preclude any fumbling motions—a variety of pose and gesture which rivets the attention. And to a prosody, which literally wrestles and hews into your ear, add a precision of diction, an arpeggio of tone which is inescapable. In a period of broadcast ovations, instructed applause, and schemed polls, I think there is only one excuse for the kind of loud, rearing, stamping homage Miss Anderson is receiving at her plain curtain-calls at the National: art.

There are further credits—some debits—and I think it's best simply to transcribe my program notes. . . . Florence Reed's support as the Nurse is no morsel of the evening. Her diction is (again) wonderful. Most of all, she is the right heroic size. I don't know whether the exact recur-

*From *Commonweal* 47 (7 November 1947): 94. Copyright Commonweal Foundation. Reprinted by permission.

rent sound of the sailed sea is due to John Gielgud's direction, or Ben Edwards's design, but it is important as a perfect effect. Mr. Gielgud's placements seemed excellent; his casting odd: the important children were awkwardly chosen and only one member of the choral trio—Grace Mills—really fitted. As for his handling of Jason, this had better be skipped. His lack of passion is almost suitable, but he hasn't the breath for the lines; and in any case, there ought to be passion in reserve. Tibor Serly's music: fine. As I am most of all interested in poetry, Jeffers's several slow ascents into the formal simile—particularly as paused and articulated by Miss Anderson—seemed to me current history. No interpolated action, no ad lib. That's all, I think. Conclusion: to be experienced.

The Double Axe and Other Poems (1948)

Transhuman Magnificence

Selden Rodman*

The appearance, after seven years of virtual silence, of a substantial collection of characteristic narrative and shorter poems by Robinson Jeffers would be an event under ordinary circumstances. But spiked, as this one is, with a belligerently "isolationist" preface by the author and on the following page with a statement of disagreement from the publishers, it bids fair to evoke as violent a reception as *Roan Stallion, Tamar and Other Poems* did in 1925. In the preface Jeffers defines his philosophical attitude as "Inhumanism, a shifting of emphasis from man to not-man; the rejection of human solipsism and recognition of the transhuman magnificence." This attitude, he goes on to say, "involves no falsehoods . . . it has objective truth and human value. It offers a reasonable detachment as rule of conduct, instead of love, hate, and envy. It neutralizes fanaticism and wild hopes. . . ." So far, except perhaps for the tone of omniscience and the misleading implication that Jeffers's driving motivation is not hatred of mankind, readers will find nothing new here. But the poet then proceeds to state that American intervention in the Second World War was "not forced but intentional"—and criminal—and he adds in poem after poem that American blood was needlessly shed at the behest of a "liar" whose motivation was "power," "ambition," and "vanity."

Before commenting further on this point of view and the poems which are inspired by it, the reviewer would like to clarify his own position in two respects. As an admirer of Jeffers's verse, he included twenty-five pages of it in his Modern Library anthology in 1938, and again this year two poems in his Penguin *100 American Poems.* As a non-interventionist in pre-Pearl Harbor days, the reviewer believed (and still believes) that failure to insist in advance on enlightened peace terms made a catastrophic third conflict almost inevitable. But from there on to assume (as Jeffers does) that Germany could have been permitted to impose total slavery on the rest of the world, that our leaders spoke only for themselves and from the vilest of motives, and that from now on we have

*From the *Saturday Review of Literature* 31 (31 July 1948): 13–14. Reprinted by permission.

nothing better to do than give our hearts to the hawks, seems to this reviewer totally irresponsible, politically, poetically, humanly.

Having said this, it remains to be said that Random House deserves credit for publishing this book. Jeffers, whatever one may think of his philosophy, remains as close to a major poet as we have. We have much to learn from him. It did not require a play (*Medea*, 1946) to establish his preeminence in dramatics. The first part of the title poem in *The Double Axe* is as gripping and powerfully paced as any of his early narratives. In the shorter pieces he retains that ability, shown sporadically by MacLeish and Sandburg in the Thirties and then abandoned by them, to speak straight (and hotly) on "hot" political issues without hedging his meaning in any of the fashionable contortions of symbolic double-talk, and without sacrificing the spare magnificence of his own style. We must respect his integrity.

Jeffers has never been a poet's poet. That is his strength, and his limitation, too. He belongs in the ranks of Dryden and Byron, Whitman and Lindsay, not in the company of Milton and Keats and Eliot. He fashioned a tool—unadorned and forceful but slack enough to contain description, speech, stage-directions, and asides—and let it go at that. Jeffers is never obscure. And by the same token he is almost never quotable. "Black-fanged rocks and high-grinning snow-teeth" is the limit of his imagery. Nuances of tone, ambiguities of meaning, felicities of language and music, are not to be looked for in his verse. But how many poets since Shakespeare have combined all these with over-all directness and dramatic power?

It is ironical that Jeffers, the philosophical heir of Nietzsche and Spengler and the spokesman of rabid isolationism, should be the only contemporary American poet capable of communicating with a wide audience in the grand manner, or apparently desiring to. It is sad that as the years go by he repeats himself endlessly; that he elects to close his eyes to human heroism and goodness and to man-made beauty; and that he feels compelled to add more than his quota of hatred and violence to the hatred and violence abroad in the world, while he sits in that properly inhuman stone tower of his waiting exultantly for the Bomb.

A Prophet of Mortality

Ruth Lechlitner*

On the jacket of *The Double Axe* Random House states that Robinson Jeffers "sees a world bent on self-destruction and takes a stand for complete political isolation"; that "his publishers cannot subscribe to such a

*From the *New York Herald Tribune Weekly Book Review*, 12 September 1948, 4. I. H. T. Corporation. Reprinted by permission.

political credo." And, in a further publishers' foreword, Random House "feels compelled to go on record with its disagreement over some of the political views pronounced by the poet in this volume." To this public handwashing Jeffers, in his preface, cheerfully consents because of his belief that history will eventually support him. He adds that his political ideas are not particularly important except as the "moral climate" of his work.

It is true that Random House, in publishing this fourteenth book under their imprint by a distinguished major American poet, does accord to it "the widest possible hearing . . . in the case of ideas on trial." But because these publishers feel "compelled" to disavow publicly "some of the political views" of their author, they thereby underline something in them that they must feel is gravely important.

From *Tamar* (1924) to *Be Angry at the Sun* (1941) Robinson Jeffers has treated, in unsocial and unorthodox ways, such subjects as sex and family relationships, religion, nature and human society. He has condemned most aspects of sexual behavior as manifestations of a "racial introversion of which culture dies," and has stressed the carnal appetites of women. He has said that family relationships are "often vicious." He has considered God as a deity of "no benevolence but only knowledge." Man, a small particle of atomic substance, is not God's primary concern: there is no personal immortality. "No life ought to be thought important in the weave of the world." And, as readers of these volumes know, he has been against war, and taken an "isolationist" stand, ever since World War I.

But Random House—although the personal beliefs of its editors probably do not coincide with these views of Jeffers—has never felt any need, up to now, to make public statements saying so. Nor do the publishers, apparently, feel impelled to repudiate his "philosophical" credo in *The Double Axe.*

Let us look, first, at the California poet's philosophical ideas presented in "The Inhumanist" (Part II of this book) through his protagonist, the old "axe-man"; a recognition of human folly in individual life, and in social war making, motivated by love, hate, envy, greed—infantile emotionalism. He wishes he might see instead adult sanity, reason, courage. Striving for complete objectivity, he beholds the history of all civilizations—their slow rise, rapid break and fall like the sea waves—as an impersonal design or beauty. When suffering individuals come to him for help, he tells himself it really isn't help they want, but "the dear pleasure of being saved." But in his hand the symbolic twin-bladed, human-voiced axe cries out: he finds himself acting, with compassion, because "that's the condition of being human. One cannot escape." He reaffirms the Jeffersian credo that only Nature (beauty) is significant and worthy of being eternal.

But just what are "some" of those political views, besides the isolationist stand, which Jeffers's publishers feel they must publicly disavow?

Jeffers' political views are most fully expressed, perhaps, in "The Love and the Hate," Part I of the opening narrative poem in this volume. Hoult Gore, soldier of World War II, returns in "rotting resurrection" from his grave on Meserole Island to avenge himself on his parents, whom he holds responsible for his disillusionment and death. For his mother, Reine, who has taken a lover while he was off defending, presumably, the sanctity of the American home, he feels bitterly "the love and the hate." Hamlet-like, he forces her confession before he kills her lover. He later avenges himself on his father, Bull Gore, "war-hound" of World War I, whose first reaction to his returned son is to want him arrested as a deserter. Hoult reminds him:

> "This is not Germany,
> Where they say sons and fathers run to the Gestapo
> To inform on each other: this is liberal America, where blood is still
> Thicker than government."

Further:

> "Tell me one decent reason
> Why the United States got into this war,
> I'll go and give myself up. . . .
> Don't say Pearl Harbor though.
> That was a trick, a dirty one. . . .
> Nor don't say freedom:
> War's freedom's killer. Don't say freedom for foreigners
> Unless you intend to kill Russia on top of Germany and Britain on Japan, and churn the whole world
> Into one bloody bubble-bath; don't say democracy;
> Don't talk that mush."

"Battle fatigue," says Gore. "I'll stick by you." But Hoult asks no pity for himself:

> "Be sorry for the decent and loyal people of America . . . For a time's coming . . . when the ends of the earth, from east and west one world, will close on your country
> Like the jaws of a trap; but people will say, Be quiet, we were fooled before. We know that all governments
> Are thugs and liars, let them fight their own battles: and the trap is closing."

Jeffers believes that the leaders of America—no better than those of the totalitarian countries—are driving us (as they did in World Wars I and II) toward a third terrible conflict:

> We shall have to hold half the earth; we shall be sick with self-disgust,
> And hated by friend and foe, and hold half the earth—or let it go, and go down with it.

These are "some" of Jeffers' political ideas.

Since *The Double Axe* is a book issued not in Russia, not under a dictatorship, but in America, a democracy, in this year of peace 1948, why, the reader may well ask, the compulsion on the part of its publishers, whatever personal disagreement there may be, to disavow publicly certain views of its author?

Oracles and Things

Robert Fitzgerald*

Robinson Jeffers, who admires Yeats, has cast a cold eye on life and death and in his best fragments has written lines, rather hugely and coldly hewn, that truthfully honor the life of rock-faces and external nature; but on a review of his work these outcroppings sink into a quagmire of appalling primitivism from which not even a pterodactyl could take wing. He has been trying to say to all men: "You are corrupted monsters, unworthy of a single mountain range," and in *The Double Axe* he outdoes himself in the violence of the saying; the two long fables of the volume are full of blood and carrion and incestuous horror.

It is easy to see why Jeffers does this: there is horror in the nature of things, nobody faces it, everybody lies about it, and this makes the poet angry. So here we have a boy—a recognizable American boy but one never presented on a magazine cover—so furious at being smashed to death on a Pacific beach that he reanimates his buried corpse and returns to California to murder his old man and make lecherous advances to his mother. The trouble is not in the poet's initial emotion; it is in the mindlessness of its working out; the sheer bombast and fantasy of it, like the vileness that small boys make up to turn each other's stomachs. If Jeffers were moved to violence by a real despair of communication, his grue would be more excusable; but I think that the exact opposite is the case. It is as if, going on his profound intimation of "transhuman magnificence"—the alien grandeur of nature—he had hammered out a big, oracular style years ago, become a big, oracular poet, and held himself thereafter absolved from the further use of his brains.

The late John Peale Bishop had a rule more or less to the effect that a poet should never write about anything that a newspaperman could understand. Taken with the salt of the aphorism, it is a valuable rule and worth recalling here, because Jeffers has not only written about what a newspaperman could understand but has written about it in a way that a newspaperman could dismiss. Most of his new short lyrics are psalms of disgust at the war and the men who "duped" the rest of us into it, of praise for the beauty and durability of mountains, ocean and starlight compared with the transient obscenity of mankind, and lofty but rather spiteful ad-

*From the *New Republic* 119 (22 November 1948): 22–23. Reprinted by permission.

dresses of welcome to all the woes to come. The attitude is childish and childishly easy; once assumed, it will turn out a Jeffers lyric an hour for anyone who wants to try it, but it is a sorry exhibition for a responsible poet to have made.

Hungerfield and Other Poems (1954)

A Grim and Bitter Dose

Louis Untermeyer*

The first poem in Robinson Jeffers's new volume, *Hungerfield and Other Poems,* begins and ends with a tribute to his dead wife, an apostrophe which is all the more moving for being uncannily calm. Between the first and last lines, however, there is a thirteen-page story, a tale of wild and tragic intensity. It is the story of Hawl Hungerfield, a war veteran who had faced Death in a hospital and had fought him off. Now he is at the bedside of his mother, who is dying of cancer, and once again he strikes at Death's throat. He saves his mother—at least he thinks she is saved.

But his mother is not grateful for the unwanted gift of a little more pain-riddled life; she longs toward Death, "her lord and lover," and resents being dragged back to misery. Death meanwhile stalks the family, kills Hungerfield's cattle, then his wife and child, makes Hungerfield murder his brother, and finally goads him into the violent act of burning down the house, while the clouds swallow "the flights of flame and the soul of a man."

Here, once more, is Jeffers's approximation of Greek tragedy transferred to the melodramatic coast of California. Here concentrated misanthropy is extended into a narrative of angry love and driving hatred. Here, too, are Jeffers's familiar similes and symbols: the beauty of hawks flying, knife-keen winds, plunging promontories, streams tearing at rocks, the black strength of the flooding tide. A Jeffers reader will be prepared for all this. But, although he will no longer be either shocked or surprised, he will not fail to be roused. Jeffers has not lost the gift of biting language and the ability to communicate the phantasmagoria of terror.

He refuses to offer false comfort to what he considers doomed and conformed mankind. This seems no more than just to him, for "there is no consolation in humanity." Defeated humanity is even cheated out of its catharsis. The mounting horrors and the successive deaths culminate in a hopelessness which Jeffers calls tranquility.

*From the *Saturday Review* 37 (16 January 1954): 17. Reprinted by permission.

It is thus (and will be) that violence
Turns on itself, and builds on the wreck of violence its violent beauty, the
spiring fire-fountain
And final peace: grim in the desert in the lion's carcass the hive of honey.

The long poem which follows *Hungerfield* is a companion piece which continues the tone, enhances the horror and lifts the dual theme of hatred and love to an almost intolerable pitch. In *The Cretan Woman* Jeffers brings the Greek tragedy back to Greece. Founded on the *Hippolytus* of Euripides, the drama is as tense, as foreboding, and as grimly eloquent as the Jeffers/Euripides *Medea.* The lust of Phaedra for the son of her husband, Theseus, is heightened by the fact that the young Hippolytus loves hunting and his own kind rather than women; Jeffers gives the old drama a new twist of the knife by making Theseus, a blind instrument of Phaedra's scorned love, murder his son and making him at the same time a fool of nature. The sickening disasters are contrasted with the detachment of the goddess Aphrodite's casual summing-up:

I am a little sorry for the lady Phaedra, his old father's young wife,
Who must go down into shame and madness to make his ruin; and I am
sorry for the old hero,
Theseus, his father: But to suffer is man's fate, and they have to bear it.
We gods and goddesses
Must not be very scrupulous; we are forces of nature, vast and inflexible,
and neither mercy
Nor fear can move us. Men and women are the pawns we play with; we
work our games out on a wide chessboard,
The great brown-and-green earth.

Jeffers's Olympian-minded spirits laugh at man's cherished virtue, love, and pretense to power. Something fatal—and usually evil—lies hidden. "There is always a knife in the flowers. There is always a lion just beyond the firelight." This is the leading theme of the shorter poems which conclude the book. The misanthropy is never without pity and seldom without a mute nobility. "One light is left us: the beauty of things, not men." "Until annihilation comes leaping like a black dog and licks the dish clean: that is atonement." "I have hardened my heart only a little: I have learned that happiness is important, but pain *gives* importance." "Good and evil are as common as air . . . Hold your nose and compromise." "Watching with interest and only a little nausea / the cheating shepherds, this time of the demagogues and the docile people, the shifts of power / and pitiless general wars that prepare the fall . . ." This is bitter medicine grimly administered—the bitterer since we are earnestly assured that the world will be well only when our sick civilization dies.

Books of the Times

Charles Poore*

Reading the poems of Robinson Jeffers sometimes gives me a feeling that his work should be declared a national park and staffed with stetsoned rangers to protect all the hawks and wild beasts in its rocky, sea-stung scenery. He makes the middle California coast a lively sanctuary of violence. It should live on, I think, when gaudy tales of other Barbarys are forgotten. His new book, *Hungerfield and Other Poems*, is written in an elegiac tone, yet it is truly Jeffers at his best, a volume of furious threnodies.

Like Webster in T. S. Eliot's poem, he is much possessed by death and sees the skull beneath the skin in endless metric variants. Although he feels life on the whole "is equally good and bad, mostly gray neutral, and can be endured to the dim end," he is enormously displeased with a variety of things that he has seen going on in the world during the past six or seven decades. He tells us:

> I have seen my people, fooled by ambitious men and a froth of sentiment,
> waste themselves on three wars.
> None was required, all futile, all grandly victorious. A fourth is forming.

This is perhaps a sentiment that can best be published by those who through other men's efforts find themselves on the "grandly victorious" side some years after a Japanese submarine has lobbed a few shells in the general direction of Santa Barbara. The opening poem, *Hungerfield*, is a wonderfully gruesome story of a grapple with death and family feuds born of several generations sharing the same roof-tree, suggesting that public war is not the only imperfection in man, modern or classic Greek. Much apparently remains to be done to improve the breed: much striking material, therefore, is continually available to the surprisingly vigorous trumpeters of despair.

Meantime, Mr. Jeffers tells us, "the hawk's egg will make a hawk, and the serpent's / A gliding serpent," each changing a little as the predestined plan unfolds.

Standing at Carmel Point, he sees "this beautiful place defiled with a crop of suburban houses." It would be idle, I imagine, to suggest that a great poet of tomorrow may now be growing up in one of those suburban houses, looking through the inevitable picture window at the same seascapes Mr. Jeffers so angrily esteems.

"One light is left us: the beauty of things, not men," he intones as he moves surefootedly from poetic commonplace to poetic commonplace, deftly refashioning the hymn's line about views where every prospect pleases and only man is vile:

*From the *New York Times*, 23 January 1954, 11. Copyright 1954 by The New York Times Company. Reprinted by permission.

Look at the Lobos Rocks off the shore,
With foam flying at their flanks, and the long sea-lions
Couching on them. Look at the gulls on the cliff-wind,
And the soaring hawk under the cloud-stream—
But in the sagebrush desert, all one sun-stricken
Color of dust, or in the reeking tropical rainforest,
Or in the intolerant north and high thrones of ice—is the earth not beautiful?

This is the best of Jeffers, isn't it, when he is making these fine hymns about what he sees? Is it not true that he is a man of limited ideas with a limitless capacity for showing us the most dramatic landscapes?

The core of drama itself he takes most readily from the creators of the past. Thus, in this book, there is a play, *The Cretan Woman,* based on the *Hippolytus* of Euripides, a tremendous theme that Euripides tried at least twice and that several other writers have in later ages used for their own devices.

Indeed, when you start counting them over (Seneca's *Phaedra,* Racine's *Phèdre,* d'Annunzio's *Fedra,* and so on) you have a longish list. Faced with a similar richness of precedents, Jean Giraudoux called his version of the Amphitryon story "Amphitryon 38," blithely acknowledging that it must have turned up at least thirty-seven varieties before he got around to it.

This is not the sort of caper that would appeal strongly to Mr. Jeffers, however. He has partly drained the supernatural element from the story, pared it down to an economical cast, given the triangle a fashionable element of perversity and added a few overtones to make it one more commentary on the bewitchments and bewilderments of man.

The Disillusioned Wordsworth of Our Age

Horace Gregory*

A man from Mars, or less remotely, a visitor from Europe might well ask those who talk of poets and poetry in the United States a pertinent question: "Why does so much deep silence surround the name of Robinson Jeffers?"

A few answers to that question are: Although his poems are read, his name has dropped out of fashion. In critical circles, right, left, or center, his candid opinions, plainly said in verse, continue to be unpopular. He is the disillusioned Wordsworth of our age who has assimilated readings in Nietzsche and Greek drama; at heart he is a compassionate Pantheist who

*From the *New York Herald Tribune Book Review,* 24 January 1954, 5. I.H.T. Corporation. Reprinted by permission.

is often misread merely as a prophet of doom and of mindless destruction. His writings cannot be analyzed by the use of critical formulae; they are at once too directly spoken and beneath their surfaces, too deeply felt and too complex.

So much then for the peculiarity of Jeffers' position and the fact that when honors and awards are given out to poets, he does not receive them. His new book, which includes a play and a narrative, both in verse, and fourteen short poems, is honorable proof of his integrity; there is no cause to pity him because of critical neglect, but perhaps a few words of further explanation are in order. These have to do with his new play, *The Cretan Woman*.

Like Jeffers' *Medea, The Cretan Woman* takes for its precedent a play by Euripides, in this instance, *Hippolytus*. In some quarters it has been assumed that some of Jeffers' dramatic poems—for they are poems, rather than plays—are adaptations from the Greek; they are not. They are Jeffers' re-creations of ancient themes. He re-created the myth itself in much the same fashion that certain Roman poets made use of Grecian precedents, and even pre-Greek fabulae. Only in broadest reference and outline has Jeffers' new play a resemblance to *Hippolytus*—he has taken the names of certain figures in Euripides' play and has followed its general course of action, but that is all. For us it is the reading of a new dramatic poem that if well produced on a television screen would be more effective than on the stage.

In the play Jeffers has never written better poetry than the speech he gives to Aphrodite; nor can I think of any living poet who given the theme of what she says could write so well. Jeffers' Phaedra, Theseus, Hippolytus are creatures of distinctly modern temper; their tragedy, however ancient the original sources of its action, is of twentieth-century revelation and interpretation.

The narrative poem, *Hungerfield,* is less successful than *The Cretan Woman,* less evenly written and sustained, probably because the figures in the poem are less heroic, and of a nearly sub-human underworld. Yet even here Jeffers summons from the scenes of "Hungerfield" a fable of man's quarrel with death and then gives the theme renewed meaning and power.

Something that is not resignation, yet has the serenity of self-knowledge, enters the fourteen short poems of the book. In taking the road beyond middle age few American poets have stepped so far with a more deeply expressed humility and courage. With this book and those that may follow it, Jeffers' contribution to the poetry of our day is of mature inspiration and accomplishment. His position is secure and singular.

The Beginning and the End and Other Poems (1963)

The Theme Is Always Man

William Turner Levy*

Fifty-one years after the publication of Robinson Jeffers's first volume of verse, this final one is posthumously issued. In the years between, we have had nearly 20 volumes, which include in their pages *Cawdor* and *Hungerfield, The Loving Shepherdess, Medea* and a sheaf of imperishable lyrics. It is on these that our judgment of his stature as poet will finally rest.

Jeffers's reputation was established with *Tamar and Other Poems* in 1924, when James Rorty and Mark Van Doren were instrumental in recognizing the verse as major American poetry. During the nineteen-thirties and forties, Jeffers's continued aloofness and pessimism in times of unprecedented national effort caused his popularity to diminish. Two other factors in the decline were loss of interest on the part of critics primarily concerned with the explication of more allusive poetry, and Jeffers's own tendency—having found what he wanted to say—to repeat himself.

What did he repeat? That man was tragic because he brought the beauty and pain of the universe to focus in a feeling brain; that only by turning away from mass corruption and living a life of individual integrity could one achieve nobility or peace; that progress was a delusion if it failed to show man the way to survival rather than to mere security. In times largely insensitive to theology, the quasi-theological quality of Jeffers's most powerful work could not be readily grasped or effectively evaluated. A new generation of critics should find him of great interest.

In these last poems, collected from his manuscripts, the themes remain unchanged. He explores man's self-destructive madness in its new dimensions. This time it is the bombs, "metal seeds of unearthly violence stored in neat rows on shelves," that provoke his searing condemnation, as in "Do You Still Make War?" Readers familiar with his work will not be surprised that his preoccupation with mankind's possible fate only strengthens his devotion to "the God who does not care and will never

*From the *New York Times Book Review*, 5 May 1963, 5.

cease." Once again he writes those wonderfully unexpected poems of personal record—as he watches his daughter-in-law cut a rose for the house, or as he looks at the portrait of a granddaughter. But for the most part his focus remains cosmic, and he sees the universe as a great heart through which pulsate all the energies that exist. To this, man must be reconciled:

> Peace in our time was never one of God's promises; but back and forth,
> die and live, burn and be damned,
> The great heart beating, pumping into our arteries His terrible life.

Robinson Jeffers in old age remains constant to the youthful vision which served for a lifetime to keep him at one with the splendor of a world he found so beautiful that man alone seemed unworthy of his Creator. His answer will not be ours, but he instructs us how our minds might be exalted in beauty—and so share in the divine quality and fabric of all creation.

Rugged Poetry Imbued with Spirit of the Hawk

Stephen Spender*

Robinson Jeffers lived in vast scenery opposite the vast Pacific on the coast of Monterey where he built with his own hands a tower in which he lived. His poetry is rugged as the hills of that landscape, with lines ragged as that ocean, and the spirit of the poet is most often likened in his poetry to a hawk. On the whole it provokes awe and enthusiasm, but it is not poetry to live with, because it lacks intimacy.

It is like a net with too wide a mesh which only catches the most cosmic experiences and the most ultimate feelings. Most of us, altho we may have such feelings, live most of our lives experiencing and feeling thru a smaller mesh, which is the scale of our own bodies, families, occupations. We do not live on rocky cliffs, under vast skies, and over great oceans. We do not act like hawks.

Death, however, is both an extreme and a universal situation, and these last poems of Jeffers, in which he is largely concerned with his own approaching death, in which he discovers a metaphor for the approaching end of the world, imminent as a result of nuclear fission, are extremely moving. They may well be his best poetry.

They are written by a poet who remains completely in command of his own technical and intellectual resources. Jeffers shows an ability to

*From the *Chicago Tribune Magazine of Books*, 12 May 1963, 3.

express ideas which are derived from reading modern scientific works, which is very rare in modern poetry.

Lines such as these about the "volcanic earth" are both exact and exhilarating:

She was like a mare in her heat eyeing the stallion,
Screaming for life in the womb; her atmosphere
Was the breath of her passion: not the blithe air
Men breathe and live, but marsh-gas, ammonia, sulphured hydrogen,
Such poison as our remembering bodies return to
When they die and decay and the end of life
Meets its beginning.

The view of life expressed here is tragic, heroic, but ultimately rather detached. Jeffers tends to see the earth in relation to the cosmos, history in relation to infinity. Destruction and defeat, indeed civilization itself, therefore, are not very important. What matters is affirmation, courage, a gesture of cosmic defiance:

Man's life's
Too common to be lamented; and if they died after a while in their beds
It would be nearly as painful—death's never pleasant.
May the terror be brief—but for a people to be defeated is worse.

I happen to disagree with this, because I think that consciousness is what gives significance to the universe, and for this reason it is not valuable to measure or weigh immensity against the littleness and brevity of man.

Without consciousness time and space would be meaningless, and meaning is what we exist for. Until it is proved that there is a superconsciousness inhabiting some other planet, the heroics of a poet such as Jeffers merely recommend the abdication of consciousness. But even if one rejects his philosophy, these poems confront one with final issues to choose among. They have imaginative grandeur.

Jeffers: The Undeserved Neglect

Winfield Townley Scott*

The little poem is called "My Loved Subject," and this is it entire:

Old age clawed me with his scaly clutch
As if I had never been such.
I cannot walk the mountains as I used to do

*From *New York Herald Tribune Books*, 16 June 1963, 10. I. H. T. Corporation. Reprinted by permission.

But my subject is what it used to be: my love, my loved subject:
Mountain and ocean, rock, water and beasts and trees
Are the protagonists, the human people are only symbolic interpreters—
So let them live or die. They may in fact
Die rather quickly, if the great manners of death dreamed up
In the laboratories work well.

And there is the Robinson Jeffers signature—peculiar, particular, willful, direct; also unmistakable and, I daresay, far more important in American poetry than the critics in later years have supposed it to be. This posthumous book gathers up his last poems, written since *Hungerfield,* 1954.

Among the startling number of deaths of American poets in the past year and a half, that of Jeffers—among the well-known names—probably went least regarded. Had he died not last year at 75 but, say, thirty years ago it would have been different. In those days there were still people calling him the greatest since the Greeks. But there has been a long hiatus of critical neglect and even at times contempt. People now write whole surveys of American poetry without finding any necessity to mention him. Other people have peered up over their little quatrains to sneer at him.

At the zenith of his reputation was Jeffers overrated? Undoubtedly he was. In the style he hammered out—loose, rugged—there are, as in his contemporary O'Neill, dull, awkward, clumsy, artless spots. And he was reiterative. He found his true style and his few ideas about simultaneously, and having in *Tamar* and *Roan Stallion* celebrated the beauty of his western coast and denigrated mankind in whom, he thought, ugliness always won out, Jeffers went on, through more narratives than we shall ever save, to say over and over again these ideas in symbols of fire and blood, murder and incest. And there is that sensational streak which may put us off.

Yet there is no question but he has been underrated in recent decades. If his reputation has suffered by his own prolixity it has suffered no less from a going and coming of fashions in verse that had nothing to do with him: fashions often, it seems to me, transitory and minor in comparison. He kept his peace. He lived and wrote with dignity and honor—honor that is likely to increase in years to come. For at his best—in a narrative or two, often in the brief poems which are the best of their sort since Whitman's—he wrote with a stern power and beauty, and he is that valuable thing, the unmistakable poet—nobody else quite like him.

If the little poem I have quoted signs all his work it also summarizes his final book, and especially in the poem's final lines. For Jeffers in many of these last poems is preoccupied with the worldwide destruction now possible to man. After all, it was Jeffers who wrote years ago that civilization hastening on hastens its own decay. But here in his lifetime had arrived a ghastlier possible climax than even he had imagined. He broods over it, thinks it "all right," thinks logically it is bound to occur, then feels unsure that it will.

And here again are his stone house and tower, his Pacific coastline, his trees and hawks; and he speaks too of poetry several times, of his own poetry and of himself. Years from now he comes back as a ghost to inspect his house. Only Yeats in modern poetry could so powerfully make himself his own protagonist. No one else in modern poetry was so little in need of an objective correlative. Jeffers could speak directly.

These are the poems of an old man; relaxed, a little prosy, strong as ever, very moving. Simply because they are his final communications it is difficult at once to assess them for importance, separately, as poems; one is too interested to be objective if one admires Robinson Jeffers.

Articles and Essays

Pagan Horror from Carmel-by-the-Sea

Anonymous[*]

Last Saturday the most widely circulated evening paper of San Francisco boasted that California has produced a great poet. Such matters must be met promptly by the *Monitor.*

Robinson Jeffers has the power of Aeschylus, the subtlety of Sophocles. Shelley and Swinburne played at being pagans. This man's work is ruggedly pagan. It is no tour de force. He is intrinsically terrible.

The first point to note is that he could not have produced such horror, had he not a pagan background in California and throughout America. Greater is our fright to note that our country has become so pagan as to produce such a writer. In college we read Greek poets, but the Greek pagans were turned to dust. The modern pagans are alive.

The second point to note is to watch and pray. Some will accuse us of advertising Jeffers. He has already been advertised by papers shamefully read in Catholic homes. This is a warning to watch and prevent our children from having their souls scarred by the reading of this modern pagan giant's corruption. This is not a matter of preventing curiosity, but of saving them from a devastating decadence.

A Tower by the Sea

George Sterling[†]

On that headland between the main beach of Carmel and the mouth of the Carmel river, once called Point Loeb and now Mission Point, lives America's latest and greatest poetic "find," Robinson Jeffers, age 38, native of Pittsburgh, Pa., and an inhabitant of Carmel for over eleven years.

It is written that it is as difficult for one to estimate genius at close

[*]Reprinted from the *San Francisco Monitor,* 9 January 1926, 8.

[†]Reprinted from the *San Francisco Review* 1 (February–March 1926): 248–49.

proximity as to note the height and contours of a mountain when one is on its lower slopes, but it is my sincere conviction that Pittsburgh will eventually owe its fame, if fame it is to have, not from its blast-furnaces and millionaires (not even the dinosaurian Schwab, Gary and Carnegie), but from its having been the birthplace of Robinson Jeffers.

Mr. Jeffers' greatness has been a longish time in becoming apparent, but its final disclosure has been as brilliant as that of a *nova,* or new star, without the latter's fate of subsequent diminution. He will grow greater with the years, both in renown and achievement, or I miss my one best bet.

As ever in the case of genius, it is not easy, even if desirable, to find other singers with whom to compare him. The most obvious criterion would be Whitman, what of their use of prosodic mediums that have something in common. Jeffers, however, is incredibly more lithe and rhythmic in his lines than Whitman, and in other details the difference becomes even more marked. Whitman slips but infrequently into beauty; Jeffers' lines glow or blaze with a thousand manifestations of it—no facile or superficial beauty, but one soaring far and high in imagination. Whitman seems to have taken, all too often, an almost perverse pleasure in stating his ideas as shabbily and awkwardly as possible. Jeffers falls into no such penurious egotism; his pace is the pace of a Titan, but not of a hobbled, stumbling one. And when one comes to deeper, if no more important matters, Jeffers immensely exceeds the gray singer in scope and depth and significance of vision. He deals with the cosmos, Whitman with the democracy of termites. His "shadow of a magnitude" far outlaps the penumbra of the older poet. And he has but hardly begun to sing!

Indeed, when I come to compare him with his contemporaries, however futile and needless the act, he seems as lonely a figure in poetry as is Dreiser in prose. By that comparison, Frost, fine poet that he is, becomes a wise New England crow, and E. A. Robinson an even sager Arctic owl! Masters is more closely akin to him in poetic blood, but Jeffers is quite as weighty of thought and beyond comparison the more radiantly clad in beauty. Well, in the House of Art there are many mansions!

It has been adduced that Jeffers, like Poe, adds an unjustified force to his artistic impact by choosing themes so horrible as to be in themselves unforgettable. It is, in fact, a harder thing to triumph poetically with the treatment of the normal. But his use of such themes is far from invariable, and we see him bring to saner and deeper matters a wisdom and divination as great as those used in *Tamar* and *Roan Stallion.* He is poet as well as philosopher in all on which he brings to bear the fierce light of his imagination, and his work abounds in poems in which crystal and granite are equally evident.

It is his use of the sterner and more sorrowful aspects of beauty that lead me to think that his work will outlive that of Whitman. The latter was primarily a sage, a philosopher occupied with visions of some future perfectibility and nonageneity of mankind. But all tastes change, and a philosophy founded on a present conception of the desirable may become the laughing-stock of generations far in the future, or may be utterly discarded and forgotten. Beauty however, seems in no such manner vulnerable. What past centuries thrilled to in the original moves us even in translations. By what mutation are future hearts to be sealed against beauty as final and inexplicable as Jeffers' superb description of a certain sunset?—"the sad, red, splendid light." Fortunate is he on whose memory that light falls unsetting!

But I am not here to quote Mr. Jeffers. That will be done more and more often in essay and review, as he rises with the years to his full poetic stature. It pleases me rather to say that I think him the most fortunate of men—a great poet, of invincible health, comparatively young, a Greek in face and form, happily and conclusively married and the father of two delightfully interesting and physically perfect boys, twins of nine! Add to that that he does not have to worry over finances, and you can see that the gods have for once gone out of their way to show what they could do for us all were they so minded. Nor does Mr. Jeffers take his poetic responsibility lightly, for though the granite Falcon Tower that he has built (with his own hands) may testify to a muscular activity, he wastes no mornings and few afternoons on the small affairs of sociability. Rather is he the hermit, guarding with jealous care the time and sensitivity necessary to his work. I wish him few callers, and windows open to the four winds of inspiration.

Shell-Shock and the Poetry of Robinson Jeffers

Floyd Dell*

The acclaiming of a poet as "great" by the intelligentsia of a given period—whether or not it affords any assurance of enduring fame for the poet—should at least give us new information concerning the psychology of the intelligentsia itself at the moment in history. The appearance of the poet Robinson Jeffers upon the literary horizon, and the enthusiastic acclaim which his work has received from many of the advanced leaders of the American intelligentsia, offer us this present opportunity for such an inquiry.

While this inquiry will not undertake any esthetic criticism of Jeffers' work, it may be said at the outset that it is certainly work of unusual and remarkable quality, and that its dramatic and narrative powers (leaving aside the perhaps debatable question of its specific poetic

*Reprinted from the *Modern Quarterly* 3 (September–December 1926): 268–73.

merits) would naturally attract attention to it. However, the attribution of "greatness" to a writer implies something more than a recognition of his possession of such powers: it implies a profound approval of his content—not necessarily his subject matter, but his treatment of it, in short his attitude toward life.

Robinson Jeffers' attitude toward life seems to be made unmistakably clear in his poems. Some documentation will be given further on, but his attitude may here be briefly assumed as follows: Mankind is a loathsome breed; an inconsiderable breed, too, mere lice on the whirling earth; and being doomed to certain extinction, its whole history in the meantime is meaningless. But there is something in the universe with which man can get into such a relation as to take him more or less outside of himself. The latter effect is gained by contact with a secondary-spiritual realm, which manifests itself in (at least what appear to be and perhaps are) ghosts, spirits, table-tipping (or chair-lifting), mediumistic utterances by the dead, and other supernatural acts and communications. This secondary spiritual world is perhaps trivial and foolish; if these spirits amounted to much, they would have no interest in our human existence at all; but there they are. There is, however, a primary spiritual realm, waiting to be discovered; this realm is the Absolute, and it is also God, we can unite ourselves with God, we can become one with God; this God is identical with the Universe, with Nature; not, however, the refined Nature of Wordsworth or the Nature-lovers, but a huge, frightful (to mere humanity, that is), indifferent, chaotic (but only from our narrow human point of view—in itself simple and grandly regular), merciless Nature that is beyond Good and Evil—the Nature that makes storms, the God that walks in the lightning. And this Nature, this God, being different from humanity, is not to be approached with human motives, is least of all to be propitiated with human deserving: it is only when one is least human, when one transcends humanity by being "inhuman," that one sees God face to face. What is ordinarily called sin and crime will serve perhaps best of all, or at least efficiently, as a means of knowing God; but it must be extreme sin, unnatural crime, and persevered in, not weakly repented. At the same time there is, or may appear to be, a Christ, who comes in glory, answering prayers, etc.; but this Christ may be a mere appearance. At all events, strong natures have no dealings with Christ; their dealings are with God only. It makes really no difference what we do, or even what is done to us, except as these tragic happenings may reveal God within us:

> When brigand powers
> Of anger or pain or the sick dream of sin
> Break our soul's house outside the ruins we weep.
> We look through the breached wall, why there within
> All the red while our peace was lying asleep.

Smiling in dreams while the broad knives drank blood,
The robbers triumphed, the roof burned overhead,
The eternal living and untroubled God
Lying asleep upon a lily bed.
Men screamed, the bugles screamed, walls broke in the air,
We never knew till then that He was there.

This does not conclude our account of the poet's attitude toward life: these theological conceptions have their direct influence upon his attitude toward science, woman, love, politics, and other mundane and familiar matters. But before going on to that, let us consider some passages in his poems, bearing on what has been said above.

In the poem *Roan Stallion* we find a woman who is in love with a magnificent stallion her husband has brought home. She woos the animal and adores and prays to it as a "God"; she is "not good enough" for sexual union with her stallion God, because her merely human husband and other men have known her sexually. These are the ideas and feelings of the character in the story, and are not legitimately to be attributed to the poet himself because he expresses them sympathetically, but only to the degree to which he "editorially" commits himself to them. There is such an editorial passage in the poem, to the effect that God is not a man, and that when man passes the limits of humanity he is praising God; humanity is "the mould to break away from, the crust to break through, the coal to break into fire"; and "wild loves that leap over the walls of nature," "unnatural crime," "tragedy that breaks man's face," vision or desire "that fool him out of his limits"—these, together with science (here conceived as humanly useless and as insulting to human dignity in its concepts), are the means of surpassing humanity and praising God. The passage may be regarded as a complete philosophic acceptance of the meaning of the fable, which fable is indeed to be taken (aside from its revelations of a temperament of interest doubtless to students of morbid psychology, but with which we are not here concerned) simply as a symbol embodying that philosophic idea. The conclusion of the tale enforces the idea dramatically: the husband offers to show the woman "what the red fellow did," i.e., to the mare, but she refuses to accept this merely human substitute for her stallion God, and goes to the stallion. The husband follows, and, with a gun in her hands, she watches while the stallion contemptuously kills the man; when that is accomplished, the woman, "moved by some obscure human fidelity," kills the stallion; at that action "the stars fell from their places crying in her mind," and she turned upon her daughter "the mask of a woman who has killed God."

In *The Tower Beyond Tragedy*, a reworking of the Greek saga of the murder of Agamemnon by his wife Clytemnestra, the prophecies of the mad Cassandra, and the revenge-murder of Clytemnestra by her children, Orestes and Electra, Cassandra has a vision which, not being strictly pertinent to the Greek drama under way, may be regarded as in the nature of an editorial utterance by the poet: a vision of the pageant of ancient and modern history as a kind of bloody farce enacted between two ice ages:

> I have seen on what stage
> You sing the little tragedy; the column of the ice that was before on one side flanks it,
> The column of ice to come closes it up on the other: audience nor author
> I have never seen yet.

She rejoices in the coming of the final ice age:

> Like a cat with a broken-winged bird it will play with you,
> It will nip and let go; you will say it is gone, but the next
> Season it increases: O clean, clean,
> White and most clean, colorless quietness,
> Without trace, without trail, without stain in the garment, drawn down
> From the poles to the girdle.

She prays to the lords of the earth to change her into grass or stone or air, "but cut humanity out of my being, that is the wound that festers in me." And: "you will heal the earth also, Death, in your time."

After the mother-murder, when Electra wishes Orestes to stay and be king, he confesses to her that in a vision he had dreamed he embraced her "more than brotherwise"; and she, thinking it is fear of these incestuous wishes that is driving him away, offers either to kill herself or yield to those wishes, to keep him. And Orestes, in going away, declares that he leaves humanity behind him; he will "go behind things, beyond hours and ages and be all things in all time" (i.e., unite himself with the Absolute, be one with God).

In *Tamar,* a story of incest between a brother and sister (involving also, aside from other incestuous relationships, communication with the dead, Indian ghosts, and what-not of the same sort, together with treachery, murder, and considerable sadism), there occurs this passage between the brother and sister—a few interpolations in brackets being put in here to make the situation clearer:

> "Go," he said, and he shut the door against them [i.e., the rest of the family] and said, "Slut, how many, how many?" [i.e., lovers] She laughing,
> "I knew you would be sweet to me: I am still sick [i.e., from a miscarriage, brought about by sexual union with Indian ghosts!] Did you find marks in the bark? [on the tree beside her window, where her other lover has climbed up to visit her in her room] I am still sick, Lee;
> You don't intend killing me?" "Flogging, whipping, whipping, is there anything male about here
> You haven't used yet? [i.e., including her own father] Agh, you mouth, you open mouth. But I won't touch you." "Let me say something,"

She answered, standing dark against the west in the window, the death of the winter rose of evening
Behind her little high-poised head, and threading the brown twilight of the room with the silver
Exultance of her voice: "My brother, can you feel how happy I am but how far off too?
If I have done wrong it has turned good to me, I could almost be sorry I have to die now
Out of such freedom; if I were standing back of the evening crimson on a mountain in Asia
All the fool shames you can whip up into a filth of words would not be farther off me,
Nor any fear of anything, if I stood in the evening star and saw this dusty dime's worth
A dot of light, dropped up the star-gleam. Poor brother, poor brother, you played the fool too
But not enough, it is not enough to taste delight and passion and disgust and loathing
And agony, you have to be wide alive, 'an open mouth' you said, all the while, to reach this heaven
You'll never grow up to. . . ."

We may now, having to this extent documented these philosophical *leit-motifs*, return to the poet's attitude toward life in its homelier aspects. Documentation here would be impossible within these limits of space, for it would require quotation of the long passages of drama and narrative in which these matters are exhibited at length, and sometimes only by implication. But the logical relevance of what follows to what has gone before will be apparent:—Since life is meaningless, it is silly to try to understand it, or attempt by unraveling its secrets to get conscious and purposeful control of it. Our moralities are pitiful fictions; the true instinctive and sexual motives of life are too large and powerful to be comprehended within any merely human scheme. In so far as our sexuality is customary and civilized, it is a despicable pretence; in so far as it exceeds these bounds, it is truly interesting, picturesque, dramatic and splendid; in this excess it relates us to the animals, who are closer to God than we are because they live instinctive lives. True sexuality, not the paltry civilized kind, is dark and terrible, stopping at nothing (that is to say, it is in the essence the "polymorphous-perverse infantile sexuality" from which incestuous, homosexual, sadistic, coprophilial and similar wishes have not yet been refined out by repression or sublimation). There is something non-human in our lives that is, from a human point of view, terrifying; we may pretend to be ladies and gentlemen, but in truth we are monsters! And what is to be done about this? Nothing. He or she who has found this out and had the courage to accept it has seen god, is one with God. Courage is needed; but wisdom is useless. (The elementary facts of modern psychology are transmogrified into bogies, which indeed they may seem to be if one has renounced science. But in renouncing science one has obviously to fall back on God.)

Human nature being what it is (in this view), it finds its most dramatic and fascinating expression in female sexuality. Women are (perhaps I should emphasize this as what we would conclude from the picture of life found in these poems—and not my own opinion), from the civilized point of view, queer and terrible creatures. They are essentially lawless, except as they obey the laws of instinct, which tell them to seduce, deceive, lie, hate, betray, kill, etc. You can never trust them, never believe a word they say. They will make love to you in the most convincing manner, hating you like poison all the while. 'Ware women! At the same time they have their fascinations, and doubtless for a man who knows how to deal with them, who can treat them as the delightful uncivilized animals that they are and not be surprised at anything they may do—for him, if he cares to trifle with them, they may provide sufficiently delightful moments, worthy even of being recorded in poems.

We have now roughly indicated the kind of world which this poet gives us to live in. It is a world in which politics are trash, revolution an absurdity (though perhaps a gallant absurdity, worthy as a spectacle of our admiration, while we wait for the inevitable ice age to wipe it all out), science a useless but impressive revelation of our human futility, art a bitterly earnest expression of the tragic quality of human existence, love a (sometimes pleasant) madness. The role of the intellect, it will be noted, is necessarily very small in this world. It can help industry to produce various practical but unimportant adjuncts to our meaningless existence. It can reveal to us, in the starry heavens and in the dancing demons of the atom, the irrelevance of all human ideals to the purposes of the universe. But it cannot discriminate between life's values to any practical human effect. It can, however, by destroying human illusions, help us to appreciate the spectacle of the universe and of human life from the tragico-esthetical point of view. The role of the intellect is small, critical and destructive; it is the humble hand-maiden of the Tragic Spirit; it can sweep clean the soul, that God may enter into us. The instincts, the passions, have us helplessly, hopelessly, in their grip. From them there is no escape, except in death; but while living we can accept them, understand their unimportance; and thus helplessly but nobly to accept our doom is to become one with God!

It might be interesting to discuss this God in all Its historical and literary aspects—to trace Its resemblance to the God of the Manichean sects, to the God of the Gille de Rois, to the God of Dostoievsky, to the Earth Spirit (whatever its name) of James Branch Cabell, and to the Devil of the Middle Ages; but all this might lead us somewhat astray from what appears to be the most important aspect of this God—that It is a God of Resignation, to which tired and baffled souls without any realistic social hopes may turn for the strength to endure the burden of a meaningless and monstrous and cruel life.

Our conclusions may be briefly drawn. The current enthusiasm for these poems would seem to indicate that the spiritual wound inflicted upon the American intelligentsia by the World War has been even greater than we have been willing to recognize.

Music of the Mountain

Loren Eiseley*

A lonely and austere man—one who took more joy in the contemplation of a hen-hawk sailing into the wind than in the chatter of any drawing room—once entered in his journal: "In literature it is only the wild that attracts us. Dullness is only another name for tameness. It is the untamed, uncivilized, free, and wild thinking in *Hamlet,* in the *Iliad* and in all the scriptures and mythologies that delight us,—not learned in the schools, not refined and polished by art. A truly good book is something as wildly natural and primitive, mysterious and marvelous, ambrosial and fertile as a fungus or lichen."

That [quotation] contains, in a nutshell, the secret of Jeffers' strength. It is not in the Greek influences about which so much has been written and said. It is not in the themes of incest and swift-stalking death, nor even in his grasp of modern science, though that is great, that the root of his power lies. It is something more simple and elemental than all these. It is that very rare phenomenon which happened once at Walden and a few other places, namely, the complete identification of the individual with his environment, or, rather, the extension of the environment into the individual to such a degree that the latter seems almost a lens, a gathering point through which, in some psychic and unexplainable manner, is projected a portion of the diversified and terrific forces of nature that otherwise stream helplessly away without significance to humanity.

This may seem like a denial of the poet's individuality. It is not so intended. The poet's peculiar temperament is the master of these forces and uses them for its own ends. That is why the various interpreters of nature have spoken with such different voices. They cannot capture it all—the goodness, the cruelty, the mystery. There is too much, and they are merely "fractions of the arc" and interpreters of their fractions. Nature is greater than her spokesmen, who were drawn out of her depth "only to be these things they are," as Jeffers himself recognizes.

This identification of the poet with his environment, the rooting of his feet into the earth, is no mere "nature writing" in the ordinary sense.

*From *Voices* 67 (December–January 1932–33): 42–47. Reprinted by permission of John A. Eichmann, 3rd, for the estate of Loren Eiseley.

In the case of Jeffers it means that his thoughts, his people, grow as naturally as the pines at Point Lobos out of the same rock. This background of the real, this communion with earth, sky and water, is what lends the illusion of reality to characters that in the hands of another poet would seem unwieldy and ridiculous. It lends, also, the sense of physical actuality which makes his every thought, his painful philosophy poignantly real and not the maunderings of a dyspeptic bookworm. In the pages of *The Loving Shepherdess* he summarizes it all—the sea rock cypress and pine, the wraiths of fog which are continually creeping over the coast rocks—and he makes his heroine say:

> The beetle beside my hand in the grass and the little brown bird
> tilted on a stone,
> The short sad grass, burnt on the gable of the world with near sun and all
> winds: there was nothing there that I didn't
> Love with my heart . . .

It is a simple thing to see a rock with the eyes; less simple to see it with the heart. And it is extremely rare that a man reared in a society whose science, even, is often anthropocentric, can take a stone in his hands and say:

> Often I have heard the hard rocks I handled
> Groan, because lichen and time and water dissolve them,
> And they have to travel down the strange falling scale
> Of soil and plants and the flesh of beasts to become
> The bodies of men; they murmur at their fate
> In the hollows of windless nights, they'd rather be anything
> Than human flesh played on by pain and joy,
> They pray for annihilation sooner, but annihilation's
> Not in the book yet.

There are critics who cry for the poet of the new science, the interpreter of our age. I think they are a little near-sighted. He is here. Moreover, he distinguishes with accuracy between the permanencies of the human background and what is ephemeral and not worth discussion. He has wasted no time eulogizing machinery and buildings that will be outmoded tomorrow. What threatens to be his only major fault, as Professor Lehman has already pointed out,[1] is, perhaps, a certain almost puritanical aloofness from his kind. Although there are occasional lines of magnificent love poetry in his narratives, one does not think of Jeffers as a writer of the love lyric; on the contrary, he has published almost nothing of that sort. He himself comments grimly in "Soliloquy" that, instead, he has "invoked the slime in the skull, / the lymph in the vessels." I do not agree with those critics who think this threatens his stature, however. Thoreau, one of the first great writers truly indigenous to America, was no lover of society, and indeed once remarked that man would take on more interest if he could be encountered in the woods like a bear or a moose. Yet, if anything, Thoreau's stature has grown with the years. With the discerning body of readers who really count, a man's reputation may rest secure on other grounds than that he was an able turner of love lyrics or that he possessed an abiding faith in humanity.

One critic has said that Jeffers expresses "the death-wish of a decadent civilization." That may be. Certainly he knows that no mere adultation of our present toys will save us:

> An end shall be surely,
> Though unnatural things are accomplished, they breathe in the sea's depth,
> They swim in the air, they bridle the cloud-leaper lightning to carry their
> messages. . . .

for:

> That pure white quietness
> Waits on the heads of the mountains, not sleep but death, will the fire
> Of burnt cities and ships in that year warm you . . . ? The frost, the old frost
> Like a cat with a broken-winged bird it will play with you,
> It will nip and let go . . .

He has been contrasted with Whitman. I do not see that Jeffers is so much the antithesis of Whitman as he is an older Whitman gone down to the land's end, grown sadder, more sophisticated, seeing: "The inhuman years to be accomplished / The inhuman powers, the servile cunning under pressure/ In a land grown old, heavy and crowded." He embodies the restlessness of a wandering, adventurous and essentially active stock now turned inward upon itself and "gnawing its famine for food." He speaks contemptuously in his latest book of verse of "the pallid pursuit of the world's beauty on paper" and envies, a bit self-consciously, the lives of his forebears. The "stone sickness" of Reave Thurso is indicative of the dilemma of this stock, caught in the trap of its own will, wasting itself away in a futile struggle with itself and its neighbors, or with phantom opponents, when there is no longer anything upon which it can worthily expend itself. Cawdor, also, had this strength, and poor Barclay, the preacher in *The Women At Point Sur* was, perhaps, a more neurotic exhibition of it in his insane and terrific effort to overleap the bounds of humanity. Yet I think this restlessness expresses something more than the thwarted will-to-action of a dynamic people. It goes deeper. It is, in the last analysis, the expression of man's dismay before the conclusions of modern science that leave him a microcosm whose deeds have no import save to himself. Though he have the power of a king there is nothing great by which to do greatly. There is left only actions *toward* humanity—the incestuous desire that Jeffers conceives as leading nowhere . . . and that somehow does not completely express that humanity nor the mind which measures itself and the stars honestly, by the same scales.

A critic reviewing Spengler's last book in a recent number of the *Symposium* remarked that the *Decline of the West*, with its overstuffed simulation of scholarship, expressed to vast numbers the despair of this generation which also finds voice in such poems as *The Waste Land.* There are those who would add Jeffers' name to this list, and the growing body of writers who see in all this feeling of futility and despair merely the death-knell of the old order of capitalism. They vision a new dawn just below the horizon—the new dawn that will sweep all these sterile prophets of despair away.

This also may be, but if we go down and the new order rises, I do not think Jeffers will suffer any more than a temporary obscurity in the flush of new enthusiasms. This was true of Thoreau, and it will be true of Jeffers so long as minds are troubled by the ache of mortality, and science, for all its conquests, can see only a universe "shining its substance away like a passionate thought." No new economic doctrine will destroy death. There will still be lonely minds surveying the night heavens, or casting forward toward our end, or lonely in lonely places finding the doctrine of acceptance and easy pleasure somehow unsatisfying.

Men misread Jeffers who find in him the cynical and superficial futility that riots across the pages of our time. He moves more painfully through that darker world known only to the student and philosopher. He knows De Sitter's theory, wrestles with the doctrine of Eternal Recurrence, with the problem of good and evil. He sees us caught

> In the one mesh; when they look backward they see only a man standing
> at the beginning,
> Or forward, a man at the end; or if upward, men in the shining bitter sky
> striding and feasting,
> Whom you call Gods . . .

He is the spokesman of the infinite hunger of mind in a universe finite and limited. "The wild fence-vaulter, science" has succeeded only in intensifying that hunger. Joy does not answer it, nor pain, though under the endurance of the latter, mankind takes on a certain glory. But, instead he yearns to: "be all things in all time . . . in the motionless and timeless center, / In the white of the fire . . ."

Jeffers' celebration of death seems, at first sight, hardly consistent with the lines just quoted. I offer as a suggestion, however, the fact that death is only a paradoxical substitute to hands reaching for the moon. It is the only gift that quite overwhelms and destroys the consciousness that our puny and limited bodies cannot long endure nor satisfy. I am not one of those who expect a poet to be always consistent. The fact that Mr. Jeffers has long been considered a nay-sayer to life does not trouble me. It is sufficient that he once wrote:

Far-flown ones, you children of the hawk's dream future when you lean
from a crag of the last planet on the ocean
Of the far stars, remember we also have known beauty.

Those are not the words of a complacent pessimist who has already set up housekeeping in his tomb. There is greater pride of life in them than in the words of many optimists. They shine the brighter coming as they do from a man who has known fully the depths of the "night side of love." I think also of his lines about the old woman who had once nursed, with Rabelaisian vigor, a motherless faun. I think it was a little wistfully that he wrote: "I see that once in her spring she lived in the streaming arteries, / The stir of the world, the music of the mountain."

Note

1. "Robinson Jeffers" by B. H. Lehman, *Saturday Review of Literature,* September 5, 1931.

The Values of Robinson Jeffers

Frederic I. Carpenter*

It is a truism that everyone who opposes the existing order of things is "dangerous." If he advocates a new order, he is a "radical"; but radicals are intellectually, at least, constructive. If, however, he opposes the existing order without advocating a new one, he is a "reactionary," and reactionaries are merely destructive. In intellectual America "radicals" are not without honor, but "reactionaries" are anathema. Perhaps for this reason Robinson Jeffers begins a typical poem: "I am not well civilized, really alien here; trust me not."[1] For he has often been called the poet of denial, the destroyer of morality and of human values. It is the purpose of this essay to inquire how far this is true. A poet may deny the authority of existing values, may be unable or unwilling to describe a new order, and yet may imply and even occasionally define the outlines of such an order.

Many critics and most readers, to whom morality looms larger than poetry, have simply dismissed Jeffers with an epithet: "Dull naughtiness," wrote Howard Mumford Jones; "Pathology," wrote V. F. Calverton; "Hysterics," said a newspaper reviewer.[2] Others, even while recognizing the beauty and power of his poetry, have been repelled by the negative implications of his thought. ". . . The most splendid poetry of my time!" exclaimed H. L. Davis. "Nothing written by this generation can begin to come up with it. . . . And yet—the poem itself is dead."[3] Comparing Jeffers to Hardy, Newton Arvin also concluded that "the appeal is to nothing affirmative . . . and, in the long run, is pure negation."[4] A reason

*Reprinted from *American Literature* 11 (January 1940): 353–66.

for this negation was suggested by Lawrence Morris: "In Jeffers the heart of an ancient mystic wars with the mind of a contemporary scientific rationalist."[5] And H. H. Waggoner blamed Jeffers's denial of existing morality on the teachings of nineteenth-century science: "He absorbed without the necessary grain of salt the implications of a science that had no place for mind or values."[6] But all of these critics, whether recognizing the beauty of his poetry or not, have opposed the "negation" of his thought, and particularly his rejection of accepted morality and human values.

The first suggestion that Jeffers might be attempting something new and constructive came from Benjamin H. Lehman in Jeffers's own California, who pointed out that "we confront simply the problem of a new approach to the universe and the individual, which shall bring into harmony the moral and the natural worlds."[7] But no writer has developed this insight, nor suggested that Jeffers, even in denying the authority of a purely humanistic morality, has sought to preserve certain of the old values, and to harmonize these with the "new" morality of the "natural world."

But, first, the question arises: Does Jeffers concern himself with human values at all? For if he does not, our inquiry is meaningless. Identifying Jeffers's thought with that of materialistic science, Professor Waggoner believes that he merely denies them: "There are no values recognized as such by man which are ultimate values; value lies only in the pre-human animals, pre-civilized activities, and the inhuman universe."[8] To this Jeffers himself replies that values are not illusory. "The belief that traditional values are divinely ordained seems to me an illusion. But to prefer—for instance—courage to cowardice or mercy to cruelty cannot be called an illusion. Traditional values may be thought of as habits or conventions, some useful, others foolish, all subject to change; but not as illusions."[9]

Jeffers, then, specifically affirms his interest in the problem of values, and his acceptance of certain traditional values. Indeed, he has proclaimed this from the beginning: "Meditation on Saviors" remains one of his most thoughtful poems. And increasingly in later years he has turned toward a purely philosophic type of poetry. Such pieces as "The Answer," "Hellenistics," and "Nova"[10] are outstanding: what they have lost in vividness of imagery, they have gained in clarity of expression. Finally, a recent letter from the poet places this problem first: "Now . . . it seems to me that some prefatory definition of values would be useful. What does the author think would be best for men? What is he working toward?"[11]

It seems clear that the problem of values is fundamental to the understanding of Jeffers's poetry. But it must be admitted that many of his statements on this subject are contradictory. Although he believes that human values are real and necessary, his poems also exclaim frequently that humanity itself is "a spectral episode," and "needless." Can human values be important if humanity itself is not? This contradiction constantly distorts his thought. Before we attempt to describe his values, our first concern must be to explain what logical right he has to values at all.

But granting the existence of contradictions, his poetry as a whole does repeatedly emphasize certain values. Some of these may be classed as "human," others as "natural." Although the human, or traditional, values are less striking, they are none the less important. Among them "freedom" will be seen to stand highest. When this is recognized as the cornerstone of his house of human values, it becomes surprising that he should so often be called "reactionary," and even "Fascist." Our second concern will be to show how the passion for freedom dominates his social philosophy.

Beyond the traditional human values, Jeffers celebrates the transcendental value of "integrity," or the unity of man and nature. Because it is mystical, this value remains somewhat vague. But more clearly in Jeffers's poetry than in any other contemporary writing, this mystic ideal has found new embodiment and definition. That it has not been recognized before is due, perhaps, to the frequent confusion between the "transcendental" and the "natural." For "integrity" transcends the old values of good and evil (as Emerson knew), but at the same time preaches the oneness of man with nature, and is thus far "natural." An idea so perennially obscure can hardly become clear all at once, but Jeffers's poetry illuminates it strikingly. Beyond the contradictions involved in his denunciation of humanity, and beyond his celebration of the traditional value of freedom, his development of the idea of integrity suggests the key to his thought.

1

According to strict logic, Jeffers's poetry is inconsistent: if man is a "spectral episode" and "humanity is needless," human values are clearly unreal and unnecessary. (Natural values may still be real and necessary, and may apply to man as a part of nature.) But Jeffers, like Emerson and Whitman before him, disclaims a purely logical consistency: "I think it is the business of a writer of poetry, not to express his own gospel, but to present images, emotions, ideas, and let the reader find his good in them if he can. Not to form a way of thought, but perhaps to activate thoughts."[12] Jeffers, therefore, usually follows the old American method of extreme statement, writing as the mood impels him, and trusting that one counter-statement will balance the other, shocking the reader into thought, and suggesting a final ground of truth.

Following this principle, Jeffers has repeatedly exaggerated the insignificance of man and of human consciousness, in order to counterbalance the anthropocentric tendency of conventional thought. Because past writers have claimed for man the supreme value, and sometimes the sole significance in the stellar universe, Jeffers, often consciously, has gone to the other extreme. In *Margrave,* for instance, he has described educated humanity at its worst, and imagined the outer stars as "fleeing the contagion / Of consciousness that infects this corner of space." But, as he explained soon after: "The poem called 'Margrave' in my latest book exaggerates. From that point of view it is just a poem. I was irritated into extravagance by the excessive value that people seem to attribute to human consciousness."[13]

In other words, Jeffers's extreme denial of the value of humanity and of human consciousness is not to be taken literally. It is purposeful, consciously intended to correct conventional errors. And always it is modified by counter-statement, often occurring in the very same poem. Thus, in *Margrave* he warns himself: "I also am not innocent / Of contagion, but have spread my spirit on the deep world;" and answers himself: "But who is our judge? It is likely the enormous / Beauty of the world requires for completion our ghostly increment." Even more clearly in "Meditation on Saviors" he grants to men:

> this advantage over their granite grave-marks, of having
> realized the petulant human consciousness
> Before, and then the greatness, the peace: drunk from both pitchers:
> these to be pitied? These not fortunate?

Jeffers's denunciation of man is often purposefully exaggerated. But he goes on to explain that all of his dramatic poetry is similarly purposeful and prophetic. Like the Old Testament prophets, he will paint vivid word-pictures of the destruction of the city. Like his countryman, Jonathan Edwards,[14] and the later evangelical preachers, he will awaken man to a realizing sense of sin. So his imagined "Redeemer" explains:

> I am here on the mountain making
> Antitoxin for all the happy towns and farms, the lovely blameless children,
> the terrible
> Arrogant cities.

And so Jeffers exhorts himself to "make fables again, / Tell people not to fear death, toughen / Their bones if possible with bitter fables not to fear life."[15]

But the final and inevitable answer to the question of whether Jeffers has, logically, the right to celebrate human values, is that every writer must have. Writing presupposes an audience. Speech, and even verbal thought, are social. Every poet has some "message," and imagines some scale of values, even if unconsciously; else he would never have written. Jeffers also admits this: he writes to influence the people. He, too, seeks power, even if only "power / After the nerves are put away underground, to lighten the abstract unborn children toward peace."[16]

Indeed, his emphasis on the insignificance of human life, combined with his significant desire to "lighten the children toward peace," merely repeats an ancient paradox. Buddha found peace under the Bo-tree, but returned to the world to preach it. The preacher of Ecclesiastes saw that all was "vanity," but nevertheless taught the people "because he was wise." Man may be relatively insignificant, and his life vain; but because no man is ever quite free of his fellows, the poet must continue to teach men their own insignificance until a true sense of values makes them also free. Therefore Jeffers denounces humanity but emphasizes values.

2

Of course, Jeffers does not believe that modern man will achieve freedom: neither his own poetry nor any other writing will accomplish much. Pessimistically, he believes that our civilization is doomed to decay. The most famous and characteristic of his poems is, perhaps, "Shine, Perishing Republic." "America," he says, is "thickening to empire; and protest, like a bubble in the molten mass, pops and sighs out, and the mass hardens." But the significant thing about this poem is that this ultimate "perishing" of the republic does not deny the sense of the social values—rather it emphasizes them. A "republic" is good; an "empire," bad. "Protest" is good; acquiescence, bad. His pessimism as to the future of these goods merely enhances the sense of their importance.

Lest anyone should misinterpret his meaning in this early poem, Jeffers has added a kind of sequel to it, entitled "Shine, Republic,"[17] in which he defines the values of Western civilization, without dwelling on its probable "perishing." For, he concludes, the true values will persist, although each successive republic may sicken and die.

But the traditional values of modern civilization, Jeffers argues, are irreconcilable. Whitman had sought to couple "independence" with the word "en masse." "—But we cannot have all the luxuries and freedom also,"[18] Jeffers replies. Choosing between the two, he proclaims boldly:

> The love of freedom has been the quality of Western man.
> There is a stubborn torch that flames from Marathon to Concord, its
> dangerous beauty binding three ages
> Into one time . . .
> And you, America, that passion made you. You were not born to
> prosperity, you were born to love freedom.
> You did not say "en masse," you said "independence."

Republics and all social groups "shine" by virtue of the freedom which they offer individuals. But all men love wealth, and many will sell freedom for an imagined security. "Freedom is poor and laborious; that torch is not safe but hungry, and often requires blood for its fuel." Therefore, he fears, even Americans may soon sell their freedom: "We are easy to manage, a gregarious people, / Full of sentiment, clever at mechanics, and we love our luxuries."[19] But even after this betrayal, the value of freedom will live: "The states of the next age will no doubt remember you, and edge their love of freedom with contempt of luxury."[20]

This doctrine is central to Jeffers's social philosophy. Individuals and individual nations and civilizations will perish, he believes, but the values which they have partially realized will persist. And whether or not these values are fully realized by later men, they remain more "real" and more significant than the human beings who realize them.

Jeffers does more than define this freedom in words. He embodies it in his dramatic poetry, illustrating it in human terms. In *Dear Judas,* for instance, this libertarian philosophy finds its clearest expression. Although tradition has always described Judas as the treacherous, self-seeking embodiment of evil—the conscious villain, Jeffers describes him as the deluded social reactionary, who betrays Jesus "to get the firebrand locked up, to save the city. . . . Oh Jesus, I also love men." To Jeffers, the reactionary is the coward who fears the dangers of freedom. And cowardice, or submission to tyranny, seems to him the ultimate evil. Therefore, "dear" Judas, even if his intentions were good, remains despicable:

> Therefore your name shall couple
> With his in men's minds for many centuries: you enter his kingdom with him, as the hawk's lice with the hawk
> Climb the blue towers of the sky under the down of the feathers.

Whatever else it is, this social philosophy does not seem "reactionary," nor "Fascist."[21] Nevertheless, many distinguished critics have so described it.[22] The reason, perhaps, is that Jeffers considers social action doomed to defeat. But his pessimism in this is not properly "defeatist." It rather suggests the pattern of fatalistic Greek thought, as opposed to Christian.

Jeffers has often compared Jesus with the Greek Prometheus. Both were lovers of man, seeking to free him by giving him one of the attributes of God—fire, or knowledge of the truth. But both were doomed to defeat for their acts—Jesus to be crucified, and Prometheus to be chained to the mountain. In *At the Birth of an Age* Jeffers identifies these two with "the Hanged God" of Norse mythology, and suggests that the symbol is universal. Man is perpetually defeated, and the leaders of men doomed to suffering. So Greek religion taught that Zeus punishes rebellion; and in this Jeffers's thought is Greek. But his thought is also Christian and modern in that he prefers the defeated rebel to the victorious reactionary. His social sympathies remain always with "the man-loving rebel: wherever there has been love or rebellion against any of the tyrannies of darkness, there is a touch of his spirit."[23] Jesus and Prometheus were rebels against God, but were greater than man: they were half-gods because of their passion for freedom. The revolutionary surpasses the reactionary, as the god-man (loving freedom) surpasses the animal-man (loving luxury and security).

These social values are clear: progress toward freedom is good, and conservative reaction is evil. But further confusion has arisen because Jeffers has always denied the ultimacy of these social values. His are rather the individual values of the mystic, beyond good and evil. For revolution breeds reaction, and power—even benevolent power—defeats itself. The man-loving rebel, be he Jesus or Prometheus, is destined eternally to suffer torment at the hands of the superhuman God. Salvation is not for society, but for the individual. For, although society can never be perfected, the individual perhaps can. By "falling in love with God," he can himself become superhuman.

But "this," Jeffers's Electra replied, "is mere death." And all the humanist and all the socialist critics have repeated—this is mere denial of social morality, denial of human values. Possibly it is. But it is also "self-reliance"—the morality of Emerson and Thoreau.[24] Fundamentally it is not the denial of social morality, but the transcendence of it. On their own levels, the social values remain valid. For the mass of mankind, they constitute "morality." But there are higher, "transcendental" values.[25]

Thus Thoreau once argued, reviewing an early book on socialism: The socialist wishes to reform the world; and then mankind will be right. The mystic wishes to reform himself; and then the world will be right.[26] The mystic sympathizes with the socialist, and wishes him well; but he seeks first to perfect himself.

3

The value of freedom is essentially social and human: celebrating man's refusal to be compelled by any power outside himself.[27] But this freedom is limited in two ways. It is (in a certain sense) negative, implying freedom from some external power. And it is dependent on life in that an external power may kill the man who refuses to submit to it, and so destroy his freedom. Since Jeffers has already declared that human life is not of ultimate importance, he must define the values which transcend it. To this problem he has addressed himself in a series of philosophical poems included in his latest book.[28] Life is good, he writes, and freedom is better than life; but best of all is integrity:

> all life is beautiful. We cannot be sure of life for one moment;
> We can, by force and self-discipline, by many refusals and a few
> assertions, in the teeth of fortune assure ourselves
> Freedom and integrity in life or integrity in death.[29]

Beyond humanity, beyond life, beyond freedom lies the value of wholeness or integrity. For it applies equally to man and the universe—to microcosm and macrocosm—uniting human and non-human under one law:

however ugly the parts appear the whole remains beautiful.
A severed hand
Is an ugly thing, and man dissevered from the earth . . .
Often appears atrociously ugly. Integrity is wholeness, the greatest beauty is
Organic wholeness, the wholeness of life and things, the divine beauty of the universe.[30]

But what is this mystic "integrity"? Old as it is, the ideal remains vague: "To thine own self be true / And it must follow as the night the day / Thou canst not then be false to any man." In the mouth of Polonius, the counsel seems platitudinous and conservative. But in the mouth of Emerson, it becomes revolutionary. "Who so would be a man, must be a nonconformist. . . . Nothing is at last sacred but the integrity of your own mind."[31] Carried to its logical conclusion, this becomes the crucial doctrine of American mysticism. For does it not deny traditional morality, and preach absolute anarchy? "He who would gather immortal palms must not be hindered by the name of goodness, but must explore if it be goodness . . . 'If I am the Devil's child, I will live then from the Devil.' No law can be sacred to me but that of my nature."[32] It is in this revolutionary and mystical sense that Jeffers develops the ideal of integrity.

Addressing "Woodrow Wilson," he explains:

you and all men are drawn out of this depth
Only to be these things you are, as flowers for color, falcons for swiftness,
Mountains for mass and quiet. Each for its quality
Is drawn out of this depth.

And his *Dear Judas* illustrates it concretely: Jesus understands his betrayer and loves him, because he knows him to be acting according to his inmost nature, and "This is the roots of forgiveness." But, he warns: "This is our secret, Judas. / For the people's hearts are not scrupulous like yours, and if they heard it they'd run on license and die." To this, however, the conservative may well reply: "If you recognize the danger, why preach so anarchic a principle?" The answer is that this principle of integrity is "true." It is the fundamental truth of mysticism, recognized repeatedly: *"Tout comprendre, c'est tout pardonner."* But although recognized, it has seldom been acted upon: "What is truth?" asked Pilate cynically. Only Jesus acted upon it, practicing the forgiveness of evil. All professing Christians, indeed, have accepted his ideal in principle, even while denying it in practice. Only the modern mystics have said: "Let us see where this logic of integrity will lead us." And they have also warned: "Beware when the great God lets loose a thinker on this planet."

Being the devil's child, Jeffers's Tamar lived from the devil. The offspring of the uttermost sin, she did not seek repentance but the realization of the logic of her evil. To her incestuous father, she explained carefully:

I'll show you our trouble, you sinned, your old book calls it,
and repented: that was foolish.
I was unluckier, I had no chance to repent, so I learned something, we
must keep sin pure,
Or it will poison us.

And so at the end, this Tamar achieved a certain tragic dignity, surpassing the other characters in the story who were less "evil" but more confused. In the poet's "Apology for Bad Dreams," her restless ghost reappears: "Someone flamelike passed me saying: 'I am Tamar Cauldwell, I have my desire.' " Self-reliant to the end, she embodies something of the absolute heroism of Milton's Satan, with "The courage never to submit or yield, / And what is else not to be overcome."

But all this is profoundly disturbing: Does the ideal of integrity lead to the lowest circle of hell? Does mysticism imply moral anarchy? If "good and bad are but names very readily transferable to that or this," as Emerson asserted, what standards remain? Even Jeffers recoiled somewhat from the implications of his early poem: "Tamar seemed to my later thought to have a tendency to romanticize unmoral freedom. . . . That way lies destruction, of course. . . . One of the intentions of *Point Sur* was to indicate the destruction and strip everything but its natural ugliness from the unmorality."[33] Yet his Barclay in *Point Sur*, lacking the tragic integrity of Tamar, failed to achieve her heroic stature, and the poem failed with him. *Tamar* remains the modern "Inferno"—the embodiment of the transcendental logic of evil.

The point is that the poem *Tamar* did not really "romanticize unmoral freedom." Although it idealized Tamar's integrity and self-realization, the poem did not pretend that these qualities—when practiced by an evil heroine—produced happiness. Always it distinguished two levels of life—the mystic and the human. In the speech quoted, Tamar said, "I was unluckier"—and she was, by the standards of human morality. She found no pleasure in her sin, and won only destruction. But she realized clearly the absolute logic of her nature. "As Blake wrote, 'If the fool would persist in his folly he would become wise.' "[34] Through her persistent folly, Tamar learned a strange new kind of wisdom.

Only if the humanistic and the transcendental levels of life are confused does moral anarchy result from the practice of this ideal of "integrity." For the morality of the mystic does not destroy the morality of traditional society, but goes beyond it to a new set of values:

For the essence and the end
Of his labor is beauty, for goodness and evil are two things and still
variant, but the quality of life as of death and of light
As of darkness is one, one beauty, the rhythm of that Wheel, and who can
behold it is happy and will praise it to the people.[35]

Going beyond good and evil, the mystic projects logically the morality of "the super-man."

But "goodness and evil are still variant." The true mystic, unlike the deluded Barclay in *The Women at Point Sur*, does not pretend that he has annulled all human laws, nor destroyed all human values. Tamar still does evil; and "dear" Judas still does evil: both remain morally despicable; but Judas is the more despicable, because he thinks he is doing good. Even Jesus does not achieve the perfect integrity, because he still seeks to struggle against God for mankind: he seeks to do good, rather than to learn the truth. But because he aims at the highest degree of human goodness, where Tamar aimed at the lowest degree of human evil, his story becomes the highest form of human tragedy, as hers was the lowest. Both realize the heroic ideal of tragedy and in so far surpass the worldly characters of human comedy.

Dear Judas, therefore, describes in detail Jesus's transcendental ideal of integrity beyond tragedy: "Life after life, at the bottom of the pit comes exultation." Through suffering and pain, endured for a purpose, man is raised above the common level of humanity. He may turn the other cheek from weakness, of course, or from strength; but if he lives "according to principle" (Thoreau's phrase) his suffering becomes creative. So Jesus lives and preaches the logic of self-sacrifice:

I having no foothold but slippery
Broken hearts and despairs . . . am yet lifting my peoples nearer
In emotion, and even at length in powers and perception, to the universal
God than ever humanity
Has climbed before.

And the parallel poem of *The Loving Shepherdess* illustrates the same principles from a different point of view.

But obviously this heroic integrity, even when practiced by "good" men, will not bring happiness, in the ordinary sense. Obviously, it will not bring worldly success. It will not bring pleasure, nor comfort, nor joy. It will set up rather a new set of values. Among these, self-realization and the discovery of truth will be primary. And secondary values will be courage, mercy, endurance, and strength.[36]

In a letter, Jeffers has suggested these post-humanistic values:

> Some prefatory definition of values would be useful. What does the author think would be best for men? What is he working toward?
>
> *Human happiness?*—If a harmless drug were invented, under the influence of which all people could be intensely and harmoniously happy, only working enough to provide each other with sustenance and the drug,—would that be a good goal for men? That would be maximum happiness, minimum pain.
>
> *Goodness?*—The modern view makes goodness a purely relative

> term. Good conduct is the conduct that conduces to general human happiness.—But then happiness is primary.
>
> *Discovery, experience, development of all powers?*—But then experience of sorrow and pain is included. And all hopes of general harmony and cooperation ought to be cancelled. For man is not only a cooperative animal, but also a fiercely pugnacious animal. Unless he annihilates a whole hemisphere of himself, universal cooperation is not possible. Do we really want to annihilate half of the powers that have carried us so far? Would a world of happy saints not be rather ignoble, if it were possible?[37]

To this Jeffers adds, "I am not answering these questions—at present." But his manner of asking suggests the answer, and his poetry has always implied it: the development of all man's powers and the discovery of truth are the new values of modern man. The experience of sorrow and pain becomes a positive value. And the old value of ignorant happiness is denied, flatly contradicting the neoclassical dictum: "Where ignorance is bliss / 'Tis folly to be wise." Only the inner integrity that transcends tragedy and defeat is final for the modern mystic.

Notes

1. "The Trap," *Solstice and Other Poems* (New York, 1935), p. 140.

2. For these references, see S. S. Alberts, *A Bibliography of the Works of Robinson Jeffers* (New York, 1933), pp. 199, 200, 217.

3. *Poetry: A Magazine of Verse*, XXXI, 274 (Feb., 1928).

4. *New Freeman*, I, 230 (May 17, 1930).

5. *New Republic*, LIV, 388 (May 16, 1928).

6. Hyatt H. Waggoner, "Science and the Poetry of Robinson Jeffers," *American Literature*, X, 288 (Nov., 1938).

7. "Robinson Jeffers," *Saturday Review of Literature*, VIII, 97 (Sept. 5, 1931).

8. Waggoner, *op. cit.*, p. 285.

9. Letter quoted in *ibid.*, p. 284.

10. All in *Such Counsels You Gave to Me* (New York, 1937).

11. Letter to the writer, dated Jan., 1938. Reprinted by permission.

12. Letter to the writer, dated Nov., 1933.

13. Letter to the writer, dated March 31, 1932.

14. For a comparison between Edwards and Robinson Jeffers, see "The Radicalism of Jonathan Edwards," by the writer, in *New England Quarterly*, IV, 637–639 (Oct., 1931). Concerning this article Mr. Jeffers wrote (Dec., 1931): "I read your essay . . . feeling a new sympathy toward your subject." Edwards has not influenced Mr. Jeffers directly (although he may have done so indirectly, through Mr. Jeffers's father, who was a theologian). But there is, I think, a clear logical relationship between the ideas of the two men.

15. "Crumbs or the Loaf." *The Selected Poetry of Robinson Jeffers* (New York, 1938), p. 461.

16. "Meditation on Saviors." *Ibid.*, p. 203.

17. In *Solstice and Other Poems*, p. 138.

18. *Ibid.*, p. 139.

19. "Ave Caesar," *Solstice*, p. 137.

20. "Shine, Republic," *Solstice*, p. 139. Cf. also "Hellenistics," in *Such Counsels You Gave to Me*, pp. 120–23.

21. Jeffers affirms that, as an individual, he would fight against Fascism in America. See *Writers Take Sides: Letters from 418 American Authors* (New York: The League of American Writers, 1938).

22. Cf. Newton Arvin, in a letter to the writer: "Jeffers's work seems to me to be increasingly shaped and colored by the kind of sentiments—negation, despair of reason, contempt for humanity, violence—that, on the political level, we call reactionary."

Benjamin H. Lehman writes: "The Fascist epithet, for me, applies only in this sense: that if we could understand it, the totalitarian, dictatorial modes are achieving because now is the time for that phase, and we may as well go along with them" (letter to the writer). Certainly Mr. Jeffers believes that the time is ripe for Fascism, but he does not, I think, for that reason believe that "we may as well go along with them." His poetry consistently denies the *value* of Caesarism, and celebrates the value of libertarian rebellion—even if each rebellion seems destined to fail.

23. See Jeffers's review of Babette Deutsch's *Epistle to Prometheus*, reprinted in Alberts, *op. cit.*, pp. 151–153.

24. Mr. Jeffers has been deeply influenced by Emerson. His first book, *Flagons and Apples*, was prefaced by a motto from Emerson. In reply to a later question, he wrote: "Emerson was a youthful enthusiasm, if you like, but not outgrown by any means, only read so thoroughly that I have not returned to him for a long time" (letter to the writer, Nov., 1933).

25. For a philosophic discussion of these "transcendental" values, see Charles Hartshorne, *Beyond Humanism: Essays in the New Philosophy of Nature* (Chicago, 1937). Robinson Jeffers is discussed in the "Conclusion." The problem is complicated by the different meanings given to "humanism" by the philosophers and by the literary critics; but even in this confusion of tongues, certain general distinctions come clear.

26. Cf. "Paradise (to Be) Regained," in *Cape Cod and Miscellanies.*

27. Of course this does not include "freedom of the will" or "freedom from *internal* compulsion."

28. "The Answer," "Nova," and "Hellenistics," in *Such Counsels You Gave to Me.*

29. "Nova," *ibid.*, p. 112.

30. "The Answer," *ibid.*, p. 107.

31. These quotations from "Self-Reliance" (see earlier note on Emerson).

32. From "Self-Reliance."

33. Alberts, *op. cit.*, p. 37.

34. Powell, *op. cit.*, p. 188.

35. "Point Pinos and Point Lobos," *Roan Stallion*, p. 241.

36. See "The Answer," in *Such Counsels You Gave to Me.* In this connection, see also Henry Alonzo Myers, "The Tragic Attitude toward Value," *International Journal of Ethics*, XLV, 337–355 (April, 1935).

37. Letter to the writer, dated Jan., 1938.

An American Poet

Gilbert Highet*

It is sad that the word *romantic* has been so misused and vulgarized. If it had not been, we could call this American poet a romantic figure. Most of the many meanings implied in the word would fit him: unorthodox, strongly individual, imaginative and emotional, daring, careless of routine success, a lover only of the material things which can be loved without desire (not money and machines, but mountains, waters, birds, animals); lonely, too, lonely. Yes, he is a romantic figure.

His name is Robinson Jeffers. He lives in Carmel, California, in a house which he and his sons built, stone by stone. He is getting on toward seventy now. When he first settled in Carmel, it was a small windswept village smelling of trees and the sea, inconveniently simple, unfrequented, unfashionable, a good place for a man to be himself and nobody else. Now—at least in the summer—it is a bright and busy seaside town, with a beach, cocktail bars, branches of very chi-chi metropolitan stores, and a rich flow of traffic from the rest of California. Why, in those quaint narrow streets there is hardly room for all the Cadillacs. This is the same kind of change which, in our own lifetime, has infected many other places: Montauk, Acapulco, Oxford, Provincetown, you can fill out the list yourselves. Mr. Jeffers does not enjoy the change. He did not expect it when he built his home there on the lonely peninsula near Point Lobos. But he is a pessimist, and he has long been convinced that mankind spoils nearly everything it touches. He does not, therefore, see much of the beauties of prosperous California. He prefers to watch the ocean which is full of life but which is too cold and powerful for us to swim in, the rocky hills which will not grow grapefruit, but have a superhuman dignity of their own.

Mr. Jeffers is not a popular poet. He never wished to be a popular poet, he has shunned every device which leads toward popularity, he avoids publicity, he will not lecture and give readings and play the guitar, he has no immediate disciples, and has formed no school. It is not that he is deliberately obscure. You can understand all his poetry, if you read it with care: far more easily than the work of his contemporaries Eliot and Pound and Valéry. It is not that he was once ambitious, and is now soured by lack of recognition: far from it. His poetry is not meant to be liked. It is meant, I think, to do people good.

But it is very remarkable poetry, and he is a very distinguished man. America has produced great statesmen, soldiers, engineers, explorers, civilizers, inventors, and actors. It has produced—in nearly two centuries—very few great poets. Robinson Jeffers may prove to be one

*From *People, Places and Books* (New York: Oxford University Press, 1953): 22–28.

of those great poets. I say *may,* because I honestly do not know whether he will or not. But if he does, he will be like some other solitary artists who were recognized during their lives as odd, provocative, masterful, self-sufficient, and eccentric; and whose work turned out to be as durable as stone. Such was Euripides, whom Mr. Jeffers admires and something resembles; such was Lucretius; such was Dante; such were Breughel, and Monteverdi, and Poe. It takes time . . . it takes at least a century for a good work of poetry to prove what it is.

If you have not read Mr. Jeffers' poems, there is a handsome one-volume edition of his *Selected Poetry.* When you look over it, what you will see is this: a single, comparatively small book about 600 pages in all. Not much for a life's work, you may think; but many of these poems are the result of thirty or forty years of thought, and they are intended to live ten times, or a hundred times, as long.

You will see that Mr. Jeffers writes three different types of poem. Some are meditative lyrics, anywhere between ten and forty lines long—a thought, a brief description of something seen, a memory or a vision. Some are long narrative poems—that is a good form which we are foolish to neglect nowadays: a story told in verse is harder to do, but often far more effective, than a story told in prose. There are about a dozen exciting, lurid, visionary narrative poems set in the wild hill-country of central California near Monterey. They are about bitter loves, and hatreds more satisfying than love. Crime, sensuality, madness haunt them. Brothers kill each other. Fearful illicit passions rage through them like forest fires.

In the same form Mr. Jeffers has also written several dramas, and poems partly narrative and partly dramatic, most of them on plots from Greek tragedy. The best known is his adaptation of the *Medea* which was (he says himself) inspired by Judith Anderson's art and personality, and which showed us her magnificent acting in New York during the winter of 1947–8. These pieces also move among the grim ideas which have long filled his mind and which are the basis of his poetry.

Both the lyrics and the stories are written in large, muscular, unrhymed lines, with an irregular pulse which is basically a new sort of blank verse, with a long rhythm (about ten beats to the line) which reminds me irresistibly of the Pacific hammering at the rocks. It is intended to echo the ebb and flow of excitement, the interchange of narrative and speech. For my taste it is usually too irregular, because I can remember poetry only when it has a fairly steady pattern; still, it is free and powerful and eloquent, anything but monotonous and conventional.

Now, if I try to explain what Mr. Jeffers' themes are, I shall risk distorting them, oversimplifying them, making them too naive or brutal, breaking up their subtle interrelations, vulgarizing a poetic statement by changing it into a Message. And yet his work is very cohesive, so that one can bring out its leading motives, as one could not do with a wayward poet like Yeats; and his ideas are so strange that unless we are boldly introduced to them, we may not comprehend them at all. He is a tragic poet; and tragedy is a truth which is hard, hard to understand.

First, let us look at one of his short poems. Through it we can see his manner and a few of his leading thoughts. It is called "Summer Holiday."

> When the sun shouts and people abound
> One thinks there were the ages of stone and the age of bronze
> And the iron age; iron the unstable metal;
> Steel made of iron, unstable as his mother; the towered-up cities
> Will be stains of rust on mounds of plaster.
> Roots will not pierce the heaps for a time, kind rains will cure them,
> Then nothing will remain of the iron age
> And all these people but a thigh-bone or so, a poem
> Stuck in the world's thought, splinters of glass
> In the rubbish dumps, a concrete dam far off in the mountain . . .

Now, there is no sex in this, while there is a great deal in Mr. Jeffers' long poems. There is no clash of personalities, while his major works are boldly dramatic. But the strong pessimism is characteristic; so is the sense of history; so is the peculiar blend of deep, long thought and deeply felt but controlled emotion; so is the sense of the earth—our mother, our home, and our grave.

You may not think this an attractive poem. But you will agree it is memorable. You will remember it. Through remembering it, you may come to admire it, and to understand more of an eminent but deliberately isolated American writer.

Mr. Jeffers, you see, believes a number of terrible things. They are not all true for Christians, who believe in redemption; but they are true for many other inhabitants of this world.

First, he believes that men and women are animals. For him, there is *no difference* between a delicatessen, or a fur store, and a pack of coyotes hunting down a deer . . . except that the coyotes hunt and devour in hot blood, whereas we breed the meat-cattle and slaughter them and trap the furry animals and skin them with a cold greedy purposefulness which is more disgusting. Many animals are cruel and noble. Their cruelty contains style and courage, the cougar and the hawk. Men and women are usually cruel. When they are cruel and mean, they are loathsome . . . animals. When they are cruel and noble, they may be noble animals.

Then, Mr. Jeffers utterly abominates war, modern war. He sees it as a symptom and a cause of what he considers the decadence of our civilization. He believes that growing populations and multiplying machines all over the world have distorted the balance of nature, and that war is now the greatest of all such distortions. His last book was full of violent isolationism. One might expect him to regard the whole of warfare as an understandable activity like the ferocity of animals: to think of the shark when he sees a submarine, to admire the flight of bombers as much as the flight of the hawks; but he cannot.

Third, he is unlike most of us in his view of happiness. Most people, I think he would say, want easy pleasure and drowsy happiness. But real fulfillment is not pleasure: it is something more powerful. Effort and suffering are more natural than rest and enjoyment. Pain lasts longer and is more real than pleasure.

Fourth—the fourth of Mr. Jeffers' themes is the grandest of all, and the most wretched, and the most difficult. It is this. *The human race is not needed.* It is an infestation from which the planet is suffering. Look at a wooded mountainside, with the bear and the deer in the forests, the badger and the fox in the brush, birds and their cousins the reptiles crawling and flying above and below. Can you truthfully say that it would improve that scene to drive a six-lane motor-highway across it? Or to put a town in the middle of it? And when people say that it would be a terrific disaster if another war blotted out the human race, do they mean it? Do they mean that the mountains would weep, the rivers run backward with grief, and the animals and the birds go into mourning? Or would the earth begin its peaceful work of purification, covering up—with falling leaves and drifting dust and sifting earth and growing plants and moving hillsides and encroaching forests—our cities, our factories, and our prisons? And then would the whole planet, with its other children, heave a single, long, unanimous sigh of relief?

These are some of the ideas which—unless I have gravely misunderstood him—Robinson Jeffers holds. He also has an extremely complex and difficult conception of sex, and the family, as a source of tragedy. He has made these themes into fine poetry. He does not think they are pleasant ideas. But he thinks they are true. He thinks that they have the truth of nature; that they are somehow part of nature. And he loves nature, wild nature. In this he is more like a primitive American than a modern man—like the Indian who climbed Chief Mountain to be alone and see visions, or the early white hunters who went west because they loved land and animals without humanity. But he is also like several distinguished American artists: Thoreau; Melville; Martha Graham; and Ernest Hemingway. Most of nature, he knows, is not pleasant; but it is—well, what is a thunderstorm? What is a forest fire? What is a north wind bringing bitter snow over the mountains? Or the ocean surging against a rocky cliff? The sound, the power, the terror, and the nobility of these things make the truth of Robinson Jeffers' poetry.

In Defense of Jeffers

Kenneth Rexroth*

In recent years the stock of Robinson Jeffers has fallen; for an entire literary generation it might be said to have plummeted and still be plummeting. He still has considerable popular following, but I believe that that too is waning. Many years ago Yvor Winters, his only serious rival to the title of "California's leading poet," wrote an essay on him in *Hound and Horn,* later to be substantially reprinted in the book *In Defense of Reason.* It was one of the most devastating attacks in modern criticism, and Jeffers's reputation, then at its height, never recovered, but entered a slow decline. Today young people simply do not read him. Few young poets of my acquaintance, and I know most of them, have ever opened one of his books, and know only the anthology pieces, which, I am afraid, they dislike. This is true even in San Francisco where I live, and where Jeffers once had a tremendous following.

Now Mr. Winters's point of view was a sort of secular Thomism; at least it was rigorously classical, and these young people are not at all so motivated. Just as such they would be much more likely to prefer the Romanticism for which Jeffers is supposed to stand. But they do not. Since I have been puzzling over how I could review Radcliffe Squires's *The Loyalties of Robinson Jeffers* and hurt a minimum of feelings I have tried the verse novels and dramas on several literary friends of the present generation. All thought them ridiculous. I myself have tried manfully to return to them with an open mind, but I like them even less than when I first read them.

In my opinion Jeffers's verse is shoddy and pretentious and the philosophizing is nothing but posturing. His reworkings of Greek tragic plots make me shudder at their vulgarity, the coarsening of sensibility, the cheapening of the language, and the tawdriness of the paltry insight into the great ancient meanings. His lyrics and reveries of the Californian landscape seem to me to suffer in almost every line from the most childish laboring of the pathetic fallacy, elevated to a very system of response. This is the sort of sensibility which calls a sunset "a picture no artist could paint." His philosophy I find a mass of contradictions—high-flown statements indulged in for their melodrama alone, and often essentially meaningless. The constantly repeated gospel that it is better to be a rock than a man is simply an unscrupulous use of language. "Better," "is," "man," "rock," are used to promulgate an emotional falsehood, but they are also used with no regard whatever for their actual meanings. This is sentimentality in the sense so long ago defined in Malachy Mulligan's famous telegram, "The sentimentalist is he who

*From a review of *The Loyalties of Robinson Jeffers* by Radcliffe Squires in the *Saturday Review* 40 (10 August 1957): 30. Reprinted by permission.

would enjoy without incurring the immense debtorship for a thing done. Signed, Stephen Dedalus."

I say all this with distaste. I do not like to put down a colleague and fellow Californian. Many friends of mine of my own or a slightly older generation, leading poets and critics of poetry, still like Jeffers, some even think he is great. I simply cannot see it.

I am afraid that Mr. Squires's case is not proven. He has labored long and hard to endow Robinson Jeffers with a coherent philosophy. He has searched the whole corpus of his work for lines that will pass muster as respectable verse. He fails. He does not seem to realize that poetic license does not mean the permission of intellectual dishonesty. In a typical passage he says, "It is easy to find fault with Spengler's history, to point to the dogmatism, the weakness of arguing from analogy, the oracular mysticism. These faults may in poetry be virtues."

It would be difficult, I believe, to make many statements about poetry that would be less true. This quotation points up the basic flaw of the whole case. You can't make an intellectual silk purse out of fustian and rodomontade.

As for Mr. Squires's examples of Jeffers's poetic gems, the less said the better. To me they sound like the rhetoric of a Southern state representative. I write this with acute awareness that people I respect will disagree and that, as the old woman said, there's no accounting for somebody else's taste.

The Double Marriage of Robinson Jeffers

Lawrence Clark Powell*

I shall approach my subject in a conservative way, as befits a middle-aged librarian, by quoting from a book which, if it is not *the* good book, is at least *a* very good book. Webster, I mean. Ours is an age of facts and statistics, of the isolation of ascertainable data. Emotion is suspect, feeling taboo. I have strong feelings about my subject, yet I also have facts to support them which I began compiling at Occidental College, thirty years ago, as a student of those inspiring teachers of English, C. F. McIntyre and B. F. Stelter. In asking the reader to share my feelings about Robinson Jeffers' poetry, I shall use some of these facts to build a footing for us as we go—a few granite steppingstones for our feet, while our minds are carried far and wide by this poet's lofty lines.

What does Webster have to say about poets? "A poet is one who makes, invents, or composes original fables, fictions and the like. One en-

*From *Books West Southwest* (Los Angeles: The Ward Ritchie Press, 1957): 110–20. Reprinted by permission.

dowed with great imaginative, emotional, or intuitive power and capable of expressing his conceptions, passions or intuitions in language marked by poetic beauty."

My approach then is two-pronged, since in addition to asking what Jeffers has made, I intend to inquire also into what has made him, to seek the major determinants in his gradual transformation from the teen-age graduate of half a century ago, enamored of sports and mountain climbing, to one of the great poets of our time who, by his devoted labor, has slowly come to occupy one of the few niches literature reserves for major poets.

A great poet does not just happen, nor can he be made to order. He is the result of powerful forces operating on a strong and a sensitive organism. Education, parentage, environment, for example; a woman, a war, economic want or security.

We are ignorant of what made Homer and Shakespeare great, for we do not know who these mysterious men were—the two greatest poets the world has ever produced—but we do know what exile did to Dante; or the effect of Italy on Browning; of the Irish revolution on Yeats; and of the Civil War on Walt Whitman. Change and growth are hallmarks of great poetry. Think of the progress from *Venus and Adonis* to *King Lear* and its supreme line "Ripeness is all"; or from "I sing the body electric" to "When lilacs last in the the dooryard bloom'd"; and from "I will arise and go now, and go to Innisfree" to "Under bare Ben Bulben's head/In Drumcliff Churchyard Yeats is laid."

Lesser poets do not change and grow, for change and growth are agonies, almost unbearable, and for a poet to be true to his genius, and write what "the tall angel" says he must write, means that he must avoid the soft sand of easy success and walk where the sharp rocks are hard and the footing firm.

To illustrate the change and growth that Robinson Jeffers experienced, I shall cite two of his short poems published only a dozen years apart. The first dates from 1912, and is called "On the Cliff"; it is about the Palos Verdes in Southern California:

> Do you remember, dear, that little house
> Built hard against the high cliff's ragged brows
> Over the emerald ocean's level floor
> Where we were sitting, while the quick day wore
> To sunset? Ah, how swiftly the day passed,
> Our day, our one sweet day that would not last.
> Altho' we did not see the sun go down,
> Nor knew till darkness that the sun was gone,
> Because our eyes were blind, while my lips drank
> Oblivious love at yours.

> But the sun sank;
> Nor all our urgent wishing had the power
> To lengthen out our day by one poor hour.

Then twelve years later this poem, "To the Stone-Cutters":

> Stone-cutters fighting time with marble, you foredefeated
> Challengers of oblivion
> Eat cynical earnings, knowing rock splits, records fall down,
> The square-limbed Roman letters
> Scale in the thaws, wear in the rain. The poet as well
> Builds his monument mockingly;
> For man will be blotted out, the blithe earth die, the brave sun
> Die blind and blacken to the heart:
> Yet stones have stood for a thousand years, and pained thoughts found
> The honey of peace in old poems.

What happened to the young bohemian athlete to make such a radical change in what he saw and how he said it? What turned the inward eye from his own emotional preoccupations outward to the external world of rock and stars and cyclical history? Two things, mainly, operating on a strong and sensitive organism, conditioned intellectually by Christianity, the classics, English romantic poetry, and travel. Just two things: a woman, and a change of environment.

Cherchez la femme, say the French, to explain almost any situation; and it is true that few creative men have achieved greatness without a woman's help. Whitman's mother, Shakespeare's Dark Lady, Browning's Elizabeth, Dante's Beatrice, Lawrence's Frieda, Yeats's Maude and Olivia and Georgie (that wild Irishman needed three), and Jeffers' Una—"more like a woman in a Scotch ballad," he said of her, years later, "passionate, untamed and rather heroic—or like a falcon—than like any ordinary person."

They met at the University of Southern California, after Jeffers' graduation from Occidental, where Una had come from Michigan at the age of sixteen. "She had a powerful ambitious mind," Jeffers wrote recently,

> Ambitious not for herself, but of life and knowledge. She was very beautiful, capable of intense joy and passionate resentment, little of stature, dowered with great blue eyes and heavy bronze hair. It is no wonder that she was married at seventeen.
>
> My first meeting with her was in a class devoted to Goethe's Faust, at the University of Southern California; for—as she told me later—she had stipulated that she must be allowed to go to college—part time—after her marriage. I have always rather disliked Goethe and his fame, thinking that Marlowe's Faustus and the Book of Job are greater poems than his great one, which derives from them. I cannot imagine why I was in that class and Una has told me that she resented my presence, because

I had learned German in Europe; she had been first in the class before I joined it.

Jeffers does not describe himself as he was in 1907. In fact, he never describes himself. "Young Greek god" is the phrase said to have been applicable to him at the time he met Una.

It was six years before divorce and remarriage were possible—impassioned years of separation, travel, reckless living, and further study. Without Una, Jeffers would still have become a poet, but not the kind of poet he became. "My nature is cold and undiscriminating," he wrote. "She excited and focused it, gave it eyes and nerves and sympathies."

For here was a marriage of educated minds as well as of beautiful young bodies, a union of two natures each incomplete and unfilled without the other. "She never saw any of my poems until they were finished and typed," Jeffers wrote. "Yet by her presence and conversation she has co-authored every one of them. Sometimes I think there must be some value in them if only for that reason."

The death of Una Jeffers in September, 1950, ended a union which was one of the most creative in all literature. The dignity with which this man has borne his loss is an example for those to whom sorrow comes in their turn.

Una and Robin were married at Tacoma in 1913. Their plan was to live in England and Ireland and on the Continent, but events somehow conspired to keep them in America until the following year, when the declaration of war changed their plans forever. According to Jeffers, "the August news turned us to this village of Carmel instead, and when the stagecoach topped the hill from Monterey, and we looked down through pines and seafogs on Carmel Bay, it was evident that we had come without knowing it to our inevitable place."

Here then took place a second marriage, of a poet and a place, and like his marriage with Una, this union with Carmel and the Big Sur coast of Monterey County was lasting and productive.

Jeffers had many opportunities to wed other women and other places, but none of them had the power to grip and to hold him. Southern California is the setting of his first book and part of his second; he never mentioned it again. As a region it was too dispersed, too hot and dry, the city superficial, the coast flat. In those early years the Malibu was closed and guarded by armed range-riders. Its coast is reminiscent of the Big Sur. If Jeffers had been able to settle on it . . . If . . . Pure speculation.

He settled instead at Carmel, and has lived there these forty-two years, with a few short absences, and the poetry of his lasting fame has been written there during uninterrupted hours each morning, on any kind of paper at hand, line after line, poem after poem, book upon book, the lyrics, the narratives, the adaptations of Greek tragedy which have made him world-famous.

In 1914, the Monterey coast south from Carmel was an isolated, unspoiled region, with precisely those elements needed by Jeffers to nourish his genius. Let him tell it in his own words, for this poet also writes prose of clarity, rhythm, and beauty:

> A second piece of pure accident brought us to the Monterey coast mountains, where for the first time in my life I could see people living—amid magnificent unspoiled scenery—essentially as they did in the Idyls or the Sagas, or in Homer's Ithaca. Here was life purged of its ephemeral accretions. Men were riding after cattle, or plowing the headland, hovered by white sea-gulls, as they have done for thousands of years, and will for thousands of years to come. Here was contemporary life that was also permanent life; and not shut from the modern world but conscious of it and related to it; capable of expressing its spirit, but unencumbered by the mass of poetically irrelevant details and complexities that make a civilization.

Writers had come to that coast before Jeffers—Jack London, Sinclair Lewis, George Sterling, Mary Austin—and many have come since. But only Robinson Jeffers has made lasting literature from that union. It was, as he said, his inevitable place, and all the subsequent poetry he has written about it has the air of grand inevitability that is one mark of major poetry.

A point I want to make now is that Jeffers was ready for this marriage to a particular environment, as he was ready, after six years of bohemianism, for a monogamous marriage with Una. He was educated by his father and mother, by his teachers and friends in college and subsequent universities, at home and abroad. He had studied history and literature and religion and medicine, forestry and astronomy. He had Goethe's universal mind.

And so when he came to Carmel and was fired by the natural poetry around him, he was ready to deal with it, to absorb the impact of one of the most overpoweringly beautiful places on earth, and to transmute it into literature by the alchemy of art. He was trained to think and to see; he had learned the discipline of metrical rhymed verse. He could write sonnets and odes in the classical form, and he knew how to construct a tragedy according to Aristotle's *Poetics*. Lucretius, Milton, Wordsworth, and Shelley were some of his masters. No great poet has ever been hurt by education; in fact, no great poet has been uneducated. For great poetry is thought and form and style, as well as basic feeling.

The Bible was another of the master books in Jeffers' education. Some student will make a book out of the influence of the Bible on Jeffers' thought and style. He was the son of a learned Presbyterian divine. His father wanted him to be, like himself, a minister—or else a doctor. His Christian education was furthered by Occidental College. It was heartbreaking not to be able to accept the dogma. All through Jeffers' verse are expressions of sorrowful regret that he could not be what many of his friends and relatives wanted him to be. Merciless honesty is another sign of his genius. Yet there are still those who want Jeffers to be what he is not, a cheerful optimist. His view of mankind and of life developed slowly, ripened gradually, and his work was founded as true and unswerving as a Roman road; and you either take it as it is, and find strength and nourishment and direction in it, or you leave it alone. It is strong stuff, not for babes or shallow optimists—for those who would have the *Oedipus Rex* in Technicolor.

"I write verses myself," Jeffers said, "but I have no sympathy with the notion that the world owes a duty to poetry, or any other art. Poetry is not a civilizer, rather the reverse, for great poetry appeals to the most primitive instincts. It is not necessarily a moralizer; it does not necessarily improve one's character; it does not even teach good manners. It is a beautiful work of nature, like an eagle or a high sunrise. You owe it no duty. If you like it, listen to it; if not, let it alone."

I have mentioned Jeffers' knowledge of Aristotle's *Poetics*. His major narrative poems are Aristotelian in their form and purpose. Constructed after classical models, the narratives *Cawdor, Thurso's Landing,* and *Give Your Heart to the Hawks* succeed in effecting a *katharsis* on the reader, showing him the burning away of destructive emotions through pain and suffering and death, even as in life, with a corresponding relief at the end.

In spite of his rejection of Christian dogma, Jeffers is a Christian moralist. Here is what he has written, *ex post facto,* about his narrative poems:

> Besides one's duty to tell the truth and one's duty to shame the devil, it seems to me there is a third moral principle for story-tellers. The story that heaps emotions or complexities and makes no thoroughfare is a weakening story and so I should think an immoral story; but the story that through whatever passes attains significant release will influence its readers in the same sense, and this is good for him, it is moral. It is a "happy ending," for something happens, whether marriage or escape or sudden death, a lysis, a freeing of some sort; and a settlement, an adjusted balance.

Jeffers' shorter poems about the Monterey coast are among his happiest work, often overlooked in the excitement created by his tragic narratives and Greek adaptations, and yet they contain many elements of his genius: feeling for history and the passage of time, precise observation of the little as well as the large things in nature—for birds and flowers and rocks—and a vivid and fluent vocabulary, and a sense of form. There is a simple nobility which distinguishes his best work. Here is a short poem entitled "Bixby's Landing," about the place where the deep canyon is now spanned by a beautiful concrete arch, and which was the setting for his long poem called *Thurso's Landing:*

They burned lime on the hill and dropped it down here in an iron car
On a long cable; here the ships warped in
And took their loads from the engine, the water is deep to the cliff. The car
Hangs half way over in the gape of the gorge,
Stationed like a north star about the peaks of the redwoods, iron perch
For the little red hawks when they cease from hovering
When they've struck prey; the spider's fling of a cable rust-glued to the pulleys.
The laborers are gone, but what a good multitude
Is here in return: the rich-lichened rock, the rose-tipped stonecrop, the constant
Ocean's voices, the cloud-lighted space.
The kilns are cold on the hill but here in the rust of the broken boiler
Quick lizards lighten, and a rattlesnake flows
Down the cracked masonry, over the crumbled fire-brick. In the rotting timbers
And roofless platforms all the free companies
Of windy grasses have root and make seed; wild buckwheat blooms in the fat
Weather-slacked lime from the bursted barrels.
Two duckhawks darting in the sky of their cliff-hung nest are the voice of the headland.
Wine-hearted solitude, our mother the wilderness,
Men's failures are often as beautiful as men's triumphs, but your returnings
Are even more precious than your first presence.

Jeffers did not follow the path of his father. He went his own way, true to his own vision, and what he has made as a poet was determined inevitably by what his heritage and education and life made of him. But I would not end with my own words; I would end with his, words charged with the magic of his own unmistakable style, sad and strong and beautiful, possessing the unfading beauty of true poetry. They are from the poem called "Post Mortem":

and like clouds the houses
Unframe, the granite of the prime
Stand from the heaps: come storm and wash clean: the plaster is all run to the sea and the steel
All rusted; the foreland resumes
The form we loved when we saw it. Though one at the end of the age and far off from this place
Should meet my presence in a poem,
The ghost would not care but be here, long sunset shadow in the seams of the granite, and forgotten
The flesh, a spirit for the stone.

Robinson Jeffers as Didactic Poet

William H. Nolte*

Though it is impossible to believe that the poets are the unacknowledged legislators of the world, Shelley spoke clearly and objectively of the major poets when he stated that they measured the circumference and sounded "the depths of human nature with a comprehensive and all-penetrating spirit, and they are themselves perhaps the most sincerely astonished at its manifestations; for it is less their spirit than the spirit of the age." It has always been true, of course, that the great poet concerns himself with subjects of lasting importance, or universal meaning, just as it has been necessary for him to interpret his materials from some philosophical viewpoint. In the work of every major poet there is a single world view apparent. The expression of that view is nothing more than a vehicle and a signature; only minor writers (or critics) believe that expression is all. If the vehicle cannot bear the freight of the philosophy, we have a misadventure of communication—an unfortunate failure. If the style of the poet cannot be distinguished from that of other poets, we may have a practiced eclectic, but no major poet.

Of all major modern poets, Robinson Jeffers came closest to expressing himself in a uniquely singular style. Among the many critics who have commented on that style, George Sterling summed up its individuality as well as any: "One could pick, unerringly, a poem by him from a stack of thousands of others. In all that collection there would be no other that could be mistaken, by a discerning eye, for one of his." In like manner, William Rose Benét wrote: "Given a short section of any Jeffers poem I think I could recognize his authorship without having any other indication that he had written it. . . . There are passages so intensely imbued with his own individuality that one could not mistake them for the work of anyone else." Nor is this individuality a result of syntactical eccentricity (as in the case of e. e. cummings) or of "studied" obscurity (as in the case of Wallace Stevens and, at times, T. S. Eliot).

But style is, as I have said, nothing more than a vehicle of the poet's meaning, the expression of his *Weltansicht*, which is at one and the same time an interpretation and a criticism of the world man inhabits, or, put another way, of man's proper relationship to the universe. In "Triad" Jeffers commented on the "affair" of the poet while at the same time criticizing Science, about which he probably knew more than any other poet in history, and Russia—the two modern "experiments" in which man placed so much hope.

> Science, that makes wheels turn, cities grow,
> Moribund people live on, playthings increase,
> But has fallen from hope to confusion at her own business
> Of understanding the nature of things;—new Russia,

*From the *Virginia Quarterly Review* 42 (Spring 1966): 257–71. Reprinted by permission.

That stood a moment at dreadful cost half free,
Beholding the open, all the glades of the world
On both sides of the trap, and resolutely
Walked into the trap that has Europe and America;—
The poet, who wishes not to play games with words,
His affair being to awake dangerous images
And call the hawks;—they all feed the future, they serve God,
Who is very beautiful, but hardly a friend of humanity.

In an earlier poem, published in 1925, Jeffers perfectly combined the expression (the awakening of dangerous images) with the criticism or didacticism which is overtly stated in many of the shorter lyrics and is always symbolically present in his long narratives, which are never the idle tales of violence that a few critics, notably Yvor Winters, mistook them for. No one, I daresay, would today dispute the prophetic truth of the following lines from "Science":

Man, introverted man, having crossed
In passage and but a little with the nature of things this latter century
Has begot giants; but being taken up
Like a maniac with self-love and inward conflicts cannot manage his
    hybrids.
Being used to deal with edgeless dreams,
Now he's bred knives on nature turns them also inward: they have thirsty
    points though.
His mind forebodes his own destruction;
Actaeon who saw the goddess naked among leaves and his hounds tore him.
A little knowledge, a pebble from the shingle,
A drop from the oceans: who would have dreamed this infinitely little too
    much?

In an extraordinary essay written in 1948, entitled "Poetry, Gongorism, and a Thousand Years," Jeffers commented on the hypothetical great poet. He was harsh on the symbolists and/or imagists because their poetry tended toward an almost exclusive concern with subjective states of mind. Their poetry, indeed, constituted a retreat from the larger questions and problems of life rather than a grappling with those issues. Jeffers might well have been thinking of Nietzsche's condemnation of the poets, which is quoted in the preface to *The Selected Poetry of Robinson Jeffers* (1938): "The poets? The poets lie too much." Having promised himself as a young man not to hide in lies, Jeffers wrote of the elemental passions which rule, and generally ruin, the lives of his characters in the long narrative poems; and in the short lyrics, he constantly passed judgment on the central events of his time. This hypothetical great poet would, Jeffers wrote, "understand that Rimbaud was a young man of startling genius, but not to be imitated; and that *The Waste Land*, though one of the finest poems of this century and surely the most influential, marks the close of a literary dynasty, not the beginning. He would think of

Gerard Hopkins as a talented eccentric, whose verse is so overloaded with self-conscious ornament and improbable emotion that it is hardly readable, except by enthusiasts, and certainly not a model to found one's work on, but a shrill note of warning." Later in this essay, Jeffers remarked that his poet "would distrust the fashionable poetic dialect of his time; but the more so if it is studiously quaint and difficult; for if a poem has to be explained and diagrammed even for contemporary readers, what will the future make of it?"

Putting his censures or warnings another way, Jeffers stated that "our man would turn away from the self-consciousness and naive learnedness, the undergraduate irony, unnatural metaphors, hiatuses, and labored obscurity that are too prevalent in contemporary verse." Rather, he would strive to say something, and say it clearly. "He would be seeking to express the spirit of his time (as well as all times), but it is not necessary, because an epoch is confused, that its poet should share its confusions." To avoid those confusions, so that he might see around as well as through his own age, the poet would of necessity have to remain detached, for "detachment is necessary to understanding."

Although Jeffers has himself been often misunderstood, by both his admirers and his detractors, he never swerved from his early belief about the proper subject matter of poetry, expressed in a poem from *Tamar and Other Poems* (1924):

> Permanent things are what is needful in a poem, things temporally
> Of great dimension, things continually renewed or always present.
>
> Grass that is made each year equals the mountains in her past and future;
> Fashionable and momentary things we need not see nor speak of.

As the years passed, Jeffers turned his talents to examining the "grass" more than the "mountains" in his verse, until in a prefatory note to *Be Angry at the Sun* (1941) he lamented "the obsession with contemporary history that pins many of these pieces to the calendar, like butterflies to cardboard. Poetry is not private monologue, but I think it is not public speech either; and in general it is the worse for being timely. . . . Yet it is right that a man's views be expressed, though the poetry suffer for it. Poetry should represent the whole mind; if part of the mind is occupied unhappily, so much the worse. And no use postponing the poetry to a time when these storms may have passed, for I think we have but seen a beginning of them; the calm to look for is the calm at the whirlwind's heart." To find that "calm" becomes increasingly difficult, for Jeffers anyhow, as the world of man passes the summit and begins the toppling decline into chaos and destruction. Nearly all the poems of *Be Angry at the Sun* are filled with the painful knowledge of man's helplessness before the gathering forces of a second world war. Refusing to subscribe to the comfortable lies on which moral indignation feeds, Jeffers viewed the sorry spectacle from a distance, from his tower, at the same time realizing that "The present is always a crisis; people want a partisan cry, not judgment." Lacking faith in any of the multifarious "causes," the poet judged the passing scene with an objectivity that only the faithless can show: "Ants, or wise bees, or a gang of wolves, / Work together by instinct, but man needs lies." In this poem ("Faith"), he then stated that truth was "more beautiful / Than all the lies, and God than all the false gods." And even Jeffers' God, the inhuman god of atoms who discloses himself in all phenomena, had become increasingly difficult to praise.

> Dear God, who are the whole splendor of things and the sacred stars, but
> also the cruelty and greed, the treacheries
> And vileness, insanities and filth and anguish: now that this thing comes
> near us again I am finding it hard
> To praise you with a whole heart.
> I know what pain is, but pain can shine. I
> know what death is, I have sometimes
> Longed for it. But cruelty and slavery and degradation, pestilence, filth,
> the pitifulness
> Of men like little hurt birds and animals . . . if you were only
> Waves beating rock, the wind and the iron-cored earth, the flaming
> insolent wildness of sun and stars,
> With what a heart I could praise your beauty.

Jeffers' refusal to take sides in the contemporary issues caused people to assume that he was simply heartless or even fascist (Yeats, too, was called a fascist). His refusal to believe that Marxism or Christianity might save mankind, that science might cure our ills, that Hitler was somehow responsible for the troubles in Europe, that the defeat of Germany and Japan would usher in a world of peace—in effect, his refusal to ascribe eternal significance to temporal circumstances caused people to call him a hater of his own kind, and a blind one at that. Such, of course, is the fate of all men who are not readily susceptible to the lures of illusion. Such was the fate of Cassandra, a favorite figure of both Jeffers and E. A. Robinson. For any man of vision—i.e., the man who views history from outside—events become parts of a gigantic fabric rather than the personal clothing one wears next his skin.

As early as 1928, Jeffers was exhorting man to deny the saviors who demanded his worship to satisfy their passion for power, saviors who baited their traps with Love, a carrot dangling before the nose of man.

> But while he lives let each man make his health in his mind, to love the
> coast opposite humanity
> And so be freed of love, laying it like bread on the waters; it is worst
> turned inward, it is best shot farthest.

Love, the mad wine of good and evil, the saint's and murderer's, the mote
in the eye that makes its object
Shine the sun black; the trap in which it is better to catch the inhuman
God than the hunter's own image.

A decade later, this constantly repeated admonition to love outward—rather than love inwardly, incestuously—has become more directly related to contemporary events. For instance, in "The Soul's Desert (August 30, 1939)":

They are warming up the old horrors; and all that they say is echoes of
echoes.
Beware of taking sides; only watch.
These are not criminals, nor hucksters and little journalists, but the
governments
Of the great nations; men favorably
Representative of massed humanity. Observe them. Wrath and laughter
Are quite irrelevant. Clearly it is time
To become disillusioned, each person to enter his own soul's desert
And look for God—having seen men.

Jeffers is not so much contemptuous of man as he is knowing of the ways of men (in reading him, I am often reminded of Swift). That the mass of men are led by lies to self-destruction may be pitiful but nonetheless a matter of eternal recurrence—and therefore necessary to accept as one accepts or anyway expects violent changes in weather. Jeffers did not, of course, converse with the mass in his poetry, but only with the individuals who possessed "the cold passion for truth [which]/Hunts in no pack." His warning was always addressed to Tom and Bill, never to manunkind:

Let boys want pleasure, and men
Struggle for power, and women perhaps for fame,
And the servile to serve a Leader and the dupes to be duped.
Yours is not theirs.

This note of warning—itself an expression of love—was most memorably sounded in Jeffers' best known poem, "Shine, Perishing Republic":

But for my children, I would have them keep their distance from the
thickening center; corruption
Never has been compulsory, when the cities lie at the monster's feet
there are left the mountains.

And boys, be in nothing so moderate as in love of man, a clever servant,
insufferable master.
There is the trap that catches noblest spirits, that caught—they
say—God, when he walked on earth.

An interesting parallel might be made between Jeffers and Yeats, the poet Jeffers most admired of all moderns. (When Donnan Jeffers showed me through Tor House and Hawk Tower some months ago, I noticed that signed photographs of Yeats hung in both the rock buildings.) Neither poet was willing, after the allegiances of youth and young manhood were past, to subscribe to any political or religious dogma or any esthetic creed. Both men attempted—with unmatched success in this century—to give to their own locale an infinitely translatable meaning. Furthermore, each was centrally concerned with the values that directed, and direct, the wayward steps of the human species. If at times Jeffers seemed to doubt that man, one of nature's more unhappy experiments, warranted the concern shown him by his own kind, Yeats' concern often took the form of fear and foreboding, as in "The Second Coming," "A Prayer for My Daughter," and "Among School Children," to name but three of his best poems. At other times Yeats begged the question by turning away from life to dwell in a world of artistic image—as in "Long-Legged Fly" and the "Byzantium" poems, again to name only three. Seeing the world tumbling into chaos, Yeats withdrew into a "mysticism of superstition," as Radcliffe Squires put it in his excellent study, *The Loyalties of Robinson Jeffers*.

In the same place, Squires remarked that T. S. Eliot tried to salve his "spiritual discomfort" by retreating into "a mysticism of the past, a slow ritualistic dance among the symbols of medieval Catholicism." While Jeffers believed that he lived in a period of decaying Christianity and misapplied science, he neither turned his eyes backward to the past nor sought escapement through the portals of mysticism. Eliot's pessimism, once thought so black, was never so deeply felt nor half so moving as that of Jeffers or Yeats, partially because his poetry has no cathartic effect on the reader. Indeed, I have never been able to rid myself of the feeling that Eliot was playing a poetic game of some sort, which the reader might watch as he watches a tennis match with indifference as to which player wins. While applauding the volleys and points, he knows that it is just a game. After all, the Waste Land of Eliot turned out to be a rather small plot of highly manicured ground from which escape was always ready at hand. Prufrock was little more than a minor actor in a play which we comfortably view from a seat in the audience, and the Hollow Men were not so much hollow as they were hungry. A few Last Suppers and they were healthy citizens again. In brief, Eliot leaves our withers unwrung. What passion he possesses and transmits is for the mind alone; the body of the reader is never shaken as it is by the great writers from the Greeks on down. Most importantly, Eliot offers too easy a way out of the human dilemma in which he found man. Actually, his "philosophy" rings hollow when you realize that his view of man extends backward only to the birth of Christ. Yeats at least included the classical periods in his world view; his view of history does not start and stop on the Christian snag at the birth of the man-god. And Jeffers, who possessed a learning in both the sciences and the classics which makes Eliot's narrow scholastic training seem paltry by comparison, saw the Christian era as little more than a moment in man's descent from the primordial past. Eliot finds reality at the "still point of the turning world," a place of hope and quiet where the faithful might lay aside their burdens. From his "small marble-paved platform / On the turret on the head of the tower," Jeffers looked out and found eternal flow:

> The earth was the world and man was its measure, but our minds have
> looked
> Through the little mock-dome of heaven the telescope-slotted
> observatory eyeball, there space and multitude came in
> And the earth is a particle of dust by a sand-grain sun, lost in a nameless
> cove of the shores of a continent.
> Galaxy on galaxy, innumerable swirls of innumerable stars, endured as it
> were forever and humanity
> Came into being, its two or three million years are a moment, in a
> moment it will certainly cease out from being
> And galaxy on galaxy endure after that as it were forever . . . But man is
> conscious,
> He brings the world to focus in a feeling brain,
> In a net of nerves catches the splendor of things,
> Breaks the somnambulism of nature . . . His distinction perhaps,
> Hardly his advantage.

It is nevertheless true that Eliot's "medieval Catholicism" has been better understood than Jeffers' Inhumanism, for the simple reason, it seems to me, that Eliot chose a standard which lies within the immediate past and which has a lingering residue of symbolic meaning to citizens of the Western world, and which, moreover, flatters the ego of man. A reader has no need to agree with Eliot that the way out of despair is the way of Christ in order to understand the causes, effects, and antidotes of the dilemma he describes. More, our understanding is not intellectual alone, but has what is far more convincing—an emotional acknowledgment of the terms of his "argument." For example, the reader has no difficulty in comprehending such "terms" as love and mercy and humility; Christian texts depend on that nomenclature for their existence. More, we are all partially Christianized whether we are believers or not. It is of little importance to the majority of men that such concepts have been impotent in the face of man's self-destructive bent, and probably even more so today than at any time in the past, since Christianity has not been a vital moving force since the Renaissance. From the hearts of men of good faith comes the old refrain, as if from a broken record endlessly repeating the now forlorn message—Faith, Hope, and Charity.

The three beams in the eye of mankind, Jeffers would say. Could man but extract the beams from his eye and look beyond the self-love which threatens to destroy him, he would see that man's place in nature is not separate from but rather a part of all phenomena. As for Hope: "Hope is not for the wise," Jeffers tells us, "fear is for fools; / Change and the world, we think, are racing to a fall, / Open-eyed and helpless. . . ." Faith, in its least harmful aspect, acts as a crutch for the weak to lean on; at its worst, it offers an outlet for fanatical cruelty:

> How many turn back toward dreams and magic, how many children
> Run home to Mother Church, Father State,
> To find in their arms the delicious warmth and folding of souls.
> The age weakens and settles home toward old ways.
> An age of renascent faith: Christ said, Marx wrote, Hitler says,
> And though it seems absurd we believe.
> Sad children, yes. It is lonely to be adult, you need a father.
> With a little practice you'll believe anything.
>
> Faith returns, beautiful, terrible, ridiculous,
> And men are willing to die and kill for their faith. . . .

When faith doesn't cause men to become "curiously ignoble," it turns them into unwitting pawns of Caesars (or Christ-figures), hungry for power. The people become "Blind Horses," turning the mill to generate power for the shepherds:

> The proletariat for your Messiah, the poor and many are to seize power
> and make the world new.
> They cannot even conduct a strike without cunning leaders: if they make
> a revolution their leaders
> Must take the power. The first duty of men in power: to defend their
> power. What men defend
> To-day they will love to-morrow; it becomes theirs, their property. Lenin
> has served the revolution,
> Stalin presently begins to betray it. Why? For the sake of power, the
> Party's power, the state's
> Power, armed power, Stalin's power, Caesarean power.
> This is
> not quite a new world.
> The old shepherd has been known before; great and progressive empires
> have flourished before; powerful bureaucracies
> Apportioned food and labor and amusement; men have been massed and
> moulded, spies have gone here and there,
> The old shepherd Caesar his vicious collies, watching the flock.
> Inevitable? Perhaps, but not new.
> The ages like blind horses turning a mill tread their own hoof-marks.
> Whose corn's ground in that mill?

Nor are the masses, the "ants," the only ones who cry out for a leader, i.e., an abstraction embodied in the person of a leader willing, and usually eager, to accept the power that comes with mass followers. Unable to cultivate their gardens in the self-reliant manner of a Voltaire or a Thoreau, "Intellectuals" also "flock into fold." Having fallen in love outward, with the "unkindly all but inhuman God," Jeffers has no need to align himself with one of man's subjective, egocentric creeds:

> Is it so hard for men to stand by themselves,
> They must hang on Marx or Christ, or mere Progress?
> Clearly it is hard. But these ought to be leaders . . .
> Sheep leading sheep, "The fold, the fold.
> Night comes, and the wolves of doubt." Clearly it is hard.
>
> Yourself, if you had not encountered and loved
> Our unkindly all but inhuman God,
> Who is very beautiful and too secure to want worshippers,
> And includes indeed the sheep with the wolves,
> You too might have been looking about for a church.
>
> He includes the flaming stars and pitiable flesh,
> And what we call things and what we call nothing.
> He is very beautiful. But when these lonely have travelled
> Through long thoughts to redeeming despair,
> They are tired and cover their eyes; they flock into fold.

It would be simple enough to list a number of other prophets (Jeffers obviously assumes the role of prophet here, as in most other of the poems I am using in this particular context) who illustrate Jeffers' point. Think of those who have passed from the Marxian stage onto the Christian (circumstances the last thirty years have not been favorable to passing the other way round). Many of the "Intellectuals" had also gone through a Freudian period before embracing Marx and then Christ—always moving from one dogmatism to another, and always revealing an ardent desire for belief, for release from the loneliness that accompanies doubt. For them the little "truths" always take the place of Truth. It might also be recalled that Mencken, who refused the comfortable chair at the foot of the saviors, remarked in the 1930s that the people who most ardently and dexterously performed the mental acrobatics necessary to good standing in the Marxian school were precisely those who had advocated the wilder theories of sexology in the 1920s, and were the ones most likely to return to Christian theology at a later date—those, in brief, who were happily blessed with believing minds.

The Hebraic-Christian worship of a personalized God, a God of human feeling, acts, and form, carries with it and even makes necessary the anthropocentricism to which Jeffers attributed the major shortcomings of our species. Unable to rely on a God outside, one capable of rewarding or punishing, Jeffers advocated a self-reliance similar to that of Emerson and Nietzsche—but with a major difference. Both Emerson and Nietzsche felt that belief in a personal God was childish superstition, but when Emerson replaced the Christian God with Self-Reliance (and thereby reliance on the God outside through the Over-soul) he actually reintroduced the belief that man was subject and the world object, a belief that eighteenth-century skepticism had challenged in all areas. Could man, whom Emerson called "a god in ruins," but fully awake, he would realize that the world was, indeed, his special oyster. Nietzsche went a step further. In offering a way out of the nihilism which modern man inherited from the scientific discoveries since the Renaissance, Nietzsche developed his philosophy of the *Übermensch*—and thereby compounded Emersonian Self-Reliance with a divine Ego.

On the other hand, Jeffers' philosophy of Inhumanism shifted the emphasis and significance from man to not-man, and rejected human solipsism while recognizing the transhuman magnificence. As he put it in the Preface to *The Double Axe* (1948), a volume that continues to be popular with poetry readers though its contents would doubtless outrage the vast majority of men were they aware of it:

> It seems time that our race began to think as an adult does, rather than like an egocentric baby or insane person. This manner of thought and feeling is neither misanthropic nor pessimist, though two or three people have said so and may again. It involves no falsehoods, and is a means of maintaining sanity in slippery times; it has objective truth and human value. It offers a reasonable detachment as rule of conduct, instead of love, hate and envy. It neutralizes fanaticism and wild hopes; but it provides magnificence for the religious instinct, and satisfies our need to admire greatness and rejoice in beauty.

Considering Jeffers' belief, so perfectly adumbrated in the long poems, that man is essentially irrational, I doubt that he considered it possible for the few rational men to avoid being pulled under by the masses, who insist on giving their accumulated power to saviors. *But there can be no doubt about his concern for the species.* If mad Ireland hurt Yeats into poetry, then ridiculous man did the same for Jeffers. At times, the exhortation in his poetry has the ring of an imperative, as in "Signpost":

> Civilized, crying how to be human again: this will tell you how.
> Turn outward, love things, not men, turn right away from humanity,
> Let that doll lie. Consider if you like how the lilies grow,
> Lean on the silent rock until you feel its divinity.
> Make your veins cold, look at the silent stars, let your eyes
> Climb the great ladder out of the pit of yourself and man.
> Things are so beautiful, your love will follow your eyes;
> Things are the God, you will love God, and not in vain,
> For what we love, we grow to it, we share its nature. At length
> You will look back along the stars' rays and see that even
> The poor doll humanity has a place under heaven.
> Its qualities repair their mosaic around you, the chips of strength
> And sickness; but now you are free, even to become human,
> But born of the rock and the air, not of a woman.

In one of the last poems Jeffers wrote, included in *The Beginning and the End* (1963), this almost painful love for the world of things, of which man is one thing, is expressed with haunting tenderness, a tenderness that in the poetry written just before and after the Second World War was often overwhelmed by the rage aroused by man's irrational behavior.

A great dawn-color rose widening the petals around her gold eye
Peers day and night in the window. She watches us
Breakfasting, lighting lamps, reading, and the children playing, and the
 dogs by the fire,
She watches earnestly, uncomprehending,
As we stare into the world of trees and roses uncomprehending,
There is a great gulf fixed. But even while
I gaze, and the rose at me, my little flower-greedy daughter-in-law
Walks with shears, very blond and housewifely
Through the small garden, and suddenly the rose finds herself rootless
 in-doors.
Now she is part of the life she watched.
—So we: death comes and plucks us: we become part of the living earth
And wind and water whom we so loved. We are they.

If Jeffers found little in man's confusion to warrant praise, he did increase our powers of perception; and his stoicism will always befriend us in the dark days when they come.

Introduction to *Cawdor and Medea*

William Everson (Brother Antoninus)[*]

1

This book places in the hands of a new generation of readers two of the long, somber and God-tormented poems of Robinson Jeffers. The first, the verse narrative *Cawdor,* is laid in the Big Sur on the California coast, the locale Jeffers knew thoroughly and used repeatedly to body forth his misgivings about the human race. The other, a redaction of the *Medea* of Euripides, is a free adaptation from the Greek written for the stage. *Cawdor* appeared in 1928 at the height of Jeffers' career, and was enthusiastically received. It is a superb example of his outlook and narrative method. *Medea,* published in 1946, was written specially for the actress Judith Anderson. The combined genius of poet and tragedienne

[*]From *Cawdor and Medea* by Robinson Jeffers (New York: New Directions, 1970): vii–xxx. Reprinted by permission of New Directions Publishing Corporation.

proved irresistible when the play was staged the following year, and it is remembered as the outstanding success of its period. Both poems have long been out of print.

The current preoccupation with mysticism, everywhere evident in the verse now being written, will gain sustenance from this reintroduction to one of the most powerfully visionary poets that America has produced. Only Whitman rivals him in this regard, though Whitman's greater universality is rather more ethical than religious; despite his range he displays nothing like the terrible intensity of Jeffers' religious passion. Nevertheless each poet presents a distinct facet of what might be called our fundamental native pantheism:[1] by the singularity of his achievement each complements the other. They define between them the positive and negative poles of the unconscious American religious spirit.

Cawdor tells what can happen when a widower past his prime, unable to relinquish youth, marries a nubile girl. It was a theme founded in Jeffers' bloodstream, for he was himself the progeny of such a union. His father, no widower indeed but a frosty Presbyterian minister, took late in life an attractive young bride. Born in 1887 in Pittsburgh, Jeffers' childhood was lonely. He was educated there and at various private schools in Europe until his parents moved to Pasadena where he entered Occidental College. Doing his advanced study in science at the University of Southern California he graduated with honors but determined to become a poet. True to his oedipal background he wooed the beautiful wife of a socially prominent Los Angeles lawyer, and when he had won her carried her off to the magnificent isolation of the Monterey coast. This was in 1914. He built there a stone tower and began the remote life that was to become legendary. His first two volumes of verse were not significant, but in 1924 he made his breakthrough with a privately published narrative poem, *Tamar,* which became an overnight sensation. It was evident that the latent American pantheistic seed had found its Californian fertility,[2] and a new breed was born. But it was not destined for tranquility: from that time on, though his productivity never abated, Jeffers' career was stormy. His verse fought with the times. After World War II the nation turned its back on him, the Eisenhower era being especially unsympathetic, and at his death he was no longer widely read. As Frederic I. Carpenter was to write in summation:

> Considered historically, Jeffers remains one of the most important poets of the years before the great depression. But in the last quarter of a century his reputation has fluctuated not only with the events and tastes of the times but with the changing tone and quality of his own successive poems. Always a few readers—including some major poets and critics—have considered his work of the greatest permanent value. Always other readers—including many major critics—have considered it beneath notice. Few authors in the history of literature

> have excited greater differences of opinion; and few have seen their reputations change so greatly in their own lifetimes. But critical praise and blame affected Jeffers himself very little. From his isolated rock tower he continued to gaze southward at the wild promontories of the coast and westward at the far horizons of the ocean, rather than eastward at his fellow men.[3]

But the times come round. An economy of affluence and a mangling Viet Nam war have conspired to prepare an atmosphere of disenchantment and risk not unlike the mood in which Jeffers himself had quickened. Perhaps a new generation, sick of the suburbs, is finding his Big Sur isolation and his westering gaze as universal in their implications as an intermediate generation found them irrelevant.[4]

2

A great deal has been written about the philosophical background of Jeffers' thought in Lucretius, Nietzsche and Spengler. However, the best way to get him in focus is as a native transcendentalist—but, it must be remembered, a transcendentalist gone West and turned inside out. As with Whitman, Emerson shaped his mind. One of the first of his recently published letters lets us see him as the ardent young poet writing to his girl: "As you remarked, most beautiful, Emerson's a great and good man. We've had only two great men yet in American literature—Poe is the other."[5] And years later, in his creative maturity, answering a query from Carpenter, he could say: "Emerson was a youthful enthusiasm, if you like, but not outgrown by any means, only read so thoroughly that I have not returned to him for a long time."[6]

Actually, it was Emerson's prose more than any other element that formed the ground for Jeffers' meditative poetic style. Jeffers emerged at the height of the Modernist triumph, but of its aesthetic tenets he utilized only one, the one that transformed him from a minor to a major artist. Against the Georgians, who looked back to the Romantics, the Modernists insisted that poetry must assimilate the techniques developed in the refinement of contemporary prose style. It was the chief break with the past that brought poetry up to date. Jeffers followed suit, and presented the resilient, massive, intellectually resonant verse idiom that enabled him to assail with such authority the complacencies of his time. When someone gets around to it, following out the implications of this particular Modernist tenet, and makes a study of the prose stylists who stand behind the major modern poets, it will be plain that for Jeffers the matrix was Emerson. Time and again his sonorous diction haunts the Jeffersian line:

> But man is conscious,
> He brings the world to focus in a feeling brain,

In a net of nerves catches the splendor of things,
Breaks the somnambulism of nature . . .[7]

What turned Jeffers' youthful transcendentalism inside out was World War I, the single most disillusioning event in our national history. Jeffers emerged from it with his idealism shattered. Under the shadow of ten million slain all the benignancy of Victorian optimism turned to dust and ashes in the mouths of thousands, and if Hemingway became their spokesman, Jeffers became their prophet. Just as he took the positive element in his father's religion and reversed it against itself, so he took the confident element in his master, and controverted it through the menstruum of his wary disenchantment. Thus what Emerson saw for a wonder:

> There is something social and intrusive in the nature of all things; they seek to penetrate and overpower, each the nature of every other creature, and itself alone in all modes and throughout space and spirit to prevail and possess. Every star in heaven is discontented and insatiable . . ."[8]

Jeffers saw for a curse:

You would be wise, you far stars,
To flee with the speed of light this infection.
For here the good sane invulnerable material
And nature of things more and more grows alive and cries.
The rock and water grow human, the bitter weed
Of consciousness catches the sun, it clings to the near stars,
Even the nearer portion of the universal God
Seems to become conscious, yearns and rejoices
And suffers: I believe this hurt will be healed
Some age of time after mankind has died,
Then the sun will say "What ailed me a moment?" and resume
The old soulless triumph, and the iron and stone earth
With confident inorganic glory obliterate
Her ruins and fossils . . .[9]

Or what Emerson, in a marvelous passage from the same essay, could rejoice in:

> A man should know himself for a necessary actor. A link was wanting between two craving parts of nature, and he was hurled into being as the bridge over that yawning need, the mediator betwixt two else unmarriagable facts. His two parents held each of them one of the wants, and the union of foreign constitutions in him enables him to do gladly and gracefully what the assembled human race could not have sufficed to do . . . The thoughts he delights to utter are the reason of his incarnation . . . Hereto was he born, to deliver the thought of his heart from the universe to the universe; to do an office which nature could not forego, nor he be discharged from rendering, and then immerge again into the holy silence and eternity out of which as a man he arose . . .[10]

This becomes, for Jeffers, in an equally marvelous passage from his same poem, a concurrence indeed but also a demur:

And have widened in my idleness
The disastrous personality of life with poems,
That are pleasant enough in the breeding but go bitterly at last
To envy oblivion and the early deaths of nobler
Verse, and much nobler flesh;
And I have projected my spirit
Behind the superb sufficient forehead of nature
To gift the inhuman God with this rankling consciousness.

But who is our judge? It is likely the enormous
Beauty of the world requires for completion our ghostly increment,
It has to dream, and dream badly, a moment of its night.[11]

In his roots, then, Jeffers retained the grandeur and scale of the transcendentalist vision, even as this quotation makes evident, regardless how deceptive his negativism appeared to those looking for sources. What they saw was that he stood as polar opposite to Whitman, and this is true enough; but of itself the fact does not establish him a nihilist.

Whitman was of the balloon age; he lived in the high atmosphere of sun and wind and buoyant clouds. Jeffers, however, broke through the stratosphere: he looked back at the earth from the blackness of outer space. Writing in 1923, when aircraft were capable of no more than a couple hundred miles an hour in a dive, he could prophesy:

Far-flown ones, you children of the hawk's dream future, when you lean
 from a crag of the last planet on the ocean
Of the far stars, remember we also have known beauty.[12]

In this, for once, he was justified in his own life. If he was not to be here to see the moon-landings, at least he was present for the space-advent of Yuri Gagarin.

3

The thing that conceals Jeffers' transcendentalism is its extremity; it is so extreme that humanity is dwarfed, reduced by the cosmic vision that has carried the poet out beyond the range of the human dimension, and gives him the eyes of God. Whitman has been called an arch-transcendentalist,[13] and indeed he is, but that leaves no term for Jeffers. Jeffers pushes the tenets of the creed beyond the point of no return. He crossed that line with his first major poem, *Tamar*, and from the break-through-position that it established for him there was no turning back. It is true that all his poems were to be involved with the life of man on earth, but that life is seen from another dimension. It is very like the gaze of an adult grown wise looking back upon a disgustingly precocious childhood.

Once Jeffers made his breakthrough he was compelled to extend its implications, and he wrote like a man possessed. After *Tamar* there followed in rapid succession *The Tower Beyond Tragedy* and *Roan Stallion* in 1925, and then, apocalyptically, *The Women at Point Sur* in 1927, where the last mask was torn from the human face as he saw it. But "*Tamar* seemed to my later thought," he was to write in explanation, "to have a tendency to romanticize unmoral freedom, and it was evident a good many people took it that way . . . one of my later intentions of the *Point Sur* was to indicate the destruction and strip everything but its natural ugliness from the unmorality."[14] There were other intentions, certainly, and their aptness is disputed, but as to this one there can be no dispute. However much the purgative of *Point Sur* relieved *him* his readers were, almost to a man, revolted. He realized that its extremity had placed in jeopardy his deeper message.

This brings us to the first of the paired poems which comprise this book, for it is with *Cawdor* that he attempted to mend his fences. His aim was to write a simple narrative, classically sound, in which his doctrine, his "Inhumanism," as he was to call it, is implicit, not obtrusive. It is, therefore, more than any other of his long poems, a "straight narrative," one with fewer allegorical overtones. Perhaps, prophet that he was, and no "teller of tales to delight women and the people,"[15] this is the real reason why he excluded it from his *Selected Poetry* when he came to compile that impressive volume nine years later.

The main point, however, is that his stratagem was successful. *Cawdor*, published the year after *Point Sur*, righted the yawing course of his career and has been widely praised. Of it Lawrence Clark Powell, the poet's first major commentator, was to say:

> This is, in my opinion, Jeffers' finest single volume: the verse in it is on a consistently high level. Whereas some of the narratives in the *Roan Stallion* volume are overburdened with doctrine, and *The Women at Point Sur* is loud with the horns of prophecy, *Cawdor* is a tale told for the telling; and though very serious in tone and marked by awful, violent acts, it is free from themes of incest and sexual perversion. Unlike the mad minister of *The Women at Point Sur*, the protagonist Cawdor is consistently sane. His tragedy, which proceeds inevitably from the postulates, is not one of abnormality, and hence is more likely to be appreciated by the general reader.[16]

Even Yvor Winters, Jeffers' most savagely hostile critic, found good in it. "*Cawdor* alone of Mr. Jeffers' poems contains a plot that in its rough outlines might be sound, and *Cawdor* likewise contains his best poetry; the poem as a whole, and in spite of the confused treatment of the woman, is moving, and the lines describing the seals at dawn are fine, as are the two or three last lines of the apotheosis of the eagle . . ."[17]

But for all Jeffers' resolution to write a straight narrative there are focal points within it from which his transcendental proclivities refuse to be excluded. These are the deaths. The first two, those of Old Frazer and the youth Hood Cawdor, are seen as disintegrative and deliquescent. They represent diffuse human consciousness incapable of achieving sufficient concentration to survive after life. The final death, that of the eagle, is integrative and transcendent. Counteracting the human weaknesses, it indicts them with an upward rush, soars into the realm of the super-real. The eagle, ancient symbol of height, of the spirit as the sun, and of the spiritual principle in general, serves powerfully to liberate Jeffers' mystical imagination. Its deathflight is one of the matchless examples of the transcendental intuition in English.

The descriptive processes shown in the human deaths have also impressed readers but they have not been so well understood symbolically. They might be called further instances of what Hyatt H. Waggoner rebukes as "the dubious taste of writing about a man by talking about the electrons and molecules that are supposed to account for him."[18] Jeffers, rather, is taking these deaths, eagle and man, as polar opposites, and using them symbolically to define the nature of the consequence that inheres in each. He is taking both the disintegrative ego-centric death of man and the trans-egoistic death of the eagle as instances in an inferred teleological ultimacy.

To Jeffers the eagle is more "real" than the man because it symbolizes a type of consciousness that is not divided within itself. It has not mis-evolved into an offshoot or sport of ratiocination as has that of man. A Catholic would say that while he sees human nature as "fallen" he sees that of the eagle as "angelic." Like an angel the eagle for Jeffers is more point-focused within its intrinsic nature, more "all there" as we would say, because it is not self-preoccupied in the flawed and divisive human way. In scholastic angelology a well-known impromptu definition has it that an angel is "a thinking thought." For Jeffers an eagle is "an acting act," and in rendering its death he evaporates language in an effort to register the intensity of his intuition. To those critics who protest that an eagle is not an angel I do not know how to reply, unable at this remove to argue the matter of how one reads poetry. At any rate it is good theology to infer that we become after death pretty much what we have made of ourselves in this life, and Jeffers reduces human desire to its normative processes in civilized life and projects from these its metaphysical consequences. Looking at man he sees in his death-act the ultimate atomization of consciousness that life had only served to accelerate in him. One way of expressing this is to particularize the disintegrating electrons and molecules of his being in physical decomposition, whether or not they really are "supposed to account for him." However that may be, the description of this process in Cawdor is, as Powell had observed, "unique in literature."

The case of *Medea* is more complex and more difficult to discuss, bringing as it does into sharper focus than *Cawdor* the whole matter of Jeffers' relation to the tragic tradition in literature. In the matter of form the two poems share a common feature. Though one is narrative and the other dramatic, though one is "modern" and the other "classical," neither originated in the deeps of his creative unconscious; both were tailored to exterior requirements. *Cawdor* was composed to the situation following *Point Sur;* in the case of *Medea* the poet was approached by a theatrical producer. This objectivity gives them greater formal restraint; they are more Apollonian than the characteristically Dionysian pieces of Jeffers' creative unconscious. "Only his adaption of the *Medea,*" writes Radcliffe Squires, "realizes Jeffers' own aim in tragedy as 'poetry . . . beautiful shapes . . . violence.' And this only because of the organic simplicity that Euripides imposes on Jeffers' restive imagination."[19] The reader of the present book, therefore, will see Jeffers "at his best" from the formal point of view. But if he wishes to touch the nerve of the master he will have to follow him into darker regions of his labyrinthine soul.[20] Squires concludes: "Almost everywhere else in Jeffers' poetry the contentions grind against each other, reducing human character to dust, destroying those very structures and relationships which recommend themselves as essential to narrative and dramatic success. I cheerfully concede these points to Jeffers' detractors. Nor do I wish to minimize these faults. Yet even after such a large loss, something larger remains, and if we do not minimize this remainder, we see that it is poetry."

4

As for Jeffers' relation to the tragic tradition in literature, he himself spoke of it as functional: "An exhibition of essential elements by the burning away through pain and ruin of inertia and the unessential." Rudolf Gilbert describes the process this way: "What to Athanasius was divinity, to Jeffers is nature—nature and divinity always separated from humanity. It is when the natural in humanity is crushed out by materialism that evil enters and tragedy begins."[21] This, however, is not really the issue as it emerges from the deepest reading of Jeffers' poems.

In order to clarify, let us set Jeffers' practice against the continuity of the tragic as it evolved in human consciousness. Emerson writes:

> The bitterest tragic element in life to be derived from an intellectual source is the belief in a brute Fate or Destiny; the belief that the order of Nature and events is controlled by a law not adapted to man, nor man to that, but which holds on its way to the end, serving him if his wishes chance to lie in the same course, crushing him if his wishes lie contrary

> to it, and heedless whether it serves or crushes him. This is the terrible meaning that lies at the foundation of the old Greek tragedy, and makes the Oedipus and Antigone and Orestes objects of such hopeless commiseration. They must perish, and there is no overgod to stop or mollify this hideous enginery that grinds or thunders, and snatches them up into its terrific system.[22]

Jeffers sometimes draws on this tradition but not to serve this reason, and certainly not in *Cawdor.* Here disaster springs from the manifest sexual vanity that leads its protagonist to wive a girl he knows does not love him, representing a kind of karmic fulfillment that, thought not lacking in inevitability, is not tragic in the above sense. The narrative, as Powell says, "proceeds from its postulates." But while karmic outworking can be recognized in the tragedies of Jeffers, as it is here, it is never his message. It is not the reason he writes.

Returning to the "classic" situation as Emerson describes it above, we must insist that, regardless how many instances occur in Jeffers' narratives which seem to verify this viewpoint—blind, mindless butcherings and catastrophes—it is not the basic Jeffersian thesis. Nor can it be ever again for man, and Emerson shows why:

> But this terror of contravening an unascertained and unascertainable will cannot co-exist with reflection: it disappears with civilization, and can no more be reproduced than the fear of ghosts after childhood. It is discriminated from the doctrine of Philosophical Necessity herein: that the last is an Optimism, and therefore the suffering individual finds his good consulted in the good of all, of which he is a part. But in destiny, it is not the good of the whole or the *best will* that is enacted, but only *one particular will.* Destiny properly is not a will at all, but an immense whim; and this is the only ground of terror and despair in the rational mind, and of tragedy in literature. Hence the antique tragedy which was founded on this faith, can never be reproduced.[23]

Because this is so, Jeffers' redactions of the Greek tragedies have often been unthinkingly dismissed as falsifications, rendered "morally and emotionally meaningless," in the words of Winters, by the differing conclusions to which he was constrained to direct them. Here we see the poet wiser than his critics. Emerson continues: "After reason and faith have introduced a better public and private tradition, the tragic element is somewhat circumscribed. There must always remain, however, the hindrance of our private satisfaction by the laws of the world. The law which establishes nature and the human race, continually thwarts the will of ignorant individuals, and this in the particulars of disease, want, insecurity and disunion."[24]

This of course is the situation of the man Cawdor, and we are wont to call it tragic, but Emerson distinguishes: "But the essence of tragedy does not seem to me to lie in any list of particular evils. After we have enumerated famine, fever, inaptitude, mutilation, rack, madness and loss of friends, we have not yet included the proper tragic element, which is Terror, and which does not respect definite evils but indefinite; an ominous spirit which haunts the afternoon and night, idleness and solitude."[25]

It is at this point that we meet the situation of *Medea,* and it compels Jeffers to the most extraordinary devices to accommodate its *dénouement* to such a view of reality and human destiny. The cloak that destroys Medea's rival is straight out of Euripides, of course, but Jeffers' employment of archetypal fire-serpents to protect her at the play's close is an acknowledged improvement upon the Euripidean device of openly driving her off in a chariot. They seem to canalize the Terror and give it concreteness in the poet's abrasive onslaught on human egoism. But there still remains the high registration of Jeffers' tragic spirit in an area that Emerson does not consider.

For at this point Jeffers parts company with his master, who now begins to subjectivize the problem of the tragic, and for its solution turns another way:

> A low haggard sprite sits by our side, "casting the fashion of uncertain evils"—a sinister presentiment, a power of the imagination to dislocate things orderly and cheerful and show them in startling array . . . And accordingly it is natures not clear, not of quick and steady perceptions, but imperfect characters from which somewhat is hidden that all others see, who suffer most from these causes. In those persons who move the profoundest pity, tragedy seems to consist in a temperament, not in events. There are people who have an appetite for grief, pleasure is not strong enough and they crave pain, mithridatic stomachs which must be fed on poisoned bread, natures so doomed that no prosperity can soothe their ragged and dishevelled desolation. They mis-hear and mis-behold, they suspect and dread. They handle every nettle and ivy in the hedge, and tread on every snake in the meadow.[26]

So pronounced is Jeffers' penchant for anguish and catastrophe that the convinced Emersonian might well be tempted to dismiss his preoccupation as no more than this. Truly, if any modern writer can be so described, Jeffers has a "mithridatic stomach." But while subjectivity might explain the emotional coloring of a tragedian it says nothing about his metaphysical assumptions or his aesthetic resolutions.

No, with Jeffers we have to go to the religious solution. He shares with the Christian both a refusal to dismiss the evils of the world and a search for an answer to tragedy in the doctrine of salvation. In this he is more traditional than Emerson, holding to an insight memorialized in all the great religions of the world. Emerson's solution is unquestionably courageous. By subjectivizing its impress ("Tragedy is in the eye of the beholder") he looks within the interplay of forces for the compensatory reaction which will correct the excess that produced the fatality. In the end he seeks for the answer in the interior life alone:

> The intellect is a consoler, which delights in detaching or putting an interval between a man and his fortune, and so converts the sufferer into a spectator and his pain into poetry. It yields the joys of conversation, of letters and of science. Hence also the torments of life become tuneful tragedy, solemn and soft with music, and garnished with rich dark pictures. But higher still than the activities of art, the intellect in its purity and the moral sense in its purity are not distinguished from each other, and both ravish us into a region whereunto these passionate clouds of sorrow cannot rise.[27]

This is indeed what might be called the modern interpretation of the ancient tragic problem. Joseph Wood Krutch writes of it as "a profession of faith, and a sort of a religion; a way of looking at life by virtue of which it is robbed of its pain. The sturdy soul of the tragic author seizes upon suffering and uses it only as a means by which joy may be wrung out of existence."[28] But this is not Jeffers. No author who ever lived was less interested in converting pain into pleasure than he.

5

For Emerson's mind was primarily philosophic, as of course is that of Krutch, while Jeffers was essentially religious, and in the most primitive and elemental sense: it is this alone that wrenched him from the beneficent solutions of the sage of Concord. Ineradicable in his consciousness is the doctrine of Original Sin. He cannot posit a "fall," with its direct moral imputations, but he does posit a past evolutionary mishap. The moral imputation enters through man's wilful adhering to his inherited liabilities in preference to ontological existence as evidenced in prime nature. Jeffers discerns, empirically enough, man's alienation from reality, and what matter if he attribute it to an evolutionary fluke, a biological mischance in the genealogy of the species? The operative point is that the evils he delineates in his narratives stem from a human penchant which is not hypothetical. As with the Christian, "salvation" lies in deliverance, and though deliverance for him amounts to assimilation into the cosmos, that cosmos is not, essentially, material. What we die into is God. Jeffers supports his torrential violence and redeems his tragedies, as do the major Christian poets, by suffusing creation—action and context alike—with a God-presence that assimilates the anguish of victims into a more intense dimension. By every poetic device at his command he sustains an elevation above the catastrophe he so graphically delineates. It is the technique of the author of Job, employing mood, imagery, rhythm, metaphor—device after device—to proclaim the God-consciousness he knows is sustaining the cruelty and which constitutes its meaning. Of these the most powerful weapon is mood, his incredible atmospherics. Despite the many faults and contradictions assailed by critics it can be fairly argued that he fails only when he fails in this.

> If complete unity of structure seems to be lacking in the narratives, unity of mood and atmosphere does not. Here Jeffers is a master. From the first to the last lines we are immersed in a tragic world, dream-laden with violence and anguish. As Dostoievski depicts a gray Russian world, Jeffers draws his with blood-images against fogs and treacherous promontories . . . The background of raging nature, together with the distorted lives of the characters, merge in turbulent images. All are underscored by the heavy, sometimes ponderous meter that supplies the muffled rhythm. Few readers of Jeffers can forget the oppressive mood he generates. It is a mood of black romanticism which brings into focus the doctrine as well as the dourness of tone, and we may be convinced, as Jeffers wants us to be, that life needs a reevaluation if things are really so bad. Through this depressing convergence of image, setting, subject and tone, Jeffers comes closest to achieving his purpose, and we begin to believe that "We must uncenter our minds from ourselves" to escape catastrophe.[29]

Thus he uses pain, as does the Christian poet, as the primary separating agent between the ego-centric human consciousness and a super-reality which heightens the pain even as it dwarfs it. This dwarfing through intensification is what the martyrs of all religious faiths have experienced time and again, and Jeffers is its great modern literary advocate. It is through his suffering that man may see God. Thus the heaping on of violence in Jeffers is proportioned to our sensual insularity, for which our multiple soporifics have rendered pain innocuous. He scours the encrustations of civilization from the nerves of his characters not so that they might know joy, but so that we, his readers, might recognize God, and die.

I observed above that in *Medea* Jeffers drew upon the aspect of the tragic that Emerson localized in the heart of unmitigated Terror. In this he followed Euripides, and said no more. If in doing so a certain organic simplicity of form was imposed on Jeffers' restive imagination, as Squires has indicated, it is done at the cost of what he himself had to say about it. For in *Solstice*, his earlier adaptation of the play to narrative verse, where no such restriction inhibited him, the deep probe of his insight is more apparent, and though it is thought to be the worst poem he ever wrote[30] his informing conviction is unmistakable. Nor can this be dismissed as one more instance of the twisting of classic themes in order to further personal ends, for even in Euripides something more is implied. In his *Greek Tragedy* H. D. F. Kitto writes:

> But if we look carefully into the last scene we shall see more than dramatic convenience in the chariot. Medea has done things which appal even the chorus, those sympathetic neighbours who had said, earlier in the play, "Now is honour coming to womankind." Their prayer now is "O

> Earth, O thou blazing light of the Sun, look upon this accursed woman before she slays her own children . . . O god-given light, stay her hand, frustrate her . . ." In the same vein Jason says, when he has learnt the worst, "After doing this, of all things most unholy, dost thou show thy face to the Sun and the Earth?" Sun and Earth, the most elemental things in the universe, have been outraged by these terrible crimes; what will they do? How will they avenge their sullied purity? What Earth will do we shall not be told, but we are told what the Sun does: he sends a chariot to rescue the murderess.[31]

Why? In *Solstice* Jeffers spells it out. His primitive religious intuition drives back behind the Euripidean implication to what must have been the deeper mythical source of this legend. He recognizes that what is at stake, what is at war in the soul of Medea, is the ineluctable contest between the Sacred and the Profane. This inexorable tension carries her beyond a human struggle between jealous rage and maternal devotion which, by Euripides' time, had for the sophisticated Greek consciousness become a point of burning concern. Rather it is a demonstration of the authority and triumph of the Sacred, and it proclaims to mankind that so crucial is this opposition that when human lives enter its arena they must be prepared to encounter the fundamental cleavage in reality. Medea is a woman in whom the archetype of the Sacred is so primitive and unadulterated that it will not permit her to accept the accommodations of normative life. Rather she is invaded by the sacral and compelled to follow its directive, which declares that children are better dead than corrupt. This is, of course, the basic Jeffersian attitude, but in this play he utilizes the dimension of Terror to render it shockingly plain.

From this it can be seen that Jeffers' solution to the problem of the tragic is essentially salvific, and that the mode of salvation is faith. Medea is saved through the capacity of the human spirit to adhere to a principle beyond itself, and by abnegation and transcendence achieve identity with that principle; to qualify for its attributes by accepting subsumption into it, even to the ultimate nullification of the individual identity, as happens to Madrone Bothwell in *Solstice* if not to Medea. Jeffers is not a gnostic in that he offers no technique by which the elect, the spiritual cognoscenti, may effect transcendence, and so escape the trap of material contingency. And he is not a Christian in that he repudiates incarnation as a synthesis between the opposed polarities of matter and spirit: the Word made Flesh.

For Jeffers, existence offers, through consciousness, one redeeming aspect: the instant of recognition, one moment in which to behold the real, and then suffer its invasion. This is not so good as the hawks, who *act* the real in a way we can't; or the rocks, who *concretize* it in a way we can't; but it is all we have. To refuse it, to pervert consciousness into self-congratulatory preening of the collective ego, is to miss the sublime opportunity of all evolution. To refuse is to fail. But to accept its moment of anguish and catastrophe is, as much as is humanly possible, to triumph. And sometimes, as on the abandoned landing above the sea where Thurso died, the challenge is grappled:

> The platform is like a rough plank theatre-stage
> Built on the brow of the promontory: as if our blood had labored all round the earth from Asia
> To play its mystery before strict judges at last, the final ocean and sky, to prove our nature
> More shining than that of the other animals. It is rather ignoble in its quiet times, mean in its pleasure,
> Slavish in the mass; but at stricken moments it can shine terribly against the dark magnificence of things.[32]

In order to arrive at this restriction he had to retrace the development of religious consciousness to the point before Abraham—that is, before Revelation, and to dismiss Revelation as phantasy: racial delusion, the anthropomorphic trap. If the Christian cannot agree it is simply because he understands that all Jeffers intuits about divinity in the cosmos he intuits *as person.* When Revelation speaks, the correspondence is not anthropocentric only, for personality is itself trans-human, that is, is also angelic and divine. Because this is so Revelation, the intelligence from person to person, speaks with such incisiveness that to the Christian all the overwhelming efflux of the divine pulsing in the cosmos becomes diffuse and amorphous compared to the penetrating Voice he hears with such directness, and to which he responds. Be that as it may, Jeffers' primitive religious spirit and his elaborate scientific training between them absolved him from the task of grappling with the ontological constitution of personality. It follows from this that the chief liability of his doctrine was that it enabled him to brush aside contemptuously the strictest problems of existence; they became irrelevant, purely mental correlates of the basic human aberration; even as the chief asset was the incentive it gave him to celebrate the magnificent superfluity of the divine where humankind rarely chooses to recognize it.

But Jeffers knew the Voice. The residual Christian elements in his verse are unmistakable. Indeed, he was later to defend himself in terms of its directive: "This is far from humanism; but it is in fact the Christian attitude:—to love God with all one's heart and soul, and one's neighbour as one's self: as much as that, but as *little* as that."[33] If he seemed to close his ears perhaps it was in order to hear more clearly, from a quarter into which his father, for whom the Voice was all, could not intrude. If this is so it follows that his quarrel was not so much with the God of Revelation as with what men have made of Him.

Still, what is important to us is the poetry, and no matter how forbidding the philosophy, or how disturbing the religion, Jeffers will be read. Because man, in Emerson's phrase, "never so often deceived, still watches for the arrival of a brother who can *hold him steady to a truth until he has made it his own.*"[34] If this is the poet's function, and I believe it is, then Robinson Jeffers has few equals in our time.

Notes

1. Tocqueville, Alexis de, "What Causes Democratic Nations to Incline towards Pantheism?" *Democracy in America* (New York, 1954), vol. II, pg. 32. "[In democracies] the idea of unity so possesses man and is sought by him so generally that if he thinks he has found it, he readily yields himself to that belief. Not content with the discovery that there is nothing in the world but a creation and a Creator, he is still embarrassed by this primary division of things and seeks to expand and simplify his conception by including God and the universe in one great whole."

2. "I am struck in California," wrote George Santayana to Porter Garnett in a letter dated August 15, 1911, "by the deep and almost religious affection which people have for nature and by the sensitiveness they show for its influences . . . It is their spontaneous substitute for articulate art and articulate religion." (Bancroft Library, University of California at Berkeley.)

3. Carpenter, Frederic I. *Robinson Jeffers* (New York, 1962), pg. 53. Written by a specialist in American literature rather than by a specialist in the content of modern poetry, this book gains from its broad approach. Coming at the moment of Jeffers' death it profits by an overall view which no previous work on the poet afforded. Its judgments are balanced rather than intensive, they present rather than argue. It is the best introduction to the whole work of the poet that has so far appeared.

4. Shapiro, Karl. *In Defense of Ignorance* (New York, 1960), pg. 227. In response to the question, "What is the pattern of the poet's life style?" the author replied: "Of course, it would be nice to say like a California poet: I live in a house on a deserted cliff. I built the house of boulders which I tore from the bed of the Pacific with my bare hands. I don't see what difference it makes." These words were uttered, presumably, in the mid-fifties. Today any spokesman for the new generation would hold that unless a poetic idiom originates in an authentic life style it cannot escape preciosity.

5. Jeffers, Robinson. *Selected Letters* (Baltimore, 1968), pg. 7.

6. Ibid., pg. 209.

7. "Margrave," *The Selected Poetry of Robinson Jeffers* (New York, 1938), pg. 365.

8. Emerson, Ralph Waldo. "The Method of Nature," *The Complete Writings of Ralph Waldo Emerson* (New York, 1929), pg. 65.

9. "Margrave," *Selected Poetry,* pg. 370.

10. *Complete Writings,* pg. 64.

11. *Selected Poetry,* pg. 371.

12. "Not Our Good Luck," *Roan Stallion, Tamar and Other Poems* (New York, 1925), pg. 242. Why Jeffers excluded this powerful poem from the *Selected Poetry* is difficult to say.

13. By Perry Miller in his *The American Transcendentalists* (New York, 1957), pg. xi.

14. Bennett, Melba Berry. *The Stone Mason of Tor House* (Los Angeles, 1966), pg. 118.

15. Jeffers, Robinson, *The Women at Point Sur,* (New York, 1927), pg. 9. "But why should I make fables again? There are many / Tellers of tales to delight women and the people. / I have no vocation."

16. Powell, Lawrence Clark. *Robinson Jeffers: The Man and His Work* (Pasadena, 1940), pg. 45. (Second Edition.) Written in the early thirties when Jeffers' reputation was at its zenith this, the first book–length study, is free from the painful necessity of defence and

justification which so strains all subsequent efforts. Powell remains the poet's most palpable reader; his first qualification is that he manifestly likes what he reads, a rare gift in a critic, and his spontaneous accessibility to the poems makes his quotations exciting as well as illustrative. It is to be hoped that the famous librarian and bookman will close his career as he opened it, with what could be the final (as this is the initial) summary of the achievement of Robinson Jeffers.

17. Winters, Yvor. "Robinson Jeffers," in *Literary Opinion in America*, by Morton Dauwen Zabel (New York, 1937), pg. 247. I have quoted from Zabel's anthology rather than from Winters' *In Defense of Reason* in order to present the essay as it originally appeared in *Hound and Horn*. Winters later retracted his approval of the lines terminating the eagle's apotheosis, and retained it only for those about the seals at dawn:

> Before the cock crew dawn
> Sea-lions began barking and coughing far off
> In the hollow ocean; but one screamed out like torture
> And bubbled under the water . . .

It is doubtful if any but the most dedicated practitioners of the late Stanford professor's method can say why these lines are better than a hundred others in the poem.

18. Waggoner, Hyatt H. *American Poets, from the Puritans to the Present* (New York, 1968), pg. 476. This book is *the* breakthrough study of American poetry done since the inception of the Modernist period. Jeffers, though, Waggoner decidedly misreads. Speaking of Lucretius' gods he says: "Like them, Jeffers' God is capricious, unconcerned, and irrelevant. Unlike them, though, He does have one function wherever He appears; He is useful for attaching ultimate blame to. What kind of a God, Jeffers keeps asking, would it be that would make *this* kind of world?" Rather, Jeffers is asking precisely the opposite: What kind of world have *we* made which in its blindness refuses to see and acknowledge so stupendous a God? Although unfriendly to Jeffers, Waggoner's overview of our poetic heritage is a tremendous corrective to the dominant school of criticism since the advent of the Age of Eliot.

19. Squires, Radcliffe. *The Loyalties of Robinson Jeffers* (Ann Arbor, 1957), pgs. 166–7. Radcliffe Squires is the youngest of the writers who have attempted book-length studies of Jeffers' work. Writing in the mid-fifties when the poet's reputation was at its nadir he strove with great perspicacity against the dominant literary prejudice to affect a rehearing of Jeffers' claims. This effort often betrays him into a kind of self-conscious critical archness. But his insights are keen, he is a practicing poet with full awareness of modern aesthetic consciousness, and his struggle to take the measure of Jeffers' intellectual sources has not been equaled.

20. These darker regions are the creative intoxication of the true dionysiac, which he enters in such masterpieces as *Tamar* and *The Women at Point Sur*. As Emerson says: "I think nothing is of any value in books excepting the transcendental and extraordinary. If a man is inflamed and carried away by his thought, to that degree that he forgets the authors and public and heeds only this one dream which holds him like an insanity, let me read his [poem], and you may have all the arguments and histories and criticism." ("The Poet," in *Complete Writings*, pg. 248.)

21. Gilbert, Rudolph. *Shine, Perishing Republic* (Boston, 1936), pg. 93. The least satisfying of the book-length studies of Jeffers' work, *Shine, Perishing Republic* is chiefly interesting for a phenomenal multiplicity of references. Were it better written it could accommodate this superfluity, but too many sentences like "The poet here has cast a final seal of approbation upon the imaginative powers of his genius" nullify his points.

22. "The Tragic," in *Complete Writings*, pg. 1370.

23. Ibid., pg. 1371.

24. Idem.

25. Idem.

26. Emerson, pg. 1371.

27. Ibid., pg. 1371.

28. Quoted by Gilbert, op. cit., pg. 122.

29. Monjian, Mercedes Cunningham. *Robinson Jeffers: A Study in Inhumanism* (Pittsburgh, 1958), pg. 88. Falling chronologically between the studies of Squires and Carpenter, this shorter treatise is a judicious summary. She tends to see the poetry, magnificent as it is, as not sustaining the philosophy, rather than seeing the philosophy, as Powell does, as essentially a catalyst in the production of such poetry. But I for one shall always be grateful for the paragraph quoted. No one else said it before, and it is an observation of the first importance.

30. Carpenter, op. cit., pg. 86. Once again I find myself somewhat apart from the "general consent" of the commentators. Whatever else in *Solstice* fails, and much does, it never fails its mood. This cannot be said for some of the other minor narratives.

31. Kitto, H. D. F. *Greek Tragedy* (Garden City, 1954), pg. 208.

32. "Thurso's Landing," *Selected Poetry*, pg. 357.

33. Bennett, op. cit., pg. 185.

34. "The Poet," in *Complete Writings*, pg. 241.

Jeffers' *Cawdor* and the Hippolytus Story

Robert J. Brophy[*]

Whatever the ultimate intricacies of its interpretation, "Apology for Bad Dreams" tells in bold statement and strong imagery Jeffers' reasons for writing "horror stories" which "inevitably ended in blood."[1] These are the narratives which dominate his poetic canon.

His poems are written, Jeffers says, to work out a personal "salvation," a salvation which seems to be three-pronged: a clarification of vision, a peace-giving therapy, and a deeper, more truly attuned participation in the cosmic life to which man should be oriented and unto which he is physically subsumed.[2] In each of his narratives, Jeffers exposes a different facet of this "salvation." In *Tamar* he reconciles a Luther-like obsessive world of corruption and human guilt with the beauty of the natural world. In *Roan Stallion* he examines the hazards, rewards, and consequences of natural mysticism. In *The Tower Beyond Tragedy* he subjects to scrutiny the human bias for power and possession. In *Cawdor* Jeffers seeks to purify the notion of "security" by reviewing the pitfalls of settling for anything less than the harsh reality of things.[3] Jeffers does this in a cosmic context of the Life-Force in which we, both the human race in general and as individuals, must find the "common sense of our predicament as passionate bits of earth and water."[4]

The title *Cawdor* is taken from *Macbeth;* Jeffers seems to have been

[*]From *Western American Literature* 7 (Fall 1973): 171–78. Reprinted by permission.

singularly moved by the vanity-of-human-wishes theme as dramatized in the Thane of Cawdor's recognition scene. All visions of power prove illusory; all security based on self-effort and calculated maneuvering is folly: "Life's but a walking shadow, a poor player / That struts and frets his hour upon the stage . . . a tale told by an idiot, full of sound and fury, / Signifying nothing" (*Macbeth,* V,v, 19–28).

The plot of *Cawdor* adapts the Hippolytus-Phaedra story. Theseus here is Cawdor, a prosperous farmer and rancher; Hippolytus is his son Hood, who has turned nomad-hunter in preference to crop-tending; Phaedra is Fera (which means "wild beast"), a girl whom a forest fire has orphaned and made homeless.

At the ritual level, which is the life-rhythm that underlies all Jeffers' narratives, the story enacts the impersonal, violent dissolution which is inevitable within the life-cycle of all being. Existence is renewed only through death and decay. *Cawdor* dramatizes this truth, the human figures acting out roles of elemental processes. All life, the poem teaches, is caged, maimed, and in pain; all life is aimed at decline and death.

Although it comprehends a complexity of many myth-motifs (Hippolytus, Labyrinth and Minotaur, Orion, Artemis, Oedipus, Christ and Mithra), the myth-pattern behind *Cawdor*'s plot chiefly concerns the more primordial cycle of life as it was personified in primitive religions. Cawdor (and, in a subsidiary sense, Hood) is the year-spirit who must in autumn turn away from the earth-mother and her fertility principle and go into fatal decline and death.[5] In the ensuing sacrificial drama the year-spirit is symbolically castrated, slaughtered and / or fragmented—thus to be mourned till his reappearance in a spring epiphany. This castration (Jeffers characterizes Hood's self-stabbing as an "Attis gesture" and has Cawdor gouge out his eyes) signifies the end of an era, a final pulse of life, a down-cycle of existence. To be renewed, the world and all its parts must be continually devastated and reduced from particularized form to formless matter—so that new forms may arise. Emasculation here is not specifically sexual in intent but symbolizes the drying up of all life-nurturing fluids—semen, sap, rivulets and rainclouds. At this level, the story repeats Jeffers' primary equation for life: BEING equals DYNAMISM equals CHANGE equals VIOLENCE equals PAIN equals DISINTEGRATION (SACRIFICE) equals RECONSTRUCTION (SACRAMENT) equals TRAGEDY equals BEAUTY equals GOD. The myth would instruct those who, like Hood and Cawdor, refuse to accept the death / risk implications of existence.[6]

Cawdor's structure is one of the most symmetrical and carefully articulated of Jeffers' art. He divides the text into sixteen sections, ranging from 180 to 360 lines. The dramatic development is separated into five act-like parts by four distinct lyric interludes which progressively comment on the action. They are: (1) the apostrophe to the kingfisher (section I), (2) the old man's death dream (section VII), (3) the young hunter's death dream (section X), and (4) the caged eagle's death dream (section XV).[7]

The first "act" (or introduction) brings the participants to the point of Cawdor's fateful marriage with Fera by which he has decided to reassert his vigor; the second act (the complication) develops Fera's frustration expressing itself in erratic seduction forays toward a baffled Hood; the third act (the crisis) encompasses the youth's self-wounding, Fera's attempted suicide (dressed in a lion's skin, drawing fire from Hood's gun), and the young hunter's death (hurled from the promontory rock by his maddened father); the fourth act (catastrophe) comprehends Cawdor's ordeal of reappraisal, endurance of guilt, and search for expiation. The final act (denouement) witnesses his public confession and self-blinding.

Through the four choral interpretations Jeffers directs his readers toward the deeper intonations of his drama. In Cawdor the deepest level of meaning is reached in the climactic fourth chorus, a fantasy on an eagle's death—the eagle which has lived in captivity on the ranch, caged, maimed, and in pain. Receiving the "gift" of death, the bird's spirit spirals toward the sun, leaving the ranch, the Coast Range, and the North American continent below. From cosmic heights the eagle sees dark night and the bright rim of dawn as light's cycle passes over the globe. Transcending even time, the bird's spectre overlooks the ebb and flow of races, emigrations, and the never-ending cycle of progress and decay in civilizations. Finally the eagle achieves a sort of ultimate vision:

> It saw, according to the sight of its kind, the archetype
> Body of life a beaked carnivorous desire
> Self-upheld on storm-broad wings: but the eyes
> Were spouts of blood; the eyes were gashed out; dark blood
> Ran from the ruinous eye-pits to the hook of the beak
> And rained on the waste spaces of empty heaven.
> Yet the great Life continued; yet the great Life
> Was beautiful, and she drank her defeat, and devoured
> Her famine for food.
>   There the eagle's phantom perceived
> Its prison and its wound were not its peculiar wretchedness,
> All that lives was maimed and bleeding, caged or in blindness,
> Lopped at the ends with death and conception, and shrewd
> Cautery of pain on the stumps to stifle the blood, but not
> Refrains from all that; life was more than its functions
> And accidents, more important than its pains and pleasures,
> A torch to burn in with pride, a necessary
> Ecstasy in the run of the cold substance,
> And scape-goat of the greater world.

We find Jeffers deep in myth-ritual terms here—archetype, body of life, scapegoat, return to sources, death beyond death, eternal return.

For Jeffers the passage establishes certain realities fundamental to his understanding of any existential situation: (1) that all history is circular, not linear; there is no "omega point," only new, absolute beginnings; (2) that the cosmic whole is God who is characteristically blind, bleeding, self-tortured, and identical with the Life-Force itself; (3) that limitation and pain are of the essence of life-participation; (4) that life is the ecstasy of matter, that life exults in and suffers the ultimate complexities of which matter is capable; (5) that peace (escape from multimorphous pain) is only available in the moment of total death (reabsorption into the "white energy") before a new experiment in "being" arises out of the old to suffer its own ecstasy.

Each of the three preceding choral lyrics has led toward this final summary vision. In the first chorus, Cawdor is mocked by the enigmatic kingfisher for refusing to accept his age and its death implications. Snatching for life in the form of a young wife, he has reneged on his own mature resolve; too he presumes on the invulnerability and security of his isolated ranch. Oblivious to his folly, he does not learn, till the final journey into darkness (when blindness and death have been accepted), that security, stability, and endurance are found only in a context of instability and the reckless process characteristic of Life-Force. Cawdor has fallen victim to *hubris*, an over-reaching pride, a presumption that he can manipulate his fate and alter life's imperatives. Inevitably the forces will reachieve their fateful balance and Cawdor will be subdued.

The second choral interlude presents the imagined brain-dissolution of Martial, Fera's father, following his death. The sequence contrasts the cruel world of pain and circumambient defeat (which was Martial's life) with a dream world of delight and illusion, made possible as the newly autonomous cells are freed from the hard, bright, cruel discipline of reality. Jeffers here writes a parable of man's wish-fulfillment fantasies—the embarrassing difference between what he *would like* the world to be and what it truly *is*. Martial's reverie significantly inverts the characteristics of the archetype Body of Life (section XV). Restriction falls away; pleasure replaces pain; grim reality is superseded; unreasoned disaster yields to a "flighty carnival" of joys never achieved in life. But the poet insists that flight from reality, no matter how comforting, is unworthy and can only be temporary. "Afterwards it [the brain nerve pulp] entered importance again / Through worms and flesh-dissolving bacteria. The personal show was over, the mountain earnest continued / In the earth and air."

The third choral meditation draws another parable out of the natural process of dissolution. Having fled his father, fearing his angry suspicions, Hood is hurled, a scapegoat figure, from the high rock into the precipice below. Far from losing its integrity thereby, the fragmented body overcomes its human isolation and enters again the "strained peace of the rock" which is "wild and shuddering" with its own desires but free of the "brittle iniquities of pleasure / And pain."

Characteristically Jeffers tells his stories on several levels simultaneously—e.g., on the levels of ritual (the underlying, inevitable process), of myth (the *humanized* dramatization of that process), and of realistic action (natural catastrophes and Freudian tensions). One less obvious level on which the narrative unfolds is that of image and symbol. *Cawdor's* apocalyptic imagery is a case in point. The hovering forces of total dissolution—flood, storm, wind, and fire—each representing the Life-Force, continually tell their tale of mutability, violence, fragmentation, and renewal to whoever will listen. In them the end is foreshadowed long before the dramatic forces sweep the participants to tragic destruction.

Apocalyptic fire is the predominant image in the poem's first section. A forest fire precipitates a realigning of lives, but it also reveals the nature of life itself—by blinding Martial, maiming him, and caging Fera in bitterness. It drives them to a sanctuary whose security belies itself, at the same time revealing the predator-victim nature of life—in the lion and fawn which flee the fire together with the father and daughter. In the next set of scenes the apocalyptic imagery changes to tidal ebb and flood, as Fera and Hood gather shellfish singularly resplendent with sacrificial features (blind forms, blood hues, constricted existences). As the couple leaves the tidal rocks, waves swell, cutting off the setting sun, gulls' wings suggesting primitive ritual scythes. This same water imagery resumes in the fourth section where torrential rains impend chaos, eroding the mountain range and washing away Cawdor's garden. As fugue-like counter-movement, apocalyptic wind enters, splintering trees, wrecking fences, littering the slopes with debris, as a "roaring chariot of storm" comes to bring Martial "home."

Scapegoat and stain imagery has already been mentioned. Fera is obsessed with stain as she prepares for her father's burial which she intends to follow with suicide and betrayal of Hood; in heating water and donning the lion pelt she becomes a priestess going to ritual purification and ceremonial rites. As scapegoat, Hood takes on his shoulders the accumulated family passions and in his death allows his father a kind of rebirth. Sacrificial imagery (variations on the scapegoat motif) permeates the drama, intimating the story's meaning and anticipating its action. It is closest to the surface in the eagle's execution, in the suppressed violence of the tidal scene, in the breaking apart of Hood's flesh, and in Cawdor's bull qualities which are slowly immolated. Perhaps the most impressive scene is Martial's interment where a blood-red, wine-purpled sky overlooks a scene of human incomprehension, ineptitude, and isolation as Cawdor and his family gather around the grave. In Jeffers' poetic imagery sacrifice is inseparable from sacrament; what is broken is broken for reintegration. Only continual fragmentation makes the world whole. Atonement is renewal. Out of dissolution "one glory / Without significance pervaded the world."[8]

Among other theme-images, animal allusions are outstanding.

Cawdor's bull-qualities mark him for slaughter. His *hubris* is expressed in "drooping eyes, like a big animal's / That never needs to look sideways." Cawdor's "blindness" involves a bull-like stolidness, precipitous anger, and solution by action. He is continually "charging" only to find an empty cape. Fera, on the other hand, is identified with the lion (animal surrogate for Dionysus whose pelt is ritual garment for his votaries). She enters Cawdor's world together with the fire-singed cat; she assumes the puma skin to lead Hood to his death. She is the Dionysian force which sends Cawdor's Apollonian world toppling; lion and bull symbolize these opposites.

Cawdor's story has an ending which Theseus' story does not share; sacrifice leads to an impressive renewal. Fulfilling the myth-motifs, Cawdor finally overcomes the challenge of the bull-monster's labyrinth—carefully groping his way out by a thread which Hood has earlier missed (section III) and which Cawdor has experienced before only darkly in a fateful tunnel of wrath (section X). Blinded for his folly as was Orion, Cawdor is led into the light by his blacksmith son George—to the ocean edge where in deep irony and paradox he receives full vision as he puts out his sinning eyes. This Oedipal act is not despair; neither is it, for a purified Cawdor, a merely melodramatic gesture. It completes his self-mastery. His eyes have been instruments of self-delusion; he makes them now symbols of unconditional submission. He has become like the eagle archetype: "Dark blood / Ran from the ruinous eye-pits . . . yet the great Life / Was beautiful, and she drank her defeat, and devoured her famine for food" (section XV). The blinding has been prefigured many times—from Martial's scarred eyes in section I to Fera's fate to be coal "between the eyelid and the eye" of Cawdor in section XVI. Freudian interpreters say that Oedipus in his rash act embodied a symbolic self-castration. This makes much sense on the ritual level which informs Cawdor's story. Cawdor is the year-god (Attis, Adonis, Osiris, etc.) from whose spilled life-fluid, sprinkled on earth, came the flowers of spring, and the possibility of a renewed self and a renewed world.

Notes

1. See "I Am Growing Old and Indolent" in Jeffers' posthumous volume *The Beginning and the End* where he recapitulates this *ars poetica*, "Apology for Bad Dreams," and admonishes his old age in terms of it.

2. The second strophe to "Apology" is crucial. The first sets up the problem of evil in almost classic terms. The second responds to this "evil" by postulating that all things demand tragedy (involvement in "evil") according to the first motion of their being. Thence the poet's concern becomes how to relate to this "evil" and how to participate in a tragic cosmos to the extent of one's powers (strophe IV).

3. *Cawdor* (*Cawdor and Other Poems*, New York, 1928) has just been re-released by New Directions after having been out of print (and available only through rare-book deal-

ers) for forty years. See Robinson Jeffers, *Cawdor and Medea* (New York: New Directions, 1970). Introduction by William Everson (Brother Antoninus).

4. Jeffers' remarks on the origins of *Cawdor* are to be found in Sidney Alberts' *A Bibliography of the Works of Robinson Jeffers* (New York, 1933), p. 50 ff.

5. Hippolytus as myth-hero is a variation of Attis, Osiris, Tammuz, Dionysus, Adonis, etc., as Gilbert Murray has shown in his "Excursus on the Ritual Forms Preserved in Greek Tragedy" in Jane Harrison's *Themis* (Cambridge, 1912), pp. 341–63.

6. The equation is an attempt to interpret the second strophe of "Apology for Bad Dreams."

According to the specifics of the Hippolytus myth, Theseus is the sun-god (or year-god) who refuses to yield to the natural decline into night-womb and grave. Instead he snatches at life in the person of a young wife, while continuing the "old man" chores of established society. His son's problem is the same kind but takes place in the other (first) half of the life cycle. This son cannot overcome Oedipal diffidence, cannot detach himself from womb-security; he refuses to grow up and thereby (through the unresolved confusion) chooses death. See the first chapter of Joseph Campbell's *The Hero with a Thousand Faces* (New York, 1949). This son's story is the story of Hood.

7. The second and third choral pieces were excerpted by Jeffers as separate poems to be included in his *Selected Poetry* (New York, 1938).

8. The scapegoat figure, common in Jeffers' myth-symbol world, ultimately has no relationship to guilt. The burden to be expiated is that of existence itself. Jeffers' Hanged God (see *At the Birth of an Age*) bears the pains of existence for the sake of continued being. Stain imagery in *Cawdor* relates to this; the stain that Fera bewails is the stain of cyclic being which is subject to corruption.

Robinson Jeffers: The Modern Poet as Antimodernist

Tim Hunt*

Sixty-four years after the publication of his first major collection, *Tamar and Other Poems* (1924), Robinson Jeffers remains a troubling figure. Neither forgotten nor fully canonized, we view him largely in isolation, and by this I refer neither to his *westerness* nor the image he cultivated of a coast-range recluse. Rather, I am pointing to the way we have taken his decision not to be part of the literary debates and community now loosely termed *modernism* as a license to conclude that he is in some way a writer without a literary context (or, at the least, a writer with a context entirely divorced from that of the other significant writers of his generation). But to separate Jeffers from his contemporaries in this manner is, speaking practically, to remove him from the canon.

In spite of their local disagreements, the modernist writers were a functioning network, a kind of neighborhood. Williams may have given Eliot the cold shoulder, but both chatted with Pound across the backyard fence. And these dialogues have made it tempting to posit the cohesive-

*This essay was written specifically for this volume and is published here with the permission of the author.

ness of modernism and assume that earlier twentieth-century poetry is significant only when (and to the extent that) it is *modernist.* Whatever the actual truth of this view (did Frost's relationship with Pound really make him a modernist?), it creates a problem for those interested in Jeffers. To argue that Jeffers is irrelevant to the general history of American poetry for the first half of the century is self-defeating, and to argue he was some sort of closet modernist (even of the Frostian sort) doesn't fit the facts. Jeffers himself chose not to become a modernist and purposefully explored a style and mode that might almost be termed *antimodernist* (if that term didn't suggest a willful attempt to revert to the perspective of some earlier period).

I have posed the question in its unanswerable form, in part because this is the form we usually give it and in part because this indicates the need to rephrase and resituate the question itself. We will not find the commonality between Pound, for instance, and Jeffers by setting passages of *The Cantos* and *Cawdor* side by side. We will not, that is, see the ways both Pound and Jeffers are *modern* and *American* by looking primarily at their products. We must look, rather, at the questions that shaped their work and at the particular heritage that shaped the questions themselves. And when we do this, we find that Jeffers's project constitutes a kind of mirror image or reversal of the modernist project. As such his work, though unique and specific, even antimodernist (though not *antimodern*), is fundamentally a part of the revolution in American poetry and poetics in the first half of this century. Recognizing this, we can begin to recognize and explore the way the work of Stevens, Eliot, and others reveals the coherence and significance of Jeffers's poetry, just as Jeffers helps extend our sense of these other writers by showing us a significant alternative they chose not to explore.

A brief consideration of Jeffers's early career shows the background, the aesthetic and cultural challenges (read *crisis* if you prefer) he shared with the modernists. He had been schooled in the same classical and modern languages, the same literary tradition.[1] He too assumed the emerging modern world—its science, its economy, its social patterns, and (ultimately) its mass violence—threatened the continuity of the culture and required a major aesthetic renewal. And like the modernists, he recognized the challenge posed by Mallarmé's symbolist practice. Ironically, Jeffers's "Introduction" to the 1935 reissue of *Roan Stallion* attests to his concern with the literary issues of his generation even as it describes his decision "not to become a 'modern.' " In the piece, Jeffers recalls an episode of 1914 when (shortly after moving to Carmel and perhaps eight years before writing *Tamar*) he was still, by his report, "imitating Shelley and Milton" even as "more advanced contemporary poets were attaining [originality] by going farther and farther along the way that perhaps Mallarmé's aging dream had shown them, divorcing poetry from reason and ideas, bringing it nearer to music, finally to astonish the world with what would look like pure nonsense and would be pure poetry."[2] Twenty years separate the episode and the writing, but the piece does seem to record Jeffers's reactions, even if its terms likely derive in part from his intervening speculations. If so, the modernism Jeffers here imagines his work to oppose is not the modernism of the mid–1930s but the work leading to imagism and early imagism itself. Appropriately, then, the one contemporary he notes, the person he suspects "must be setting the pace," is Pound.

The *Roan Stallion* "Introduction" points to Jeffers's concern with his own literary generation at a moment when he was intensively considering the direction for his own work (even if he was not to find that direction for at least another six or seven years and even if the searching was still to involve much imitation). Significantly, though, Jeffers bases his rejection of modernism (or more properly his rejection of imagism) on a critique that parallels Pound's own reasons for moving beyond imagism a few years later. For Jeffers, the path of "Mallarmé and his followers" required for "every advance . . . the elimination of some aspect of reality," and Jeffers was not willing to follow the "austerities" of "originality by amputation."[3] Jeffers returned to this point a few years later in the "Foreword" to *The Selected Poetry:* "It became evident to me that poetry . . . must reclaim some of the power and reality that it was so hastily surrendering to prose. The modern French poetry. . . . was becoming slight and fantastic. . . . This feeling . . . led me to write narrative poetry, and to draw subjects from contemporary life; to present aspects of life that modern poetry had generally avoided; and to attempt the expression of philosophic and scientific ideas in verse. It was not in my mind to open new fields for poetry, but only to reclaim old freedom."[4] In *The Tale of the Tribe,* Michael Bernstein describes Pound's own dissatisfaction with Mallarmé as he began working on the early cantos. Bernstein suggests Mallarmé and poets like him appealed to Pound because they had "purged" the "accumulated weight of neo-classical or romantic rhetoric," opened new rhythmic possibilities, and made possible new "areas of consciousness." But, he suggests, their attempt to create a " 'pure' poetry" "of the *word*" by "deliberately abandon[ing] the *world* 'to novelists' " also threatened to leave poetry "totally self-reflective" and "emptied of all 'outside' content." Finally he suggests that Pound by 1917 no longer wished to be "confined to a . . . single, intensely felt perception . . . crystallized into a timeless pattern" and had begun searching for a way to incorporate Mallarmé's stylistic advances while yet being able to refer to the world of daily reality and narrate (albeit elliptically and allusively) what he termed (borrowing a phrase from Kipling) the "tale of the tribe."[5]

That Jeffers and Pound both sought ways beyond the narrowing influence of Mallarmé (and apparently did so within several years of each other) does not mean that they were, finally, similar. It does mean, though, that they shared similar questions and that Jeffers cannot be dismissed simply or primarily for having chosen not to become an imagist any more than Pound can for leaving imagism behind. And yet, whatever the parallels, Jeffers's rejection of Mallarmé and imagism both was a more radical break than Pound's, and this, too, is important. If Pound and Jeffers both wished to rescue "the world" for poetry, they wished to rescue a different world. For Jeffers, the world meant natural phenomenon, and human culture was simply one of its elements. For Pound, the world meant human culture with natural phenomenon as its material and backdrop. In Jeffers, the significant human act is to acknowledge and contemplate the interaction of the world's forces, a world within time and within which human action per se is largely insignificant. In Pound, the significant human act is to take part (through appreciation or creation) in the texture of culture and art, a world that in some way transcends time and nature both and celebrates human power.

Such differences should not be ignored, even if finally we end up shrugging and invoking "differences in temperament" for what we can't explain. Still, one factor in the difference between Pound and Jeffers may simply have been education. In addition to his training in languages and literature, something he shared with Pound, Jeffers (like Williams) had spent several years in medical school where he seems to have developed (in contrast to Williams) a deep interest in modern science and its vision of the world, and the impact of this is apparent in his response to such matters as the depth psychology of Freud and others and the then still-new anthropology popularized by Frazer's *The Golden Bough*.[6] For someone like Eliot, Freud's work seems to have revealed the psyche as the source of an imagination requiring the aesthetic act to order and redeem it; for Jeffers, Freud seems to have demonstrated the psyche as *natural* force and the essential unity of nature and imagination as analogous forces or energies. Similarly, Frazer's work on primitive myth seems to have suggested for Eliot that the structures for imaginative experience might be implicit in cultural groups, while for Jeffers, Frazer's emphasis on primitive ritual seems to have demonstrated these same groups participating in, and acting as, natural force. Together Frazer and Freud, viewed against the backdrop of Darwin, seem to have helped shape or confirm Jeffers's sense of the human species as a social organism responding to natural force as natural force, and this in turn perhaps suggested to Jeffers that he could treat (as he seems to do in the narratives) social units such as the family as forms of nature. Here again, Jeffers's reading of Freud and Frazer sets him apart even as it defines a larger dialogue.

I should note as well that Jeffers's *scientific* use of perspectives such as Freud's and Frazer's seems to leave little room for human autonomy, and this, coupled with his sense of humanity's insignificance at a cosmic level, has at times led to charges of nihilism. But Jeffers's sense of Freud and Frazer is probably more precise and sympathetic than that of Eliot and the other modernists who deflected Freud's and Frazer's *science* to support their own visions of art and culture. More importantly, even though Jeffers's perspective undercuts the value of *imagination* (perhaps *the* value for symbolists and modernists alike), this same perspective in turn elevates the importance of *consciousness*, the faculty that allows us to attend to our participation, however problematic and contradictory, in the larger world around us, and such attention is more properly a struggle for meaning than its denial.[7]

The dichotomy between what I have termed *imagination* and *consciousness* is readily apparent in Jeffers's early poem "Credo," and it is tempting to see it as in part his commentary on the direction of his modernist contemporaries.

> My friend from Asia has powers and magic, he plucks a blue leaf from the
> young blue-gum
> And gazing upon it, gathering and quieting
> The God in his mind, creates an ocean more real than the ocean, the salt,
> the actual
> Appalling presence, the power of the waters.
> He believes that nothing is real except as we make it.
> I humbler have found in my blood
> Bred west of Caucasus a harder mysticism.
> Multitude stands in my mind but I think that the ocean in the bone vault
> is only
> The bone vault's ocean: out there is the ocean's;
> The water is the water, the cliff is the rock, come shocks and flashes of
> reality. The mind
> Passes, the eye closes, the spirit is a passage;
> The beauty of things was born before eyes and sufficient to itself; the
> heart-breaking beauty
> Will remain when there is no heart to break for it.[8]

In "Credo," Jeffers in no way denies the power of imagination or the beauty it can create. He does, though, insist that the world outside the "bone vault," outside the eye, has its own and more fundamental beauty and that the act of attending to such beauty is itself an emotionally rich and complex act, a complexity even more apparent in "Oh Lovely Rock," in spite of that poem's simple descriptions and seemingly clear statements. The second and final stanza reads:

> We lay on gravel and kept a little camp-fire for warmth.
> Past midnight only two or three coals glowed red in the cooling darkness;
> I laid a clutch of dead bay-leaves
> On the ember ends and felted dry sticks across them and lay down again.
> The revived flame
> Lighted my sleeping son's face and his companion's, and the vertical face
> of the great gorge-wall
> Across the stream. Light leaves overhead danced in the fire's breath,
> tree-trunks were seen: it was the rock wall

That fascinated my eyes and mind. Nothing strange: light-gray diorite with two or three slanting seams in it,
Smooth-polished by the endless attrition of slides and floods; no fern nor lichen, pure naked rock . . . as if I were
Seeing rock for the first time. As if I were seeing through the flame-lit surface into the real and bodily
And living rock. Nothing strange . . . I cannot
Tell you how strange: the silent passion, the deep nobility and childlike loveliness: this fate going on
Outside our fates. It is here in the mountain like a grave smiling child. I shall die, and my boys
Will live and die, our world will go on through its rapid agonies of change and discovery; this age will die,
And wolves have howled in the snow around a new Bethlehem: this rock will be here, grave, earnest, not passive: the energies
That are its atoms will still be bearing the whole mountain above: and I many packed centuries ago
Felt its intense reality with love and wonder, this lonely rock.[9]

Here, again, the speaker attends to the reality beyond the self, but in this case he becomes progressively aware of the different temporal dimensions implicit in the scene, until his consciousness has come to comprehend (in the most fundamental sense of the word) a past, present, and future that paradoxically includes and excludes him, fulfills and annihilates him.

Jeffers's decision to view poetry as a way of attending to the world, rather than a way of remaking or transcending it, has a number of implications. For one, it places him in a line of descent from Wordsworth rather than Coleridge.[10] It also means that we should not be surprised that his sense of language stresses its referential powers, nor that his poems often dramatize a speaker in the act of apprehending or struggling with the implications of a problematic scene, nor that he assigns an independent life to the material world, nor that he is willing to make direct statements about that world. In each of these ways, Jeffers differs from most of his modernist contemporaries who tend to emphasize the power of language to create aesthetic products that transcend time and the ordinary, and to that extent, in each of these ways Jeffers is unfashionable. But, as a poem like "Oh Lovely Rock" indicates, Jeffers' various devices and gestures do match and serve his aesthetic, and (more importantly) when viewed on their own terms they can evoke and explore a complex, significant, and "intense reality."

In spite of the differences between Jeffers and the modernists apparent in such poems as "Credo" and "Oh Lovely Rock," these differences, finally, point as much to what he shared with the modernists as to where he differed. In her recent study, *Victorian and Modern Poetics*, Carol T. Christ suggests that the modernist poets, like the Victorians before them, feared that the subjectivity of romanticism would limit them to "arbitrary and personal meanings" unless they could "objectify the materials of poetry" by forestalling the reader's "identification of the speaking voice of the poem with the poet" and by formulating "theories of the image in poetry which [would] establish some objective ground for the feeling it generates."[11] Christ's claims hold with equal justice for Jeffers. He, too, mistrusted the solipsistic tendency of the romantic mode, but instead of seeking to make poetry the contemplation of images to discover "a radiant truth out of space and time," as Christ suggests the modernists did,[12] Jeffers made poetry the contemplation of process in which the radiant truth *is* space and time (or perhaps more accurately, the self becoming aware of space and time). Similarly, instead of objectifying his poetic means, Jeffers objectified his poetic matter and retained the drama of the speaking voice—but used it to enact an awareness of the broader world rather than an awareness of the self. (In this sense, Jeffers inverts Stevens by decreating the self rather than decreating nature.) But Jeffers did not turn poetry into a kind of science; rather he used it to attend to science (or rather nature as modern science had revealed it), and if his means were less radical than Pound's, it may be that he applied them to a more radical project. But whatever we choose to make of this final claim, Christ's model indicates that Jeffers's transformation of the romantic and Victorian modes should be seen as parallel to, and potentially in conversation with, the transformation represented by modernism. If this is so, the time may have come to begin considering Jeffers and his modernist contemporaries as a single matrix, an attempt that would sharpen our sense of Jeffers's achievement and deepen our sense of the modernist episode.

Notes

1. For a brief discussion of Jeffers's background, see "Introduction," in *The Collected Poetry of Robinson Jeffers, Volume One, 1920–28,* ed. Tim Hunt (Stanford: Stanford University Press, 1988), xv–xxii.

2. "Introduction," in *Roan Stallion, Tamar and Other Poems,* ed. Robinson Jeffers (New York: Modern Library-Random House, 1935), viii.

3. "Introduction," in *Roan Stallion,* ed. Robinson Jeffers ix.

4. "Foreword," in *The Selected Poetry of Robinson Jeffers,* ed. Robinson Jeffers (New York: Random House, 1938), xiv.

5. Michael Bernstein, *The Tale of the Tribe: Ezra Pound and the Modern Verse Epic* (Princeton: Princeton University Press, 1980), 6–9.

6. John B. Vickery discusses Jeffers and Frazer in *The Literary Impact of "The Golden Bough"* (Princeton: Princeton University Press, 1973), 157–61, and Robert J. Brophy develops Jeffers's use of mythic and ritual elements more fully in *Robinson Jeffers: Myth, Ritual, and Symbol in His Narrative Poems* (Cleveland: Case Western Reserve University Press, 1973). Jeffers's letter of 24 April 1926 to his editor Donald Friede is also relevant. Referring to *Point Alma Venus,* the precursor to *The Women at Point Sur,* Jeffers wrote, "The story, like Tamburlaine or Zarathustra, is the story of human attempts to get beyond humanity. But the superman ideal rather stands on top of humanity—intensifies it—ends in 'all too

human'—here the attempt is to get clear of it. More like the ceremonial dances of primitive people; the dancer becomes a rain-cloud, or a leopard, or a God. . . . The episodes of the poem are a sort of essential ritual, from which the real action develops on another plane." See *The Selected Letters of Robinson Jeffers*, ed. Ann Ridgeway (Baltimore: The Johns Hopkins University Press, 1968), 68.

7. Tim Hunt, "A Voice in Nature: Jeffers' *Tamar and Other Poems*," *American Literature* 61 (May 1989): 230–44.

8. Jeffers, *The Collected Poetry, Volume One*, 239.

9. The text used here is from *The Collected Poetry of Robinson Jeffers, Volume Two, 1929–38*, ed. Tim Hunt (Stanford University Press, 1989). The poem appeared originally in *Such Counsels You Gave to Me and Other Poems* (New York: Random House, 1937), 124–25.

10. Hunt, "A Voice in Nature," 235–236.

11. Carol T. Christ, *Victorian and Modern Poetics* (Chicago: Univ. of Chicago Press, 1984), 2–3 and 11–12.

12. Christ, 4.

Spheral Eternity: Time, Form, and Meaning in Robinson Jeffers

Robert Zaller*

Aristotle, that famous law-giver, laid it down that the action of a tragedy should occur within twenty-four hours. He was thus the first to inscribe an arrow in a circle—the accomplishment of a perfected sequence of events in the orbit of a day's passage. Robinson Jeffers has been faithful, in his fashion, to this dictum; and part of the fascination with ancient tragedy that appears both in his retelling of the Greek stories and in the California narratives that evoke them[1] lies in the tension between human praxis and natural process that Aristotle found in tragedy and saw, with unerring insight, as its essence. To be sure, Jeffers's narratives do not keep to the single alternation of day and night prescribed by Aristotle, but his world is wider, and his notion of human fate and cosmic necessity is far less rigidly deterministic than that of the ancient poets. The essence of his art is still, however, like theirs, the inscription of human meaning within natural process.

If Jeffers owed his basic perception of the tensions between the human and the natural to the Greeks, he expressed it within a consciousness informed by Christian eschatology and the language of modern science. For the ancients, the relation of human time to that of cosmic process, however problematic, was linked by a shared nature. With the Christian appropriation of Neoplatonism, however, the temporal drama of human salvation was imposed on the natural world, subjecting it to a transcendent order that implicitly devalued and ultimately subsumed it.[2]

*This essay was written specifically for this volume and is published here with the permission of the author.

Jeffers regarded this as a vast and corrupting mistake, a myth that did not reflect or interpret reality but usurped it. The result was to obscure men from themselves no less than from the world. The Greeks had dealt frankly with incest and *familicide* as generically human violations of the natural order, and they sought to expiate them through tragic reenactment. Christianity repressed this painful but necessary consciousness as sin, subordinating all drama and ritual to the rite of redemption, as it had subordinated the temporality of natural process to that of divine history.

As Christianity had been (at least from this standpoint) a corruption of Neoplatonism, so secular humanism was a corrupted form of Christianity. Christianity had replaced the ancient relation between man and cosmos with a radical dichotomy between matter and spirit, self and world, time and eternity. The humanism which replaced a decadent Christianity in turn did not abandon the promise of salvation but recast it in political terms (from "Mother Church" to "Father State," as Jeffers sardonically put it).[3] By making humanity the author of its own salvation, humanism fed what the ancients would have recognized as hubris, whose symptoms Jeffers described as introversion and the denial of temporal succession—in its extremest form, the denial of time itself—and which he depicted, as the Greeks had, by incest, sexual inversion, and familicide.

Humanism had captured not only politics (in the form of mass democracy, fascism, and communism) but philosophy as well. Kant had made reality a construct of the human intellect; by suppressing the transcendental pole of his thought, Marxists, utilitarians, pragmatists, and positivists made the real itself a product, in John Passmore's phrase, of the "community of finite selves." Set against this, however, was the enterprise of modern science. As humanism had contracted reality to the social organism, science expanded the cosmos forward in space and backward in time, dwarfing human presumption with a scale so vast as to humble the imagination. Jeffers saw science as ethically but not ontologically neutral, for it proclaimed the cosmos as value, and by grounding itself in empirical observation and experiment it affirmed its material substratum as well. But science, too, was corruptible, and partook of its epoch; in "Prescription of Painful Ends," Jeffers linked "the immense vulgarities of misapplied science and decaying Christianity," and, in a moment of disgust, he likened the human race to a "botched experiment."[4] Harnessed to the destructive impulses of cultural introversion, science could only hasten the impending collapse. It afforded, perhaps, a refuge, but no escape.

Nonetheless, science provided Jeffers with a perspective that, like the cosmogonic speculations of Lucretius and Empedocles before him, was the basis of a redemptive vision. The perception of beauty and the contemplation of order, he contended, afforded satisfaction to the senses and the intellect, discipline to the will, and peace to the mind. Yet truth to tragedy—fidelity to lived experience—demanded that human time be related to sidereal time, demanded narrative. Between the individual and the cosmos, however, stood a third term, the measure of collective human activity called history. History gave perspective to the individual act as cosmic evolution did to the world's daily occasion. As humanity was comprehended in nature, so history was assimilated in the wider entelechy of the universe.

Broadly speaking, the three major modes in which Jeffers wrote—narrative, meditative, and lyric—corresponded to the three tropes of time—personal, historical, and cosmic—in which the drama of being had its play. The three modes were freely woven through the fabric of individual poems; the narratives were punctuated by lyric or meditative strophes, while the predominantly meditative poems frequently took lyric or dramatic observation as their point of departure, and the lyric ones seldom lacked a meditative or didactic point. Some of the poems—"A Redeemer," "An Artist," "Steelhead," and "Going to Horse Flats" come to mind—are deliberately hybrid, consisting of lyric meditations set off by dramatic scenes. While particular poems may resist categorization, however, the modes remain distinct.

As the modes are mixed within the poems, so, consequently, are the temporal tropes that correspond to them. It would be difficult, if not bootless, to say which element was structurally primary, since temporal differentiation is always so present in Jeffers's consciousness. A mere glance at his titles will confirm not only his preoccupation with time but also its importance as an ordering principle in his verse and thought: "The Year of Mourning," "Dream of the Future," "Ante Mortem," "Post Mortem," "Solstice," "The Cycle," "At the Birth of an Age," "At the Fall of an Age," "Birth and Death," "Birthday," "Return," "Now Returned Home," "Resurrection," "No Resurrection," "Time of Disturbance," "Believe History," "The Day Is a Poem," "Moments of Glory," "New Year's Dawn, 1947," "End of the World," "The Beginning and the End."[5]

As we have noted, Jeffers keeps to no set time scheme in his narratives, but their action tends to follow seasonal patterns and variations, often with a high degree of specificity. Thus, the opening of *Tamar*, depicting the drunken, near-fatal fall of Lee Cauldwell, is set not with calendral but sidereal time: "grave Orion / Moved northwest from the naked shore, the moon moved to meridian."[6] It is only several stanzas later that this is converted into calendral time: "he that fell in December / Walked in the February fields" (*CP*, 20). But Orion is invoked again as Lee's sister, Tamar, recalls that their aunt, Stella, had foreseen him lying injured under Orion's sky in a vision. (The association of the name *Stella* itself with the sky is too obvious to require comment.)

Lee dismisses Stella's prophecy as without significance, just as he interprets his accident as banally as possible, seeing it as a call to abjure his youthful sins and become "decent." It is Tamar who returns to the shore where her brother had fallen to undergo a symbolic purgation of her humanity, rising for an instant beyond good and evil to bear "a third part / With the ocean and keen stars in the consistence / And dignity of the world" (*CP,* 49). The twist of perspective recalls Jeffers's comment in *Thurso's Landing* that humanity could shine "at stricken moments . . . terribly against the dark magnificence of things" (*SP,* 357), and the observation on tragedy in a late poem, "The World's Wonders": "Lear becomes as tall as the storm he crawls in."[7] The willingness to suffer extremity, and even, as in Tamar's case, to willfully seek it, is tied to the sense of human destiny that tragedy reflects. Humanity is pathetic and admirable for the same reason, pathetic in its vulnerability to pain, but admirable, in singular individuals, in its ability to endure it. To quote the previously cited passage in full:

I have learned that
happiness is important, but pain *gives* importance.
The use of tragedy: Lear becomes as tall as the storm he crawls in; and a
tortured Jew became God.

But pain is never properly sought for itself; it is the by-product of action, and action is the product of desire. Only in the tragic poet are these instrumentalities welded together. For the tragic protagonist, in Jeffers's view, the satisfaction of desire is the end of action; for the poet, it is the means whereby the revelation of suffering is accomplished. Suffering in itself, of course, has no value, but suffering plus endurance—the tragic virtue—*is* value.

So central was the notion of accepted suffering to Jeffers that he conceived of God himself as ultimately Promethean, and being—the material emanation of Godhead—as a condition of pain. He expressed this vision most directly in the speech of the Hanged God in *At the Birth of an Age*:

Without
pressure, without conditions, without pain,
Is peace. . . .
I have chosen
Being; therefore wounds, bonds, limits and pain; the crowded mind and
the anguished nerves, experience and ecstasy.
Whatever electron or atom or flesh or star or universe cries to me,
Or endures in shut silence: it is my cry, my silence; I am the nerve, I am
the agony,
I am the endurance.

(*SP,* 559)

In God alone, however, was willed suffering a value for Jeffers, since God alone could not suffer *except* by willing. Suffering, he thought, was all we can know of God, since it was only in this attribute that he was intimately revealed to us, only this attribute that we could share, and only by participation in it that we could aspire towards him: "a tortured Jew became God."

We can thus begin to understand Jeffers's conception of humanity's place in the cosmos. Each person was, he said, one of God's sense-organs, "immoderately alerted to feel"; but his distinguishing characteristic was consciousness:

> But man is conscious,
> He brings the world to focus in a feeling brain,
> In a net of nerves catches the splendor of things,
> Breaks the somnambulism of nature . . .
> ("Margrave," *SP,* 365)

Consciousness represented for Jeffers a principle of return from the created world towards its creator. In consciousness, the "splendor" of creation became apparent for the first time in the form of beauty, which Jeffers described as "the human mind's translation of the transhuman / Intrinsic glory."[8] But beauty posed, inevitably, the question of derivation, and, with that, the quest for origin. Thus consciousness took God as its ultimate subject, while God, by the same token, objectified himself in humanity as well. Consciousness was in this sense a participation in the divine, and a vehicle of its self-transformation. The import of this process was not to be fathomed; as Jeffers remarked succinctly, "[God] being sufficient might be still."[9] But the task it imposed on consciousness was not mere contemplative understanding but tragic action, the *imitatio Dei.* This was fulfilled—could only be fulfilled—in suffering.[10]

We may now put Jeffers's vision of tragedy in perspective. The setting of his narratives is the California coast, but their space implies cosmic depth. Indeed, the coast itself assumed for Jeffers the aspect of a cosmic stage whose grandeur seemed to reflect the immanence of the divine agon:

> The platform is like a rough plank theatre-stage
> Built on the prow of the promontory: as if our blood had labored all around the earth from Asia
> To play its mystery before strict judges at last, the final ocean and sky . . .
> ("Thurso's Landing," *SP,* 357)

> This coast crying out for tragedy like all beautiful places,
> (The quiet ones ask for quieter suffering: but here the granite cliff the gaunt cypresses crown
> Demands what victim? The dykes of red lava and black what Titan? The hills like pointed flames
> Beyond Soberanes, the terrible peaks of the bare hills under the sun, what immolation?)
> ("Apology for Bad Dreams," *CP,* 209)

Similarly, while strictly narrative time was the duration of accomplished action, significant time was the time necessary for the tragic protagonist to assume the burden of pain that bound him to the divine agon. The prototypically tragic figures for Jeffers were Oedipus and Lear, and, historically, Jesus:

King Oedipus reeling blinded from the palace doorway, red tears pouring
from the torn pits
Under the forehead; and the young Jew writhing on the domed hill in the
earthquake . . .
I saw the same pierced feet, that walked in the same crime to its
expiation; I heard the same cry.
("Meditation on Saviors," *CP*, 397–98)

Jeffers's tragic exemplars were Cawdor in the poem that bears his name, Reave Thurso in *Thurso's Landing*, and Lance Fraser in *Give Your Heart to the Hawks*. These protagonists—the first middle-aged, the other two young but prematurely grave—are all ranchers, bluff and stolid men who not only have no desire to transgress limits but seem almost obsessively determined to live within them. They seek not power but only control, and what betrays them is not hubris but jealousy and resentment.

Cawdor, a man of fifty, unwisely takes a young wife, Fera Martial. Fera falls in love with Cawdor's son Hood, who rejects her advances. Vengefully, she tells Cawdor that Hood has raped her, and he kills him in a fit of rage. Consumed by grief and despair, he becomes monumental in his anguish, and threatening to those around him. When Fera at last confesses the truth, he admits his own guilt, and forestalls the judgment of others by putting out his own eyes. Even this, however, seems to him "mere indulgence": " 'I'd not the strength,' " he says, " 'to do nothing' " (*CP*, 521).

A similar tale is told in *Give Your Heart to the Hawks*. Lance Fraser surprises his brother Michael making love to his wife Fayne after a drunken picnic, and he hurls him over a cliff. Lance's instinct is to confess, but Fayne persuades him to keep silent: " 'What we have done / Has to be borne. It's in ourselves and there's no escaping, / The state of California can't help you bear it' " (*SP*, 392). Fayne hopes that time will ease his sense of guilt, and Jeffers, in an ironic passage, seems to agree:

Oh, ignorant penitents,
For surely the cause is too small for so much anguish.
To be drunk is a folly, to kill may call judgment down,
But these are not enormous evils,
And as for your brother, he has not been hurt.
For all the delights he has lost, pain has been saved him;
And the balance is strangely perfect,
And why are you pale with misery?
(*SP*, 390)

Lance's guilt only intensifies, however. He seeks judgment from his father, but, finding none, gashes his hands to the bone on barbed wire in an attempt to divert himself from his moral agony, and finally leaps to his own death.

Reave Thurso, like Fraser and Cawdor, has an unfaithful wife, Helen. Reave's crime is not against law but against nature; wanting to control what he cannot possess, he forces Helen to return to a loveless marriage. His punishment is physical: attempting to cut the cable of his father's abandoned lime kiln that hangs like a symbol of his own failure above him, he is crushed and left paralyzed when it swings back on him. Lying helpless in a pain he can only assuage by the drugs he refuses to take, Reave discovers that "pain is the solidest thing in the world, it has hard edges, / I think it has a shape and might be handled" (*SP*, 340).[11] In Fraser and Cawdor, pain is mixed with guilt, and thus it distracts the will; for Reave, however, it becomes the will's very project, the most difficult and therefore the most necessary thing in the world to master. Paralysis has stripped away all else in his life, and pain is the only meaning left: if it ever ceased, he says, "I'd have to lie and burn my fingers with matches" (*SP*, 323). Reave in fact dies unconquered; he is slain by Helen, who takes her own life in turn.

Cawdor, Thurso, and Fraser are all men on whom pain descends as a burden to be ceaselessly and immitigably borne. Their endurance is not passive, however. It requires all the fortitude of which these supremely willful men are capable; it is, for all of them finally, the ultimate project of the will. In virtually all the narratives of Jeffers's classic phase, the action of the story may well be called a pretext for the occasion of pain; the crippling blow, be it physical or psychological, is the crux of the drama, and the remainder of the poem—in the extreme case of *Give Your Heart to the Hawks*, sixty-nine of eighty pages—is in each case devoted to the protagonist's struggle with pain and its effects on others. It is, needless to say, the moral character of this struggle that concerns Jeffers, and gives his depiction of agony the redeeming power of art.

With this in mind, we can more fully understand the choral apostrophe from *Give Your Heart to the Hawks* quoted above. Jeffers, addressing his own characters as "ignorant penitents," tells them that Lance Fraser has not "hurt" his brother in slaying him, for he has spared him the pain that would inevitably have been his lot in this life. These remarks seem to undermine the moral coherence of the poem, for they suggest that pain has no redemptive value and that grief should be temperate. But tragedy is precisely what exceeds the norm of life, and, by means of transfiguring pain, gives access to the divine. Were not certain natures predisposed to suffer this excess, the tragic epiphany, the *imitatio Dei*, would not be possible. Thus, while Jeffers's counsel to temper grief and avoid pain is entirely appropriate from an ordinary human perspective—indeed, is the only appropriate counsel from such a perspective—it has no applicability in the tragic realm; and the very function of the apostrophe is precisely to set off the merely human action of the poem from its tragic consequences.

In terms of our earlier distinction, Jeffers's tragic protagonists step from the arena of ordinary, personal experience—the place where, in the words of the prophet, there is to every thing a season—into the unbounded cosmos of the divine agon, where pain, as a manifestation of the divine essence, is inexhaustible and indivisible.[12] Their suffering, that is, remains rooted in material cause—the act or event which, slight in itself from a cosmic perspective, casts them beyond atonement, and separates them from humanity. To those around them, their steadfast self-punishment seems monstrous and perverse. They seem fixated on a single deed that excludes all other meaning; in other words, they refuse to let time flow, and thereby heal. In the tragic realm, however, their acts *are* immitigable, because in this realm, the realm of epiphany, time does not flow, succession does not exist, and the divine wound is never stanched.

Tragic consciousness in this full and final sense, as the revelation of divinity, is beyond such men as Cawdor, Thurso, and Fraser, blunt skeptics who are, if anything, confirmed in their unbelief by the experience of suffering.[13] They participate in the divine agon without realizing it, and their rejection of all consolation is the quality that perfects their suffering. They are "ignorant penitents," or, as Jeffers suggests elsewhere,[14] the apes of God; and, like apes, their function is to mimic without understanding.

In so defining his heroes, Jeffers remained faithful to the spirit of Greek tragedy, in which the cosmic order can only be fully revealed by the acts which defy it. On the plane of history as well, he contended that the great religious founders were driven by inner shame or conflict, the epistemic equivalent of the tragic flaw. His paradigm was the figure of Jesus, which he explored in a number of poems, most notably the verse drama *Dear Judas*, a work contemporary with the California narratives we have considered here.[15]

Dear Judas is set in the suspended time of Noh drama, whose protagonists enact their passions in the form of ritual.[16] They are "nearly unfleshed of time," "fading" into eternity, Jeffers says; yet the Jesus-figure notes with exactitude that nineteen hundred years have passed since his passion first transpired, which places the poem in the historic present as well (*DJ*, 9). This apposition seems to indicate the waning of Christian belief, whose final eclipse will release Jesus and his fellow performers from their purgatorial ritual. Jesus exists in both dimensions; he suffers his passion as if for the first time, and yet is conscious of it as repetition, repetition with a term.

This perception encapsulates Jeffers's view of historic time, which he saw, with Nietzsche, as a form of cyclical recurrence.[17] Jeffers's concern was not whether exact persons or events would recur, but rather to assimilate historic time to cosmic process by showing homologous *patterns* of events. On the level of personal experience, this took the form of the archetypal passions incarnated by individuals; on the historic one, of the ebb and flow of great civilizations. Jeffers in fact pursued parallel projects in the 1920s and 1930s designed to illustrate this symmetry, alternating the narratives of the California coast, which depicted the fate of individuals, with the verse dramas (*Dear Judas*, *At the Fall of an Age*, *At the Birth of an Age*, *The Bowl of Blood*), which portrayed the crises of Western civilization.

At the same time, Jeffers commented on the relation between the great religious founders and their civilizations in such poems as "Meditation on Saviors" and "Theory of Truth," and, in a series of meditative and didactic poems from "The Broken Balance" (1929) to "Prescription of Painful Ends" (1941), on the cyclical nature of historical experience and impending decline of the West. He was thus able to link personal to historical time, and the historical cycle to cosmic process, in an overarching pattern of recurrence. The latter relationship is evoked with particular effectiveness in "Prescription of Painful Ends":

The future is a misted landscape,
no man sees clearly, but at cyclic turns
There is a change felt in the rhythm of events, as when an exhausted horse
Falters and recovers, then the rhythm of the running hoofbeats is
changed: he will run miles yet,
But he must fall: we have felt it again in our own life time, slip, shift and
speed-up
In the gallop of the world; and now perceive that, come peace or war, the
progress of Europe and America
Becomes a long process of deterioration—starred with famous
Byzantiums and Alexandrias,
Surely—but downward.

(*BA*, 101)

The image of the horse, with its portent of fatigue and collapse, is checked by that of the stars, whose duration is indefinite, though their extinction is certain. Jeffers thus combines gathering force and momentum with protracted duration, thereby suggesting the great scale of the event, and assimilating it to the cycles of cosmic change. At the same time, he suggests that the nature of historical process is necessarily concealed; the acceleration toward doom is portrayed as a mechanized advance ("slip, shift and speed-up"), and, by a deliberately archaized usage, "progress," the promise of improvement, is stood on its head as the process of decay.

The suggestion that historical decay inevitably masked itself as progress and enlightenment was the most radical aspect of Jeffers's cultural pessimism. In the modern world, this decadent progress manifested itself most clearly in the post–Nietzschean injunction to overthrow conventional restraints and personal inhibitions. The result was an exaltation of the will, portrayed by Jeffers in the personae of Tamar Cauldwell, the Clytemnestra of *The Tower Beyond Tragedy,* his verse adaptation of the *Oresteia,* and Arthur Barclay in *The Women at Point Sur.* If Cawdor, Thurso, and Fraser represent the negative exercise of the will as endurance, these earlier protagonists embody it as an assertion against the limits of existence as such. Tamar seeks nothing less than a reversal of the temporal ordinance itself. "All times are now," she declares, "to-day plays on last year and the inch of our future / Made the first morning of the world" (*CP,* 63). Tamar not only assumes the temporal perspective of divinity, seeing the world as simultaneity and recurrence, but asserts a divine potency: "I am the fountain" (*CP,* 63).[18] When her megalomania (inevitably) collapses, she consumes the small world of her family and farmstead in a holocaust.

These key images of fire and fountain are repeated by Clytemnestra in her address to her lover, Aegisthus: "I'd burn the standing world / Up to this hour and begin anew. You think I am too much used for a new brood? Ah, lover / I have fountains in me" (*CP,* 144). Aegisthus, a merely conventional sinner, counsels moderation: "We may pass nature a little, an arrow flight, / But two shots over the wall you come in a cloud upon the feasting Gods, lightning and madness" (*CP,* 140). The "arrow" of individual action, even of vengeance and murder, must remain inscribed within the sphere of prescription. To come upon the gods is a catastrophe; to aspire towards them, unthinkable. But this is precisely what Clytemnestra does, and when she acknowledges that "It's not a little / You easily living lords of the sky require of who'd be like you" (*CP,* 139), it is only to steel herself further for whatever may be necessary.

Unlike Tamar and Clytemnestra, who ultimately seek power on a merely personal level, Arthur Barclay is a savior, a man who would become a god *for* others. Such men—as Jeffers asserted in "Meditation on Saviors"—were the founders of great civilizations, which flourished as long as the metaphor of divinity they provided remained vivid. But the decadence of founding myths was as essential as their ripening; renewal could not come until the full course had been run. *The Women at Point Sur* was written in the aftermath of World War I, when Jeffers's sense of the West's decadence was particularly acute: "You kept the beast under till the fountain's poisoned, / He drips with mange and stinks through the oubliette window" (*CP,* 241). But Jeffers imagined Arthur Barclay as a product of his time's sickness, not as its cure. The West, as Jeffers had concluded by the time of "Prescription of Painful Ends," had its Byzantiums and Alexandrias yet ahead of it, and many false prophets to follow before a new messiah might, perhaps, appear.[19]

Jeffers was skeptical whether civilization could transcend its need for myth, the apprehension of the true by means of the false. Communal truth, he felt, would always be partial, distorted, and transitory; and history followed from that fact. But if every man were obliged to endure history, it did not follow that he was necessarily bound by it. Again and again, Jeffers counseled what he called finally a "reasonable detachment" from the historical moment (*DA*, xxi). This detachment was not to be gained by denial of or indifference to the world. One had to live the life of one's time no less than the times of one's life, and quietism was no more acceptable a response on the historical plane than suicide was on the personal one.[20] Rather, detachment was the fruit of a deep, contemplative engagement with the natural, nonhuman world, and the perception of divinity that was its basis:

> Things are so beautiful, your love will follow your eyes;
> Things are the God, you will love God, and not in vain,
> For what we love, we grow to it, we share its nature.
> ("Signpost," *SP*, 574)

Jeffers's own verse was the best testimony of his conviction that "Things are the God." For more than four decades, he celebrated the beauty of his chosen coast and the divinity he found manifested in it with the direct lyric earnestness of a religious witness. But if the natural world was the most immediate revelation of value, humanity too—as Jeffers never ceased to insist—was part of it, and to ignore the human pathos within the transhuman splendor was as much an error as the cultural self-absorption that had cut man off from his root in nature, and blocked the sight of God. The coast, as Jeffers noted, "cried out" for tragedy; man was implicated in landscape, and in a special (though not salvific) way, in divinity as well. Only by living all the times of man—the personal one of passional experience, the collective one of history, and the cosmic one of natural process and divine immanence—could the human condition be seen in proper perspective, and its terms accepted.

Jeffers did create one character who attains fully to such a perspective through purgative suffering and religious exaltation. In *The Tower Beyond Tragedy,* Clytemnestra represents the misdirected passion for power, and the prophetess Cassandra, who is punished by seeing divine motion through human eyes, the terror of an unmediated perception of cosmic process (*CP*, 146–50). The hero Orestes experiences both trials, and emerges with a vision of final cosmic order:

> I entered the life of the brown forest
> And the great life of the ancient peaks, the patience of stone, I felt the changes in the veins
> In the throat of the mountain, a grain in many centuries, we have our own time, not yours; and I was the stream
> Draining the mountain wood; and I the stag drinking; and I was the stars
> Boiling with light, wandering alone, each one the lord of his own summit; and I was the darkness

Outside the stars, I included them, they were a part of me. I was mankind
also, a moving lichen
On the cheek of the round stone . . . they have not made words for it, to
go behind things, beyond hours and ages,
And be all things in all time, in their returns and passages, in the
motionless and timeless center,
In the white of the fire . . . how can I express the excellence I have found,
that has no color but clearness;
No honey but ecstasy; nothing wrought nor remembered; no undertone
nor silver second murmur
That rings in love's voice, I and my loved are one; no desire but fulfilled;
no passion but peace,
The pure flame and the white, fierier than any passion; no time but
spheral eternity . . .

(*CP*, 177)

Orestes' experience is not of a static order, but of one whose "eternity" is manifested in the flux and reflux of phenomena and bound by the sphere of recurrence. It is the vision of Jeffers's temporal beatitude, of a world that, perfected in God, is never finished. Such a world can only be expressed in terms of contradiction because it *is* a contradiction, a world which is both endless and bounded, active in repose, and "passionately at peace" ("Night," *CP*, 115). The contradiction remains, too, between the individual and the historical community. "Let each man make his health in his own mind," Jeffers counsels in "Meditation on Saviors," and Orestes, alone among all his creations, perhaps does this; but he writes as well in "The Beaks of Eagles" (*SP*, 607) that "It is good for man / To try all changes, progress and corruption . . . not to go down the dinosaur's way / Until all his capacities have been explored"; to remain, to the last, the ape of God.

Notes

1. *Cawdor* (1928) is based upon Euripides' *Hippolytus*, and Greek references can be found throughout the narratives (e.g., Lance Fraser's association with the laurel bush, or the apostrophe at the end of "Thurso's Landing"). On the subject of Jeffers's use of myth generally, see Robert J. Brophy, *Robinson Jeffers: Myth, Ritual, and Symbol in His Narrative Poems* (Hamden: Archon Books, 1976).

2. Karl Lowith, *Meaning in History: The Theological Implications of the Philosophy of History* (Cambridge University Press, 1950). On ancient theories of time and its relationship to cosmology, see Pierre Duhem, *Le Système du monde*, 2 vols. (Paris, 1954, 1974), and Richard Sorabji, *Time, Creation and the Continuum: Theories in Antiquity and the Early Middle Ages* (Ithaca: Cornell University Press, 1983).

3. In "Thebaid," in *The Selected Poetry of Robinson Jeffers* (New York: Random House, 1959), 593. Henceforth cited as *SP.*

4. *Be Angry at the Sun* (New York: Random House, 1941), 102 (henceforth cited as *BA*); "Orca," in *The Double Axe and Other Poems* (New York: Liveright, 1977), 144 (henceforth cited as *DA*).

5. Before and during World War II, Jeffers began to date poems in his titles—e.g., "Contemplation of the Sword (April, 1938)," "The Soul's Desert (August 30, 1939)," "The Day Is a Poem (September 19, 1939)," "Helsinki Bombed, November 30, 1939," "Battle (May 28, 1940)"—or *as* titles, e.g., "February, 1940" and "June 14, 1940" in Robert Ian Scott, ed., *What Odd Expedients and Other Poems by Robinson Jeffers* (Hamden: Archon Books, 1981). In his prefatory note to *Be Angry at the Sun*, Jeffers lamented what he acknowledged to be the "obsession" with contemporary events "that pins many of these pieces to the calendar, like butterflies to cardboard." Some of the poems in the posthumously published Scott edition are more in the nature of diary jottings or drafts (e.g., "June 14, 1940" is a draft of "I Shall Laugh Purely," *BA*, 96–100). They are nonetheless valuable in indicating the state of mind of a poet whose best work—as he knew—achieved the largest perspective.

6. Tim Hunt, ed., *The Collected Poetry of Robinson Jeffers, Volume One, 1920–28* (Stanford University Press, 1988), 18 (henceforth cited as *CP*). Cf. other references to Orion, e.g. in "Night" (*CP*, 115) and "Dawn" (*DA*, 135).

7. *Hungerfield and Other Poems* (New York: Random House, 1954), 108. Jeffers weaves personal chronology in this poem ("Being now three or four years more than sixty") with historical time and cosmic process to skillful effect, using an ascending numerical scale ("twenty-five hundred years," "ten thousand years," "half a million flies") to suggest a steadily widening scale.

8. "De Rerum Virtute" (*Hungerfield*, 95). Cf. the almost identical formulation in "The Double Axe" (*DA*, 56).

9. "Apology for Bad Dreams" (*CP*, 211).

10. Cf. Arthur Barclay's comment in *The Women at Point Sur*: " 'God thinks through action, how shall a man but through action?' " (*CP*, 253). The suppressed term in the copula suggests that a man can be as God or (in Barclay's ultimately more radical case) become God only by imitative action.

11. Reave's speech prefigures the action in Jeffers's last narrative, *Hungerfield*, whose hero grapples with the embodied figure of Death: "He reached Death's monstrous flesh . . . It had looked like a shadow, / It was harder than iron" (*Hungerfield*, 10).

12. Cf. Barclay's final speech in *The Women at Point Sur*, where his deranged identification with the Godhead completes itself: " 'I want creation. The wind over the desert / Has turned and I will build again all that's gone down. / I am inexhaustible' " (*CP*, 367).

13. The crippled Reave Thurso: " 'I'll tell you / What the world's like: like a stone for no reason falling in the night from a cliff in the hills, that makes a lonely / Noise and a spark in the hollow darkness, and nobody sees and nobody cares. There's nothing good in it / Except the courage in us not to be beaten. It can't make us / Cringe or say please' " (*SP*, 341–42).

14. "Apology for Bad Dreams"; and cf. "Meditation on Saviors," where Jeffers speaks of "the apes of Christ."

15. *Dear Judas* was first published together with another California narrative, *The Loving Shepherdess*, whose heroine, as Jeffers himself explained, formed a trinity in his imagination with Jesus and Judas (Jeffers to S. S. Alberts, in S. S. Alberts, *A Bibliography of the Works of Robinson Jeffers* [New York: Random House, 1933], 57). "The Loving Shepherdess" was linked in turn to *The Women at Point Sur* and *Thurso's Landing* through the character of the visionary Onorio Vasquez, although its theme—selfless love—is sharply at variance with the narratives of heroic will contemporary with it. These elements of continuity and recurrence underscore the unity of Jeffers's creative project from the mid–1920s to the mid–1930s, and the connection between the stylized historical verse dramas and the "realism" of the narratives.

16. On Jeffers's use of Noh, see the remarks of Robert Brophy in the Liveright edition of *Dear Judas and Other Poems* (New York, 1977), 135–37 (henceforth cited as *DJ*).

17. On Nietzsche's view, see Sorabji, *Time, Creation and the Continuum*, 189–90, and references cited.

18. Cf. the use of the fountain as a symbol of divine creativity in "Night" (*CP*, 115).

19. Cf. "Hope is Not for the Wise" (*SP*, 596): "But this is only / The August thunder of the age, not the November"; "Decaying Lambskins" (*SP*, 610): "Our civilization, the worst it can do, cannot yet destroy itself; but only deep-wounded drag on for centuries." The advent of atomic weapons modified this view without, however, displacing it.

20. The distinction between detachment and indifference is made in a poem of the 1930s, "Rearmament" (*SP*, 565): "I would burn my right hand in a slow fire / To change the future . . . I should do so foolishly." Jeffers used the same figure in responding to a query from the League of American Writers on his attitude toward the Spanish Civil War: "I would give my right hand, of course, to prevent the agony; I would not give a flick of my little finger to help either side win" (Ann N. Ridgeway, ed., *The Selected Letters of Robinson Jeffers 1897–1962* [Baltimore: The Johns Hopkins Press, 1968], 266). The source of the figure is the classical story of Mucius Scaevola, who burned his hand to show loyalty and fortitude. Cf. the late poem, "Local Legend": "But most of us, one time or another, / Have taken unhappy causes or hopes to heart, and gotten well burnt" (*Hungerfield*, 96).

Suicide figures in virtually all of Jeffers's narratives, particularly *Thurso's Landing*, *Give Your Heart to the Hawks*, *Such Counsels You Gave to Me*, and *Mara*, as well as in many of the shorter poems ("Suicide's Stone," "Give Your Wish Light," "The Deer Lay Down Their Bones," "Vulture"). It was clearly a matter Jeffers wrestled with on a very personal level, and in a sense his entire oeuvre can be read as a bulwark erected against it. Suicide severed the link between the divine agon and human tragedy; it was a repudiation of value as such. As one should suffer history, without the illusion that its conflicts could ever be resolved, so, too, Jeffers averred, one should suffer the hard gift of life, understanding that pain was its essence.

SUPPLEMENTARY SELECTIONS

Ackerman, Diane. "Robinson Jeffers: The Beauty of Transhuman Things." *American Poetry Review* 12 (March–April 1983): 16–18.

Angoff, Charles. "Three Towering Figures: Reflections on the Passing of Robert Frost, Robinson Jeffers, and William Carlos Williams." *Literary Review* 6 (Summer 1963): 423–29.

Beers, Terry. "Robinson Jeffers and the Canon." *American Poetry* 5 (Fall 1987): 4–16.

Boyers, Robert. "A Sovereign Voice: The Poetry of Robinson Jeffers." *Sewanee Review* 77 (July–September 1969): 487–507.

Cunningham, Cornelius Carman. "The Rhythm of Robinson Jeffers' Poetry as Revealed by Oral Reading." *Quarterly Journal of Speech* 32 (October 1964): 351–57.

de Cassares, Benjamin. "Robinson Jeffers: Tragic Terror." *Bookman* 66 (November 1927): 262–66.

Drew, Fraser. "Carmel and Cushendun: The Irish Influence on Robinson Jeffers." *Eire-Ireland* 3 (Summer 1968): 72–82.

Gelpi, Albert. "Yvor Winters and Robinson Jeffers: The Janus-Face of Anti-Modernism." In *A Coherent Splendor: The American Poetic Renaissance, 1910–1950.* Cambridge: Cambridge University Press, 1987.

Gilbert, Rudolph. "Robinson Jeffers: The Philosophic Tragedist." In *Four Living Poets.* Santa Barbara, California: The Unicorn Press, 1944.

Gioia, Dana. "Strong Counsel." *Nation* 246 (16 January 1988): 59–64.

Glicksberg, Charles I. "The Poetry of Doom and Despair." *Humanist* 7 (August 1947): 69–76.

Gregory, Horace. "Poet without Critics: Robinson Jeffers." In *Spirit of Time and Place: Collected Essays of Horace Gregory.* New York: W. W. Norton & Co., 1973.

Hass, Robert. "Introduction." In *Rock and Hawk: A Selection of Shorter Poems by Robinson Jeffers,* edited by Robert Hass. New York: Random House, 1987.

Hesse, Eva. "Poetry as a Means of Discovery: A Critico-Theoretical Approach to Robinson Jeffers." *American Poetry* 5 (Fall 1987): 17–34.

Hotchkiss, Bill. "Afterword." In *The Double Axe and Other Poems* by Robinson Jeffers. New York: Random House 1948; rep. Liveright, 1977.

Houston, James D. "Necessary Ecstasy: An Afterword to *Cawdor*." *Western American Literature* 19 (August 1984): 99–112.

Jarman, Mark. "Robinson Jeffers: 'The Love and the Hate.' " *New England Review and Bread Loaf Quarterly* 8 (1985): 90–97.

Kafka, Robert. Explanatory notes. In *Where Shall I Take You To: The Love Letters of Una and Robinson Jeffers,* edited by Robert Kafka. Covelo, California: The Yolla Bolly Press, 1987.

Lagayette, Pierre. "L'engagement solitaire de Robinson Jeffers." *Revue Française D'Etudes Américaines* 40 (May 1986): 251–62.

Macdonald, Dwight. "Robinson Jeffers: I and II." *Miscellany* 1 (August and September 1930): 1–10, 1–24.

Milosz, Czeslaw. "Carmel." In *Visions from San Francisco Bay,* translated by Richard Lourie. New York: Farrar Straus Giroux, 1975.

Moss, Sidney. "Robinson Jeffers: A Defense." *American Book Collector* 10 (Summer 1959): 9–14.

Nickerson, Edward H. "Robinson Jeffers: Apocalypse and His 'Inevitable Place.' " *Western American Literature* 12 (August 1977): 111–22.

Perkins, David. "Robinson Jeffers." In *A History of Modern Poetry: Modernism and After,* 52–59. Cambridge: Harvard University Press, 1987.

Schweizer, Harold. "Robinson Jeffers' Excellent Action." *American Poetry* 5 (Fall 1987): 35–58.

Scott, Robert Ian. "The Great Net: The World as God in Robinson Jeffers' Poetry." *Humanist* 46 (January–February 1986): 24–29, 46.

Staley, Gregory A. " 'But Ancient Violence Longs to Breed': Robinson Jeffers's *The Bloody Sire* and Aeschylus' *Oresteia*." *Classical and Modern Literature* 3 (Summer 1983): 193–99.

Vaughn, Eric. " 'Dear Judas'—Time and the Dramatic Structure of the Dream." *Robinson Jeffers Newsletter* 31 (July 1978): 7–22.

Vendler, Helen. "Huge Pits of Darkness, High Peaks of Light." *New Yorker,* 26 December 1988, 91–95.

Waggoner, Hyatt H. "Melodies of Chaos." In *American Poets: From the Puritans to the Present,* Revised Edition. Baton Rouge: Louisiana State University Press, 1968.

INDEX

0 00 02 0499774 6
MIDDLEBURY COLLEGE